FOOTPRINTS
a sri lankan family story

Donald Wijasuriya

© Donald Wijasuriya 2020

All rights reserved. No part of this book may be reproduced or transmitted in any form or by any means whatsoever without prior written permission from the author.

2nd edition, revised and enlarged

ISBN 978-0-646-95327-4

National Library of Australia Cataloguing-in-Publication entry

Creator: Wijasuriya, D. E. K., author.

Title: Footprints : a sri lankan family story / Donald Wijasuriya.

ISBN: 9780646953274 (paperback)

Subjects: Wijasuriya, D. E. K. – Family.
Families – Western Australia – Biography.
Sri Lankans – Western Australia – Genealogy.
Sri Lankans – Malaysia - Genealogy
Sri Lanka – Genealogy. Western Australia – Genealogy.

Dewey Number: 929.20994

Cover design by Peter Schenk against a backdrop of a recent painting by a Sri Lankan artist.

TABLE OF CONTENTS

Prologue	1
Acknowledgements	6
Sajak	8
Ancestral Threads	10
Don Clement	11
James Peter	25
Ancestral Country	31
Historical Milieu	32
Socio-economic conditions	34
Railways	35
The Malay States	35
When my parents got married	52
Growing Up	64
My school days in Malaya	75
Japanese Occupation	80
The Japs are coming	80
The jungle hideout	84
Emerging from the jungle	85
Back to Bukit Nanas	87
Japanese school	88
Learning to survive	89
The Kepong wilderness	95
The ending of Rule Britannia	103
Rejoining the family	103
The move to Klang	111
The Riverside Road house	112
Nanny	114
Nanny's rubber plantation	115
Diabetic strands	118
Rekindling links with Ceylon	119

Cultural footprint	121
The communist insurgency	123
Our little world	127
Societal wedding	129
Neighbourhood games	131
Reading and story telling	133
Socialising	134
Living within our means	135
Sojourn in Ceylon	138
The holiday interlude	138
The bombshell announcement	144
The trauma of parting	145
Coming to terms with reality	146
Boarding school	149
Grandma's house in Kossinna	154
The Rajakadaluwa walauwa	163
Journey's end at boarding school	168
Uncle Noel's visit	170
Visit home	171
A taste of campus life	173
Birthdays	173
Kandy bus depot	174
Career choices	176
College friends	176
The University of Ceylon	178
An up-country holiday	185
Soccer tournament in India	189
Pilgrimage to Thalawila	189
Health concerns	190
Gampola floods	191

Trincomalee	192
Looking back	193
Underlying ethnic tensions	195
Farewell Ceylon	198
Sibling Pathways	203
The Federation of Malaya	212
Joining the Workforce	216
The Methodist Girls' Afternoon School	217
The University of Malaya in Kuala Lumpur	219
My early working life	220
Post graduate studies in London	222
Life in Malaysia	226
Getting to know you	226
Annette's eyesight	227
Getting hitched	229
Back to the salt mines	235
Our very own family	237
Bringing up our boys	237
Our own home in PJ	245
Corneal graft	247
Changing course	248
Sabbatical	249
Back in Sri Lanka	254
Back to work	255
Career and Family	259
Planning for a National library	259
The Public Service	262
Pilot project for educational television	263

Managing without Annette	264
Swimming lessons	269
Piano lessons	269
Bayu	270
Teaching stint at Aberystwyth	271
Fascination with flying	273
Pulau Pangkor	274
Boating and fishing	276
Travel abroad	277
Travel within the country	281
Trauma in Trengganu	282
An unforgettable holiday	284
Severing ties with academia	285
Developing the infrastructure	286
Doctoral studies	291
National accolades	294
Malaysian nationality	298
Malayanisation	300
The migration option	301
Dad's passing away	304
Mum's twilight years	306
The family's departure	309
The continuing saga	309
Surviving in officialdom	311
Official farewells	319
The future	321
The National Library revisited	322

Family Doings	324
Culinary tradition	324
Christmas celebrations	327
Life without the family	329
Catholic heritage	331
Home ownership headaches	332
New Horizons	336
Our Australian family home	336
School and university	338
Annette's work life down under	340
Post retirement blues	344
Consultancy work	346
The cloisters of academia	346
International commitments	348
Commemorative publication	348
Holidays together	349
Golf	349
Volunteering	351
Painting	351
Supporting aid programmes	352
Annette's illness	353
An ending and a beginning	359
Music in our lives	360
Barbershop singers	363
A new generation	364
The Jayatilaka lineage	365
Epilogue	374
Additional Information	376

Appendices	378
Wijasuriya Family Tree	378
Jayatilaka Family Tree	381
Birth Certificates	383
Baptism Certificates	387
School Leaving Certificates	389
Marriage Notices and Certificates	391
Statutory Declarations	394
Pension Records	397
Certificates of Registration / Citizenship	398
Marriage Advertisements	401

Prologue

I have written the story of my life primarily for my sons. It is a descriptive or narrative account and is on the whole chronological. I have however taken the liberty of digressing and taking the story forward and sometimes back to earlier times, as the story line dictated.

I simply called my literary efforts 'Footprints' – not because I left behind an indelible footprint or mark of my passage on this earth but because it took many footprints – mine and others before me, which have brought me to where I am today.

I need to emphasise that 'Footprints' is not a work of fiction. It is essentially factual and was never designed to be entertaining. My main concern throughout the work was to give my sons as full a picture as I possibly could of my life story. The first edition of the book had a very limited print run and was distributed to family and friends only. Based on the positive feedback I received from some of them – both family and friends – who said 'they simply could not put the book down', I decided to work on a revised edition which will be available to a wider readership.

I knew so little of the life of my own father – he was a rather quiet man and rarely talked about himself, not even to his children but I did know a bit more about my mother – who talked so much more. I sometimes wondered whether my sons – I have three of them – really know me? I am now in the twilight of my life and it may be that there are aspects of my life that they know little about. Quite apart from that,

I am sure that they know very little about their ancestry or the country their ancestors came from. This is something that needs to be corrected.

What is my legacy to my sons? I certainly do not see it in terms of worldly wealth I can bequeath to them. They have enough of that anyway which they have earned by the sweat of their own brows. I would rather see my legacy not in terms of what I leave for them at my death but rather what I have been leaving for them by my life.

Amid all the stresses and strains of life; of bringing up a family whilst grappling with career and ambition; whilst striving at the same time for fulfilment and peace, I hope I have, together with their mother, given our sons a stable home environment – a place where they felt safe; where they were loved; where they would always be welcome and where they could grow and be free to find their own place in the sun.

Although our lives have been and still are separated by great distances and may be even more so in the future, it is a very great comfort that whenever we meet the encounters are joyful and whenever we are unable to meet we keep in touch by whatever means are available to us. I hope that we have left them many pleasant memories of times gone by. And if by chance I got to know that they think warmly of us from time to time as they journey on through life, I would smile and say to myself, 'hey, we did not do too badly after all!' Needless to say, their mother would have been over the moon!

When I reflect upon my life, I realise that I may not always have taken the time to explain my actions or keep the family fully informed. My sons need to know the decisions as well as the choices I made especially when they became a part of my life and to know that they were always in my focus and that of their mother. If we have left behind some wisdom and common sense from our own life experiences that they can learn and benefit from, it would indeed be an added bonus.

Where my own parents were concerned, I would have liked to have known much more about their lives and that of their own parents. Alas when one is young one tends to show little interest in one's ancestry. But when interest finally awakens, the subjects have long passed away. This is exactly my predicament. Life is so very fleeting. Just like footprints, they fade away – here today and gone tomorrow.

Perhaps the family story could over a period of time be continued, enlarged and even corrected as new information comes to hand and new strands of the family are traced to the far corners of the earth. Even at the present time, the strands of both sides of the family stretch to four continents – to North America, Europe, Asia and Australia.

While I have included some photographs at various points within the text to add some colour and interest to the narrative, I have relegated all documents, including the family trees, to the Appendices so that they (or the originals there-from) could be referred to, if necessary, and further deductions drawn from them that I may have overlooked. I do realize that in the pursuit of career, I may have placed too heavy a burden on Annette – the boys' mother, to keep the home fires burning. She did an excellent job to be sure.

There were indeed national accolades and some sense of achievement for me personally, as well as for their mother, but these are soon forgotten and are really of little consequence – in the ultimate analysis, it is family that is the most important.

All persons mentioned in the book are real and have mostly been identified by their first names. Most of the older generation in my family have passed away. I have told the story as it is and without malice to anyone.

"I now see that stepping into the unknown isn't about being blind or uncertain. There's no need to let go of everything that got me to this point. Quite the opposite is true. Embracing the unknown is about accepting every aspect of the past. It comes from acknowledging the footprints of your life without wanting to retrace your steps"

Simon Peter Moxham – Ripples of Stillness, 2016, p 70

Donald Wijasuriya

Acknowledgements

I am greatly indebted to my father, James Robert Solomon Wijasuriya for carefully preserving over the years a collection of documents, papers, photographs and other memorabilia from which I was able to build my ancestral links.

For the rest of my life story, I had to delve into the inner recesses of my mind. Karen Gourley who came into my life the year after Annette died, listened with great interest to reminiscences of my past life, wrote it all down in her own handwriting and even prepared the Wijasuriya Family Tree. I am greatly indebted to Karen for pages and pages of her invaluable notes which helped me to get started with the writing of Footprints and putting together a coherent account of my ancestry and my life.

I am also indebted to Annette who prepared the Jayatilaka Family Tree nearly 15 years earlier but did not get to write more than a few pages before illness struck her down. Understandably, the Jayatilaka component is somewhat sketchy as Annette wrote so little of her own life.

A special word of appreciation to my eldest son Rohan for his continued interest in my writing as well as feedback from time to time which kept me going and helped with some additions and corrections. Despite his busy travel and work schedule, he dropped in on business trips to Perth to sort out computer glitches and help me in setting up backup copies as the work progressed.

Rienzi, my second son – usually the silent one and not especially known for his interest in books or reading, actually read through the entire manuscript. This gave me further encouragement.

Finally, I am especially grateful to Renan, my youngest son for scanning photographs and documents, adding in captions, inserting the photographs at appropriate sections in the manuscript and redrawing the Family Trees. In addition, Renan painstakingly read through the entire manuscript, gave me the benefit of so many helpful comments, created a new Title Page and reformatted the entire manuscript for the printers.

I would indeed be remiss if I failed to also acknowledge the work put in by Peter Schenk of Graphic Elements, not only for the cover design but also for fine tuning the manuscript and facilitating its transmission to the printers.

To all of you, I say thank you. I could not have completed Footprints without your help.

Sajak

Naungan Baru

Dalam samar-samar hening pagi
Mentari, kau mengintai dicelah dedaun
Nan melambai kehadiranku
Angin pagi bertiup sepi
Sepi sesunyi hatiku ini

> *Perjalananku berlalu bagai angin*
> *Kelilingku hingar bingar tak menentu*
> *Tiba-tiba...*
> *Oh...*
> *Terhenti sejenak daku terpaku*
> *Hai!!! gerangan siapakah itu?*
> *Ah...*
> *Tampannya dia*
> *Namun kau terus berlaku*
> *Tanpaku tahuarah mana tujuan mu*

Masa berlalu
Pertemuan berulang lagi
Kini, setelahku temui pencarianku
Rupanya aku bernaung di bawah bayu

Musripun Nangin
Perpustakaan Negara Malaysia

The Shelter of the Breeze

In the haze of the morning stillness
The sun, you peer between the leaves
To note my presence
The morning wind blows lonely
As lonely as this heart of mine
    My journey passes like the wind
    Around me the commotion is bewildering
    Suddenly...
    Oh...
    I stop rooted
    Oh!!! who may that be?
    Ah...
    Handsome he is
    But you move on
    And I don't know where you go
Time passes
We meet again
Now, I've found what I'm looking for
Truly I shelter under the breeze

Musripun Nangin
National Library of Malaysia

Translated by Ungku Maimunah Mohd Tahir

Poem composed by Musripun Nangin and recited by her at my official retirement.

Excerpt from The Information Challenge: a Festschrift in honour of Dr. Donald Wijasuriya. Edited by Ch'ng Kim See. Kuala Lumpur, Knowledge Publishers, 1995.

Ancestral Threads

But where should I begin? How far back can I go? The dearth of documented evidence is a serious stumbling block. All those earlier generations in our family tree have long since departed from this earth. My siblings who are still alive may have some recollection of our childhood years but on the whole I feel I have to dig deep into my mind to tell you this story.

I may have to speculate, make deductions and draw conclusions on those parts of the story that are unclear but I shall try to weave as full a picture as I possibly can and leave my readers to draw their own conclusions.

To me the story of my own life seems somewhat mundane and I often questioned those who read earlier drafts of the manuscript as to whether it came across as a boring account. Most of them thought otherwise - those who know me a little or think they do.

I have never maintained a personal diary - recording events, happenings, feelings or reactions to anything or anyone on a daily basis. My diary has always been in my mind. I may not remember specific dates as such but it is quite amazing what I have been able to call back to mind. However, writers sometimes suffer from a maladay known as selective amnesia - to blot out what has been unpleasant or embarrassing. I am no different.

I can only trace back, albeit somewhat sketchily, family links to my grandfathers - for my sons it would be their great grandfathers.

I never knew my paternal or my maternal grandfather – they both died long before I was born. Coincidentally, both my grandfathers were born and grew up in Matale – in the hill country of Ceylon, in the late 19th Century. I am unable to trace the family story any further back.

I never knew my maternal grandmother either. I very much doubt that my mother did as well, since she never spoke of her own mother and neither did her own siblings – I must conclude that their mother died when they were toddlers and hence they scarcely remembered her. My paternal grandmother however lived with the family in my youth and I got to know her.

Ours is the story of a Sri Lankan family – a simple, ordinary Sri Lankan family. Much of the story is factual and is based on real persons, many of whom I have known but have long faded away. Since the family story can be traced back to our ancestral homeland (Ceylon/Sri Lanka), I have attempted to provide a brief backdrop of the country setting in the times of my grandfathers to provide a better understanding of the ancestral roots.

In narrating the family story, it is more than likely that I may have to speculate, make deductions and draw conclusions on those parts of the story that are unclear. However, I shall try to weave as full a picture as I possibly can and leave my readers to draw their own conclusions.

Don Clement

My maternal grandfather Don Clement de Silva was born in Matale, Ceylon on 23rd November 1881. (It is interesting to note that my mother was born on 22nd November 1910 in

Colombo, Ceylon while I was born on 22nd November 1934 in Kuala Lumpur, Federated Malay States). My mother's Certificate of Birth, Ceylon (or Birth Certificate as it is commonly referred to) is really not an original document but an extract from the records at the Registrar-General's Office, Colombo dated 2nd June 1939 – an extract of the official record which was requested nearly 29 years later, long after my mother was born, had married and left her homeland. This is a story in itself and one could speculate as to the circumstances that necessitated it. Nevertheless, it is my main documentary source.

Since then, I have obtained additional information from my first cousin Sybil in Sri Lanka – information which she herself obtained from her mother (my Aunty Sally – who was my mother's younger sister). Nothing is known about Don Clement's parents but it is known that he had three other siblings – an elder sister who was known as Matale Aunty and two younger brothers named Henry and Raphael.

Arranged marriages appeared to be the order of the day in the late 19th and early 20th centuries as the three de Silva brothers – Clement, Henry and Raphael – married the four Fonseka sisters (Josephine, Cecilia, Maggie and Matilda). Clement married the two elder sisters – both of whom died after bearing several children – my mother was the eldest of Don Clement's second wife, after which he married a third wife – Gladys Perera.

In my mother's Birth Certificate (or extract), it is recorded the grandfather's rank or profession was 'Estate Clerk' while my mother told me that her father was in charge of the New Peradeniya Estate. However the information I have obtained from Sybil indicated that grandfather was Superintendent of the New Peradeniya Estate. A further detail that I was unaware of was that grandfather did not die of natural causes. My mother only told me that her father died when she was 11 years old – she must have known what actually happened but chose not to reveal any of this to me. However I now understand that grandfather died rather young as he was poisoned by the tea taster on the Estate. Sybil's mother (my Aunty Sally) remembers her father throwing up blood as a result of the poisoning and that the priest had to be called in to administer the last sacraments as grandfather lay dying.

It seems more than likely that grandfather was actually Superintendent of the Estate rather than just the Estate Clerk – as otherwise, who would simply want to poison the Estate Clerk? An Estate Clerk was unlikely to have much clout and therefore not worth disposing of. While such an analysis, so very long after it happened may seem somewhat cold and dispassionate today, it must have been a traumatic event then. Whether the perpetrator was apprehended and sentenced is not known.

It does appear that grandfather as well as his brothers were in the tea business and were superintendents or managers on tea estates or plantations in Peradeniya and Mawanella. I doubt very much that any of them owned these tea estates. It is more than likely that the tea estates were British owned while the labour force was comprised largely of Tamils who were brought in from South India as tea pickers. This is perhaps why the Superintends or Managers on the estates were often referred to as PDs – Peria Dorai (Big Boss) - in Tamil.

According to my mother, her father was educated, cultured and bi-lingual and spoke English and Sinhalese equally well. She also said her father spoke a little Tamil. Apart from that, grandfather also lectured to agricultural students at the botanical gardens in Peradeniya and served as accountant and book keeper on the estate as well. The New Peradeniya Estate was a tea plantation in the environs of Peradeniya, which was very close to Kandy, in the very heart of the hill country. My mother's childhood home – the estate bungalow her father was assigned – still stood on the sloping hill-side, on the outer fringe of the University of Ceylon. My mother pointed this out to us when the family visited Ceylon in 1950.

Don Clement was somewhat of an entrepreneur as well. He recognised that the tea pluckers and other workers on the estate would need access to provisions and other basic necessities for everyday living and accordingly set up a sundry provision store on a piece of land he owned close by. My mother often stopped by her father's little shop for sweets or lollies.

In tracing my Sinhalese or Sri Lankan ancestral roots, some clarification of the Sinhalese or Sri Lankan naming system is necessary. In the times of my grandparents and great grandparents – the Western concept of a surname was unknown. Instead, there is a clan name which appears before the given names. This is called 'vaasagama' which literally means resident village. The clan name ends with the 'ge' followed by the given names. Hence everything before the 'ge' is the clan name while 'ge' also means 'gedera' or house as well as possession.

In the late 19th Century, the upper class elites or native peoples (called Ceylonese by the British) formed a second class group in their own country serving their colonial masters. The elites maintained their status – such as it were – on the basis of landholdings inherited over many generations and being given posts in the colonial administration. Initially, these posts were limited to 'Rate Mahattaya' in the highlands and 'Mudaliyars' in the coastal lowlands.

The next level of social stratification were the upper middle class of native professionals – doctors, lawyers. academics, senior civil servants, traders and merchants – many of whom had the benefit of an English education in missionary schools as well as study in British universities. Ceylon's aspiring political leadership largely came from this group. Then came the lower middle class, consisting of individuals who were also educated in English but were not well-heeled enough to attend British universities – public servants, policemen, teachers, estate clerks. My maternal grandfather probably came from this group.

The whole subject of caste and clan in Sinhalese society is very complex and further research into my ancestral 'ge' names will be necessary in order to show social status, association with a trade and occupation or place name. At this stage, my remarks in this regard are indicative, but not necessarily conclusive.

The very long Sinhalese names, incorporating both the clan and the given names came to be progressively shortened with the clan names being shown only by initials. With increasing western influence, particularly the British, the surname concept was adopted and clan names, even its initials were gradually dropped.

When I was born, my Birth Certificate did not record any clan or 'ge' name, neither was it recorded as part of my parents' names. But I had three given names – Donald, Earlian, Kingsley. I was always Donnie at home and simply Donald to my friends. In my professional life my name was cited in full as D.E.K. Wijasuriya. In more recent times I have simplified my name to Donald Wijasuriya. I never ever used the names Earlian or Kingsley.

In my parents' generation and perhaps in the generation before them too, it was the norm to conform or emulate the British in almost everything – becoming proficient in the English language; adopting western table manners and western dress. My aunts (Dad's sisters in the Malay States) kept up with the latest fashions – high heels, stockings, long gloves and fashionable hats. Photographs of my aunts in the family album in the fashionable attire of the early thirties attest to this fact. By contrast, my mum's sisters in Sri Lanka dressed in more traditional garb – in sarees, worn in the Kandyan style.

Many of us, not only in my generation but the previous generation too, were saddled with English names or even Biblical sounding names. I would have been far more comfortable with a Sinhalese name – I was never given one. I am eternally grateful to my parents however for not naming me Abraham or Moses. I am also grateful that I was not given any of my father's forenames – James Robert Solomon – especially Solomon. I surely would not have survived that!

Getting back to my maternal grandfather, it is a matter of record that in my mother's Birth Certificate, her father's name is given as Kelaniya Hettiarachige Don Clement de Silva. The name is quite intriguing. The surname in particular, 'de Silva' (it could well have been 'da Silva') seems to suggest, way back in the dim mists of history, some linkages or perhaps indiscretions of my Sinhalese ancestors with the Portuguese mariners who came to Ceylon in the 16th Century.

Whether these liaisons were formalised in marriage to local maidens or were casual indiscretions we will never know. But it is quite true that Portuguese men were encouraged to take native Sinhalese women as their wives.

The Portuguese seafarers who came to the country in the 16th Century were quick to see that the island was a major centre for the cultivation and trade in the exotic spices of the East – cinnamon, pepper, cloves, cardamom, fennel and cumin – to name but a few. The Portuguese wanted to acquire a major slice of the spice trade and set up a virtual monopoly – especially in relation to other countries in Europe.

But to establish and maintain a monopoly, it was necessary to take control – and that the Portuguese did – at the behest and with the cooperation of the King of Kotte – mostly in the littoral or coastal areas of the country, except the Kandyan Kingdom. However it is not part of my story to detail the power intrigues of Sinhalese 'royalty' at that time – history buffs will need to look elsewhere.

In the wake of the Portuguese came the Christian missionaries, especially the Franciscans and the Jesuits. As a result, many Sinhalese and most probably my grandfathers were 'Christianised'. This did not go down too well with the Buddhists, who constituted the majority of the population at that time.

Sri Lanka has mesmerised the West since ancient times and has variously been called Serendip, Taprobane, Zeilan, Seyllan, Ceylon and other names. Arab, Indian and Chinese traders have visited the island over the centuries but only the Europeans claimed and took possession by the power of the gun and sword – as they have done throughout history in many parts of the world.

Don Clement was born in Matale in the heart of the hill country. The snobbery of categorising an individual as 'up country' Sinhalese as contrasted with their 'low country' countrymen based on their place of birth was quite meaningless as they were all part of the same ethnic group without any dialect or cultural differences. The more significant social grouping however was based on caste and clan. Don Clement was most likely of the Govigama caste. The Govigama are traditionally associated with land ownership and cultivation. While Don Clement was educated as far as was possible under the British yoke, the family were certainly not wealthy landowners.

Making further deductions from Don Clement's name, the initial part of the name 'Kelaniya' is a place name in the environs of Colombo while 'Hettiarachige' may refer to a

(**footnote**. The religious composition of Sri Lanka's population, according to the 2011 Census was as follows: Buddhist 70.02%; Hindu 12.6%; Muslim 9.7%; Christians 7.4%. It is likely that the overall percentage of the Buddhist population in the late 19th Century would have been even greater – although the total population was so much smaller; the 1901 census only recorded a total population of 3,565, 954. Decennial census taking was introduced by the British from 1901)

clan name and shows affiliation to household, trade or a 'ge' name. Even the term 'Don' for the male and 'Donna' for the female may also suggest Portuguese linkages. Clement was his very own or personal name and it smacks of Christian or more specifically, Catholic connections. Could the Portuguese - Sri Lankan inter ethnic mix within the family have produced any progeny who were spirited back to Portugal ? Who knows, but it is an intriguing thread to explore.

Don Clement was probably the scion of the house of Hettiarachi of Kelaniya. But what of my grandmother – who was she and where did she come from? Gleaning once again from my mother's Birth Certificate, my grandmother's name was Weera Narayanna Mudalige Cecilia Fonseka. The "Hettiarachi" and "Mudalige" in my maternal grandparents names may suggest some social standing within a caste or clan but it is unclear whether it was within the dominant castes of the time – namely the Salagama, the Govigama or the Karave. Grandmother's forename Cecilia suggests a Christian or Catholic background. The surname Fonseka itself may point to some Portuguese connections. Without further research, however, all this is conjecture.

My mother, Donna Cecilia Mabel Florinda de Silva was born on the 22nd of November 1910. She was born in

(**footnote** : In the sixteenth Century, when the Portuguese began to establish their dominance in the spice trade in Ceylon, the Salagama rose in importance as the caste mainly responsible for the collection of cinnamon. The cinnamon peelers (kurundukara) were a grade within the Salagama. Rivalries between the Salagama, the Govigama and the Karave elite seemed to have continued even to my grandparents generation. Many of the elite within these castes were Christianised and accumulated wealth and landholdings. I have heard my mother mention in discussions with Nanny her own Govigama background while my father was Karave. By the early decades of the 20th Century, when my parents got married, caste distinctions had greatly blurred)

Kotahena (Colombo) but her birth was only registered on the 10th February 1911 in the Register of Births, Registrar General of Births, Deaths and Marriages in the Island of Ceylon. After her came her brother Theodore (Tiddy) and two sisters – Celine and Stella. My grandmother was actually grandfather's second wife whom he married after his first wife (who was grandmother's elder sister) died. There were two sons by the first wife – Percival and Stanley (my step-uncles so to speak).

The marriage photograph of grandfather (in top hat and tails) and grandmother is in the best traditions of the day – very Western and very British. It is more than likely that it was a church wedding in Colombo – specifically in Kotehena (where my mother was born). According to the fashion of the day, grandfather sported a luxurious moustache.

But did grandfather call it a day then? Oh no! He got married a third time to a much younger woman (my step-grandma whom I got to know) who bore him three more children – Trixie, Gerry and Gladys. All in all, grandfather fathered nine children. Had it not been for his premature death (he was not even 40) he could well have fathered a few more – a veritable Sri Lankan cricket team, except that most of his children were girls while the males never played cricket as far as I know! The whole of my maternal brood have long since passed away.

(**footnote**. When my step-grandma died in the 1970s, the Kossinna estate was sold and my mother's share of the proceeds of the sale was handed to me by Aunty Sally on one of my visits to Sri Lanka. Since at that time it was not possible to convert Sri Lankan Rupees to US Dollars or Malaysian Ringgit and take it out of the country, I gave the money to Aunty Sally to be shared between her and Aunty Girlie as theirs were the two homes I spent some of my semester breaks in. I subsequently gave the equivalent sum in Malaysian Ringgit to my mother.)

All Mum's sisters in Sri Lanka were very nice – Aunty Sally(Celine) and Aunty Stella (who became a nun and was called Sister Mary Clementa) as well as Mum's step sisters, Aunty Trixie and Aunty Girlie (Gladys). All my uncles whom my aunts married – Uncle Francis (Navaratne), Uncle Jacky(Perera), Uncle Norbert(Manatunga) and Uncle George(Jayasinghe) were very nice too. I never met Mum's step brothers Stanley or Gerry while her own brother Theodore (Tiddy Uncle) was a bit of a pain. Mum's step brother Percy was the doyen of the family. I also got to know members of my step-grandma's family – she had two brothers who were married with children – Uncle Wilfred and Uncle Godwin and two unmarried sisters.

It is to be noted that grandfather married three times and it is more than likely that all these marriages were arranged and that a dowry was paid every time – for these were the norms and conventions of the time. It is more than likely that the Kossinna property was grandfather's legacy to the family. I never knew what happened to the rest of grandfather's estate.

From the stories my mother related, grandfather was a rather jolly soul who liked a tipple from time to time and sometimes came home in the evening, somewhat inebriated. He would line up his children and sing a little ditty to them, which my mother used to sing to us. My mother simply loved to sing – and in my mind's eye, I can still picture her – slim and beautiful – singing to us.

The lyrics of the ditty went like this:

> *"I walked into my parlour to see what I could find*
> *I found there three gentlemen hats, one by two by three*

I called to my loving wife, wife come here and see
How came these three gentlemen hats without the leave of me
You blind fool, you silly fool, can't you very well see
They are the three flower pots mother sent to me
Ho'b- nob, here is one flower pot with whiskers on
A thing I never did see
And now and then when I go out the sight when I come in"

While my grandfather was still alive, my mother's life was pleasant and comfortable enough. My mother schooled at the Kandy Convent and related how she travelled to school in a horse drawn buggy. However, grandfather died when she was only eleven and her schooling came to an abrupt end.

My mother also mentioned the trips with her family to the Madhu Church festival. The Madhu Church which was a shrine dedicated to the Virgin Mary, is located in the Mannar district in the North West of the country, virtually in the wilderness. The family travelled by bullock cart and the journey took 1-2 days. The family group usually comprised 2-3 bullock carts. My mother really enjoyed those trips. The bullock cart 'drivers' did most of the heavy work while the women folk prepared all the meals on open fires.

Sleeping on mats in the open under clear moon-lit skies was unforgettable. My mother described the flickering oil lamps (kuppi lampuwa) hanging from the thatched roofs of the bullock carts as well as the aromatic smells which wafted from the bubbling curries in chutty pots placed over make-shift stone fire places. The bullock cart 'drivers' were quite resourceful. The Madhu festival was attended by thousands of Catholic devotees but also attracted Buddhists, Hindus and Moslems. During the civil war in Sri Lanka, access to Madhu was restricted as it was in the heart of the conflict zone.

It is rather curious that in my mother's growing up years in Ceylon in the early decades of the 20th Century, my mother never mentioned travel within the country by train, considering that the rail network was well in place by then. It is quite possible that in her growing up years (after the death of her father) – serving virtually as hand-maiden in the homes of her relatives – she would not have been given any opportunity to travel.

Considering that my mother lived in Peradeniya, schooled in Kandy and got married in Matale – all in the hill country, she never ever mentioned visiting Nuwara Eliya – the hill resort the Brits and the native elites frequented, to escape from the heat and humidity of Colombo and the lowlands. The Brits often took their horses along to be entered in the Nuwara Eliya Cup. Horse racing was very popular all over the country. I very much doubt that my mother travelled to Nuwera Eliya even when her father was alive – as she never spoke of it.

Although my mother said that she was taken to school in a horse drawn cart. I very much doubt that her father maintained a stable of racehorses or participated in horse racing. It is more than likely that the horse and cart were hired and that the horse was long past its racing days.

In the early years of the twentieth century, it was unusual for legal provisions to be made to ensure that the estate of a deceased person would pass on to his legitimate heirs.

I greatly doubt therefore that grandfather had a Last Will and Testament. He left his estate in the hands of his brother Henry, with the expectation that his family would be looked after. But little of this ever happened.

My mother spent the next ten years of her life being shunted from pillar to post in the homes of her relatives where she had to do the cooking, cleaning and other household chores– and thus she grew into adulthood.

Don Clement de Silva and Cecilia Fonseka
Maternal grandfather and grandmother

My mother never mentioned what happened to her siblings but did say that her step-mother (the step- grandma I later came to know) took care of her own three children.

James Peter

Moving now to my paternal grandfather, the lack of documented evidence is again a major impediment. I knew very little of him. I have no recollection of my father ever mentioning him. I wonder why? Admittedly, my grandfather died young too – my father was barely 15 years old and was still in school then. Regrettably, I only have a single photograph of my paternal grandfather which I recently obtained from my cousin Bernard Wijesuria (note difference in spelling).

James Peter Wijasuriya
Paternal grandfather

In tracing my ancestral forebears, much information was gleaned from my mother's birth certificate, but in the case of my father, I have been unable to trace his own birth certificate, which could have yielded much information. It appears that my father's birth certificate had been misplaced or lost, but when exactly is anybody's guess. It does not also appear that birth certificates were as crucial documents of identity then as they are today.

What is most interesting is that my father applied for and obtained an 'Extract' in respect of his own birth records from the Register of Births, Negeri Sembilan (part of the Malay States) on 24th March 1955 – nearly fifty years after he was born. I am sure that this was done to prove that he was born in the Malay States, as this would have been a pre-requisite in applying for Citizenship of the Federation of Malaya. Malaya obtained its Independence from Britain in 1957.

Even more astonishing is the information shown on the 'Extract' as it is replete with errors. Firstly, my father's name is given as 'Saliman' and his father's name is simply recorded as Wijasuriya, J R. Who is this J.R.? In other documents – more reliable perhaps, (which I shall cite later), my grandfather's name is given as James Peter. Hence where the J.R. comes from is a matter of conjecture. Even my grandmother's name is grossly misspelt and is recorded as Mary Joskpere Jayatelaka!

It is not at all clear whether these errors were introduced when the 'Extract' was written out or whether the errors were in the original birth records. Clearly, clerical support at the Office of the Registrar of Births, Deaths and Marriages in the Malay States was seriously wanting.

It must be remembered that British Colonial policy in the Malay States was only designed to train locals to fill subordinate clerical positions. The bosses were all 'Orang Puteh' or white men. Other errors in the Extract in regard to my father will be touched upon later.

All that is known about James Peter is that he was born on 13th May, 1870 in Matale, Central Province, Ceylon; that he enrolled as a contributor to the Widows and Orphans Pension Fund (WOPF) (in the Malay States) on 1st January 1904; that he retired on 11th August 1919 and died on 29th October 1919. Interestingly, these facts only came to light in a signed Memo from the Secretary, Widows and Orphans Pensions Office, Kuala Lumpur dated 26th June 1954 – well over thirty years after James Peter died. One wonders why an excerpt of these records had to be solicited nearly 50 years after grandfather became a contributor to the WOPF.

While these facts about grandfather refer to records in the Malay states, the only details sourced from Ceylon – the Notice of Marriage, St Thomas' Church, Matale dated 18th July 1931 (when my father and mother got married) – only mentions grandfather's full name as – Wijesundara Arachige James Peter Wijesuriya. This bit of information could only have been furnished by my father himself and may have been obtained from his mother (our Nanny) who was present at the wedding along with my father's sister (our Aunty Gladys). Nanny however was not included in the wedding photograph.

Nanny (who JP later married in Kuala Lumpur, although no records exist of this marriage either) could have been an excellent source for tracing the Wijasuriya branch of the family in Ceylon. Alas, this does not appear to have ever been explored and has been lost forever.

In Sri Lanka, most persons with the surname Wijesuriya spell the name as 'Wijesuriya'. However the variant spelling of the surname (Wijasuriya and Wijasuria) in my father's birth records resulted in all of us (his children) being saddled not only with a somewhat un-Sinhalese version of the surname but also with an inelegant pronounciation of the name. I have learned to live with the surname as rendered in my own birth records but pronounce it with a softer rendering of the 'ja'.

It is rather curious that Nanny never spoke of grandfather to any of us and as I stated earlier, neither did my Dad. I wonder what my Dad called his parents. I am quite sure it was never Daddy and Mummie; more likely it was Tahtha or Appa and Amma. I have heard Aunty Baby (Dad's youngest sister) call her mother Mumma – but all of us called her Nanny.

Since it has been documented that grandfather was born in Matale, Central Province, Ceylon in 1871, any attempt to trace James Peter's own parents or siblings will require research and travel in Sri Lanka in order to trace relatives who may still be alive. It is to be noted that compulsory registration of births and deaths was only introduced by the British in 1895. However, Church records have also existed in Ceylon since the 17th century and could be a source of information, but such records were mostly for the Dutch and the 'Christianised' Sri Lankans. These records were maintained by the Dutch Reformed Church.

In the late 19th century, the revival of Buddhism led to increasing clashes with the Christians and introduced further uncertainties as the country struggled to come to terms with its colonial masters. The Buddhist revival was spearheaded by laymen – mostly wealthy landowners, traders and entrepreneurs, most of whom were members of the Karava, Salagama and Durawa castes.

Wijesundara Arachige James Peter Wijesuriya – my grandfather – was part of the Karava Suriya Clan. The majority of Karava 'ge' names reveal military, naval or allied occupations. Whether James Peter took his clan and caste seriously; whether he felt any sense of superiority because of it or was simply irritated by all of it, we simply do not know.

The question of clan and caste has bedevilled the island for centuries. Numerically the largest group have been the Govigama – the people associated with the land, mostly as tillers of the land rather than as land owners. Govigama people provided the backbone of 'rajakaraya' or service to the king.

The Karava, on the other hand, were more exclusive. Karava people, unlike service castes are completely independent and do not owe any loyalty or service to royalty – they chose their own allegiances to kings and kingdoms.

Karavas in the 19th century, had not only a distinct clan name and identity but also their own flag and standard. Such identities are still strongly evident in Negombo, Chilaw and towns north of Colombo. The wealth of the Karavas led them to challenge the Govigamas for social supremacy.

Clan and caste rivalries in the late 19th century have spilled over into the 20th century and were effectively exploited by the British. British policies did promote ethnic competition by suggesting that 'Dravidian' Tamils and 'Aryan' Sinhalese were racially distinct, simply because the Tamil and Sinhalese languages belonged to different linguistic families.

This was but a reflection of the familiar British practice of 'divide and rule'.

Despite the socio-political complexities of the times, the clan and caste rivalries as well as the Buddhist/Christian clashes, there were no lack of career opportunities in Ceylon for James Peter. Assuming further, that James Peter came from a reasonably wealthy Karave background, it is difficult to fathom the reasons that made him leave his seemingly idyllic homeland.

Taking up the story line once again it, is reasonable to deduce that around 1895 grandfather left Ceylon and took ship to the Malay States. It is more than likely that grandfather did so in response to a British Colonial recruitment drive for skilled workers for the construction of railway track in the Malay States. These job advertisements appeared in the local newspapers in Colombo and it would have seemed to James Peter that he was not only assured of a job in the Malay States Railways (if selected) but that he would also receive free steamship passage to get there. It would have seemed like a win-win situation.

It is unlikely that the British were looking to recruit railway engineers from the ranks of the locals. Not only were steam engines or locomotives brought in by steamship to the Malay States, but key technical personnel were invariably recruited from the Colonial Service in British India. Local recruits (from Ceylon) were in demand mostly for the construction of track and the laying of sleepers and rails. This is where James Peter may have fitted in. It was hard work with extended periods spent in campsites along the track.

The tasks ahead would have been challenging if not downright daunting. The Malay Peninsula was densely forested and the central mountain range constituted a major barrier to east –west communication. There were also the swamps, floods, heavy downpours and landslides to contend with not to mention the major rivers to be crossed, the bridges to be built, the trees to be felled and the land surveyed. The political landscape with different states under the authority of individual rulers (Sultans) would have thrown up other challenges as well. James Peter would most likely have been a very small cog in this developing landscape – he lived, worked and died in the Malay States – with only a terse record in the Pension Office to attest to his presence in his adopted country.

Whatever motivated grandfather to leave his homeland for greener pastures abroad remains a complete mystery. Could it simply have been the challenge of youth and the driving urge to explore the world that motivated him? Or could it be because of the social changes taking place in Ceylon in the late 19th Century and the cultural and societal norms he was subject to which he found to be quite irksome. We will never know. But by doing so, he 'condemned' his progeny to live, work and seek their livelihood in the Malay world – away from their motherland.

Ancestral Country

It does seem appropriate at this stage to provide a thumb-nail sketch of Ceylon in the late 19th Century as a backdrop to understanding why my paternal grandfather left his motherland in his youth and as far as I know, never ever returned, not even for a visit.

My grandparents and generations before them were ethnic Sinhalese who lived out their lives on the Island of Ceylon. Although the British referred to the natives of the country as Ceylonese, the population of the country comprised not only of the ethnic Sinhalese majority but also of the minority Tamils who have lived in the North and East of the country for centuries. In the 19th Century however significant numbers of Tamils from South India were brought in by the British to work on the tea estates as well as the rubber and coffee plantations. Also to be included in the country demographic are the Moors (Indian Muslim traders), who have also lived in the country for centuries. There is also a small community of Malays who have made Ceylon their home.

The overall picture, however, would be incomplete without mention of the Burghers, a term collectively used to refer to the descendants of the Portuguese, Dutch and English who occupied the country in successive stages from the 16th Century and intermarried with the locals. The surnames of Burgher families gave some indication of their European heritage – British, Dutch or Portuguese.

Historical milieu

Both my paternal and maternal grandfathers were born in Matale, Ceylon in 1870 and 1881 respectively – they could well have attended the same school. It is unlikely at that time that there would have been more than one school to choose from – at least in the hill country. Matale was situated in the heart of the hill country, not far from Kandy – the Capital of the Kandyan Kingdom.

Colonial Ceylon

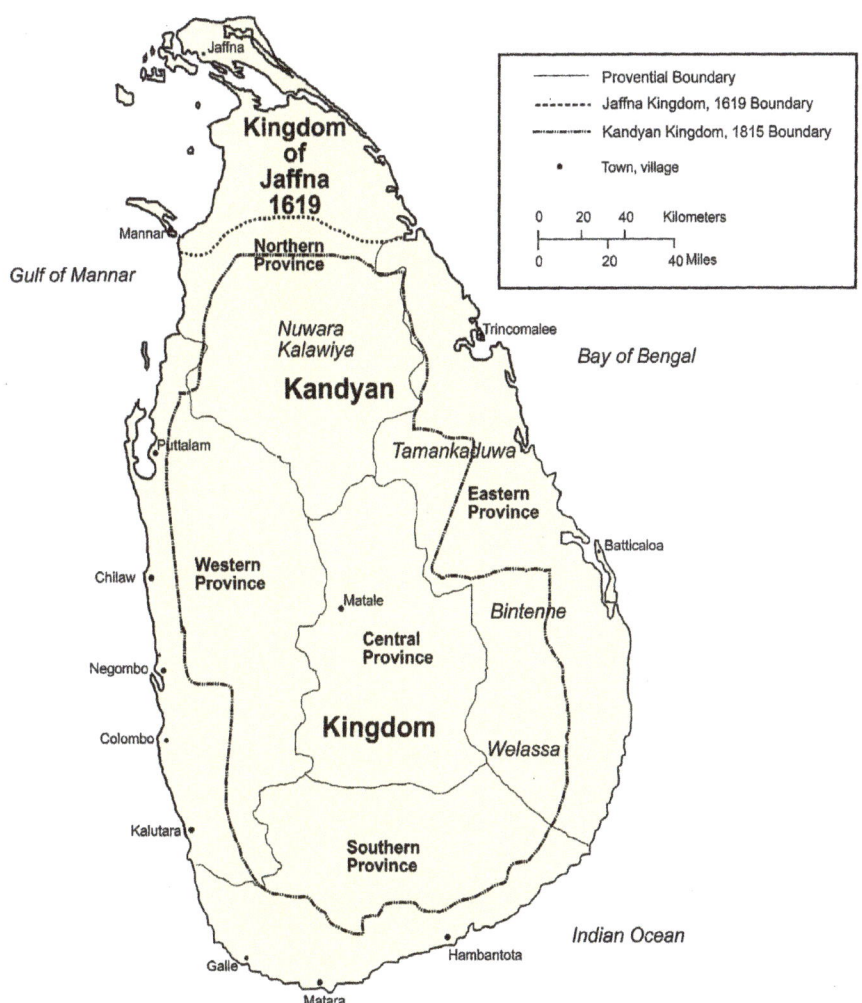

The Kandyan Kingdom was the last bastion of the Sinhalese who viewed the British with great suspicion and engaged in a bloody guerrilla warfare with the British in the early 19th Century. The rugged nature of the Kandyan Kingdom kept the British at bay – but not for long. The first and second Kandyan wars were soon over and by 1815, the Kingdom was formally ceded to the British. The whole island was now under British control and became a Crown Colony. The 'sudhas' (white man) were now in control. But simmering discontent led to the great rebellion in 1817-1818, which was the most formidable insurrection during the whole period of British rule in Ceylon. After a long and ruthless campaign the back of the resistance was broken and the British gained full control of the whole island.

Socio-economic conditions

In the late 19th Century, when my grandfathers were young men, the country was at peace. The coffee and tea estates continued to expand and British planters grew rich from the bounties of the land.

Financed by commercial enterprises in the British Isles, the Brits in the local colonial service purchased large acreages of crown land in the hill country at rock bottom prices for tea planting and leaned on the Colonial Government to bring in large numbers of indentured labour (mostly Tamils from South India) to work on the estates.

In the last quarter of the 19th Century, there was a significant recovery of the plantation sector after the coffee blight and the 3 major plantation crops – tea, rubber and coconut – became the basis of the country's economy. This in turn led to the progressive development of the road and rail network as well as the Port of Colombo, to facilitate the transport and export of these commodities. At the same time concerted efforts were made to repair the 'tanks' or reservoirs and restore the ancient irrigation systems of the country in order to revitalise peasant agriculture, especially rice cultivation.

Railways

The railway network in the country developed after the middle of the 19th Century. The Ceylon Government Railway(CGR) was established in 1858. By 1864, the line from Colombo to Ambepussa had been completed. In the years following, the rail service was extended to Kandy, Nawalapitiya, Nanu Oya, Bandarawela and Badulla. The line to Matale was added in 1880, the coastal railway line in 1895 and the northern line in 1905.

When James Peter was in his early twenties, there would have been ample opportunities for work in the rapidly expanding plantation sector, traditional agriculture and irrigation, the expanding road and rail network or even in commercial enterprises, export and shipping. It does appear however that James Peter may have obtained work in the developing railway network and acquired some experience in railway track construction and maintenance in Ceylon. This may have motivated him to venture abroad to further his career in the same line of work.

The Malay States

The Malay States in the first half of the 20th century, comprised of the Federated Malay States (FMS) and included the States of Perak, Selangor, Pahang and Negeri Sembilan; the Unfederated Malay States (UFMS) which included the States of Perlis, Kedah, Kelantan, Trengganu and Johore and the Straits Settlements (SS) which included Penang, Malacca and Singapore. The Straits Settlements came under direct British control as a crown Colony in 1867. Originally, the straits settlements were a group of British territories in southeast and east Asia controlled by the British East India Company.

The British presence in the Malay States was a logical progression of the trading activities of the British East India Company from the beginning of the 19th Century. In 1874, the Governor of the Straits Settlements, Sir Andrew Clarke concluded a treaty with the Sultan of Perak called the Pangkor Treaty which provided for a British Resident to advise the Sultan on all matters concerning the administration of the State while residual powers concerning Malay culture and religious matters remained in the hands of the Sultan. This pattern of local British Residents was later established in the States of Selangor, Pahang and Negeri Sembilan and these 4 protected Malay States were constituted as the Federated Malay States(FMS) in 1895.

The northern Malay states of Perlis, Kedah, Kelantan and Trengganu which functioned as vassal states of the Kingdom of Siam were ceded to the British in 1909. These states, collectively referred to as the Unfederated Malay States, (UFMS) included Johore in 1911.

By the turn of the century, real power in the Malay States or Tanah Melayu was in British hands – the terminology of the chief executive changed over the years from Governor, Resident General, High Commissioner and Chief Secretary. In fact little or nothing could be effected in the Malay States without their endorsement. In all reality, it was British Malaya and remained so until the Japanese Occupation of the Malay peninsula, 1942-1945.

The immediate aftermath of the war, saw a brief period of British Military Administration (BMA) followed by the establishment of the Malayan Union(MU) in 1946 which brought together all states in the Malay Peninsula but excluded Singapore. The MU was dissolved in 1948 and replaced with the Federation of Malaya which achieved independence from Great Britain in August 1957. Singapore remained a British crown colony. Modern day Malaysia was established in 1963 with the addition of Singapore and the British territories of Sarawak and North Borneo. Singapore however seceded in 1965 and became a fully independent Republic.

James Peter did work on the railways in the Malay States. In the Selangor Establishment List (which is a list of government employees in the State of Selangor <Malay States>) grandfather's name: James Peter Wijasuriya is recorded as Foreman Plate Layer.

It must be pointed out however that being a plate layer is one of the lowlier jobs within the railway system. A plate layer is responsible for the laying of track – which is back breaking work while a foreman is responsible not only for overall supervision in the laying of sleepers and lines but also in inspecting and maintaining a section of railway track. Being a foreman may have been just a notch up the totem pole but it was a hard life and certainly nothing to crow about.

It does appear that moving from idyllic Ceylon to a low paying job in the Malay States may have been a jump from the frying pan into the fire! At the very least, it was a move from one tropical country to another – but still under the British yoke.

Very little is known of grandfather's personal life. However, it is known that in his early years in the Malay States, grandfather had a relationship with a young Japanese woman. We do not know her name, where she came from and what she was doing in the Malay States. She came into grandfather's life as mysteriously as she faded away. For ease of reference I have named her Akiko. Here again, one sees the unconventional nature of the man – instead of seeking refuge within the confines of his own little community in the Malay States, he chose to look beyond.

James Peter's relationship with Akiko was unusual to say the least. It would have raised many eyebrows in his day – particularly within the Japanese community who would have strongly disapproved of one of their fair daughters getting romantically involved with a 'gaijin' or foreigner. The same sentiments would have prevailed within the even smaller Sinhalese community.

While Imperial Japan has long had designs on lands beyond its insular borders – designs carefully camouflaged – which culminated in Japan's military thrust into South East Asia in the Second World War, Japan had hardly emerged from the dark ages in the late 19th Century. It was only decades later that Japan began to flex its military muscles – mostly in

China in the Sino Japanese War as well as the Russo Japanese War when Japan captured Port Arthur from the Russians in 1905.

It is quite interesting to note that in the early years of the 20th Century, there were Japanese business enclaves in the Malay States. It is reported that over 1776 Japanese were employed in the rubber plantations and Japanese companies owned 170,000 acres of rubber plantations in Negeri Sembilan (where James Peter worked) and in Johore.

It is quite unlikely that Akiko was in the Malay States on her own. It is possible that she may have been visiting members of her family engaged in trade and commerce in the Malay States. Or, one might even speculate that Akiko was brought in to tutor children within the Japanese community. There are so many possibilities. It must be noted that in the 1911 Census, there were 2029 Japanese living in the Malay States, the greater percentage being females.

My speculations about Akiko could be pure fiction of course – just a fanciful notion on my part to add a measure of glamour and mystery to the ancestral threads. But to come down to earth, James Peter and Akiko had a daughter born on 9th January 1899, named Ada.

Were James Peter and Akiko really married in the legal sense or was Akiko simply his consort? If they were married, was it a church wedding or were they married in a Shinto ceremony in accordance with Japanese custom. Alas, we will never know. What impact this had on James Peter is also not known. It is most unusual for little Ada to be with her father rather than her mother, unless something untoward happened to her mother.

Not surprisingly, with a little daughter on his hands, James Peter married Mary Josephine Jayatilaka (our Nanny) on 21st December 1904, in Mission House, Bluff Road, Kuala Lumpur. Nanny readily took in little Ada and brought her up as one of the family.

Mission House no longer exists while Bluff Road was later renamed Jalan Bukit Aman. Little is known of grandfather's life. He died on 29th October 1919 and was buried at the Venning Road Cemetry. The Venning Road Cemetry is no longer in existence as the site has been taken over for the National Mosque or Masjid Negara. Venning Road has been renamed Jalan Perdana.

To return to my story – Mary Josephine was about 23 when she got married. She was born on 28th May 1881. It is logical to assume that Mary Josephine was born in Ceylon – possibly in a suburb of Colombo called Grand Pass (since several of her sisters are known to have lived there and owned property there). It would also be quite logical to assume that the marriage was 'arranged' as this was the prevailing practice at that time. Who did the arranging and whether a dowry was paid is not known.

To digress a little, Aunty Ada later married Dan Leardam and they had several children. I remember a few of them – Gwen, Nita and Geoffrey. I also remember that Dan Leardam – their father – simply disappeared before the war ended.

Uncle Dan's disappearance must have been a very traumatic experience within the Leardam family. While Aunty Ada, Nanny, my Dad and Mum and members of the older generation may have been in the know as to what really happened, the matter was never discussed within the family. Now that I reflect upon it all, it may explain why Geoffrey – Leardam's eldest son, came to live with us in Bukit Nanas and attend school at SJI. I do not know what happened to Geoffrey's sisters. It is likely that the older girls were placed at the Convent in Bukit Nanas leaving Aunty Ada to cope with the little ones only. Aunty Baby was then at the Convent too.

When the family were living in Port Swettenham, Nita used to be 'going out' or dating Uncle Roy. They almost got married but it fizzled out. Over the years, we lost track of the Leardams, most of whom migrated to Australia. We did stay in touch with Aunty Ada, who died in the sixties. I remember driving Dad and Mum to Taiping, Perak for her funeral. Uncle Roy (Dad's younger brother) and his wife, Aunty Lennie also attended the funeral. Over the years, Dad and Mum kept in touch with Gwen and her husband who worked in the Pudu Prison services while Geoffrey Leardam and his wife visited us in Rockingham in the late 1980s.

It never occurred to me in my growing up years that Geoffrey and his siblings were my cousins – we had the same grandfather. Geoffrey was very kind to me and from time to time took me along to watch football matches at the Selangor Padang. I remember that Geoffrey wanted to undertake medical studies after finishing at SJI. But my Dad was unable to help financially.

My father, James Robert Solomon, was born on 21st September 1905 in Seramban, Negeri Sembilan (in the Malay States). After my father came six other siblings, some of whom may also have been born in Seremban but it is likely that the three youngest were born in Ipoh, in the State of Perak:

Joslyn Gladys Rita	5th Mar 1907
Gertrude Hazel Beatrice	2nd Jul 1909
Mable Irene Esme	13th Nov 1910
Roy Charles Lester	26th May 1912
Grace Merline Jennet	29th May 1916
Dorothy Margaret Jinadari	24th Sep 1918

It is interesting to note that all my father's siblings had English forenames, except the youngest who also had a Sinhalese forename. Relatively isolated as my grandparents are likely to have been in the Malay States and noting the even smaller Sinhalese community, one wonders where or how these names came about. I very much doubt that grandfather was a scholar who was familiar with English literature or had access to printed sources to choose names from.

Sadly, my father passed away on the 21st November 1982. Most of my father's siblings passed away in the last quarter of the twentieth century while the youngest (our Aunty Baby) passed away in 2013. She was 95. Aunty Baby passed away in her sleep, barely a fortnight after Uncle John – her husband, who also passed away in his sleep.

I have very few photographs of the Wijasuriya clan from the previous generation. They appeared to be a typical middle class family. Aunty Ada does not appear in any of these photographs. It could well be that she had married and moved away before these photos were taken.

I remember Aunty Ada – she was slim, tall, black haired and fair skinned – harking back to her Japanese mother and quite different in appearance from the rest of the Wijasuriya clan. I am proud to say that I have known two from the clan – my grandmother and Aunty Ada who were born in the late 19th Century.

I was unable to find any photographs of grandfather and grandmother together. But there were a few of Nanny taken between 1946 and 1949.

Nanny

It is interesting to note that despite Nanny's Buddhist background, all her children attended Catholic schools. This may simply have been because the mission schools were the best schools at that time. Government involvement in schools and education only came after independence.

When I look back on the life of my own father, I have to admit that I know very little of his childhood and home circumstances. Admittedly, my father was a rather quiet man and was not overly communicative, least of all about himself. My father attended St Michael's School in Ipoh, Perak (part of the Federated Malay States) from 2nd December 1918 to the 10th January 1927 (dates specified in his School Leaving Certificate).

The dates are rather curious as it indicates that my father attended St. Michael's School when he was about 13 years old and left School when he was 22, the reason given that he was going to work. The School Leaving Certificate also stated that the previous school attended was the Ipoh Convent – which was a girls' school, very unusual indeed!

Assuming that my father began his primary education when he turned six or seven (presumably at the Ipoh Convent), it does seem that he had nearly six years of primary education followed by a further nine years of secondary education. This does seem to be a rather long period spent in school, based on present day time periods spent in primary and secondary school.

In his School Leaving Certificate, Dad's conduct and general progress in school was reported to be 'Excellent'. He was also Vice-Captain of the School Football Team, School Librarian and Assistant Scout Master of the Ipoh 3rd. Troop. From Dad's School Leaving Certificate, it is recorded that Dad passed the Junior Cambridge Examination and enrolled in the Senior Cambridge class – but left to go to work

---

(footnote : St. Michael's School was set up in Ipoh, Perak State by the La Salle Order of Christian Brothers on 4th December 1912)

without taking his Senior Cambridge Exam. This may have been a necessity – the family needed a bread winner and Dad was it, as he was the eldest son. Grandfather had died nearly 8 years earlier.

One wonders how the family managed after grandfather died. The family was quite large – 9 in all, counting Nanny and Aunty Ada. It is known that James Peter contributed to the Widows and Orphans Pension Fund. Nanny therefore received a pension and managed to keep the family schooled, fed, clothed and housed – but it must have been difficult. Small wonder that my Dad had to go to work without completing his studies in order to help support the family. Dad never complained or moaned about the hard life he may have had growing up.

While deductive reasoning may suggest the above scenario, the story is also told that Nanny wanted my Dad to undertake medical studies and become a Doctor. This seems to suggest, not only that Nanny had the financial resources to underwrite my Dad's medical studies, but that my Dad had the basic qualifications and the discipline to undertake a career in medicine. If there is any truth to this story, it is difficult to explain why my Dad 'left school to go to work' (as stated in his School Leaving Certificate) without even sitting for his Senior Cambridge Exam.

Another curious fact is that my father was born in Seramban, Negeri Sembilan yet he went to school in Ipoh in the State of Perak. Alas there is no one left alive to explain how this came about. As an employee of the Malay States Railways, it could well be that grandfather was transferred to Ipoh and hence it was quite logical for the family to have moved there, too.

The fact that Dad carefully preserved his School Leaving Certificate in its original form for so many years is possibly reflective of its importance in relation to future job prospects. By contrast, I have to admit that although I attended two schools in the Malay States – St. John's Institution in Kuala Lumpur and the High School in Klang followed by St. Anthony's College Kandy, in Ceylon, I only preserved my School Leaving Certificate from my very first school but not from subsequent schools.

This may have been because of the perception that such documents were quite unimportant as most young people of my generation who had the intelligence and the means, went on to tertiary studies and aspired to careers in law, medicine or other professional fields.

In my Father's Day, the School Leaving Certificate was a crucial document for subsequent employment. The locals were on the whole expected to fill subordinate positions in government service or commercial enterprises. Only the affluent and those with links to royalty who had a modicum of intelligence could aspire to tertiary study and to a higher calling and this invariably meant study abroad in England.

I have little to add about my father's working life. The family were well aware that he served in the General Clerical Service in the Forest Department, mostly in Kuala Lumpur, followed by a stint in the Forest Research Institute in Kepong, Selangor (part of the Malay States) during the years of the Japanese occupation (WW II) and then at Klang, followed by a final stint at Forest Department Headquarters in Kuala Lumpur. His final stints at Klang and Kuala Lumpur were as Chief Clerk. Dad never shared any details at all of his working life with his family – his achievements, frustrations, aspirations – nothing at all. I even doubt my mother knew much at all.

Soon after leaving school, Dad attended short term courses in book keeping and in health inspection and sanitation. However he did not complete his studies in either line but instead joined the General Clerical Service (GCS) and remained in it all his working life. According to Dad's Statement of Service, Government of the Federation of Malaya, he was first appointed to the GCS on 13th February 1928 and retired within the same service on 18th September 1960 on Tinkatan Khas or Special Grade. Dad's starting salary was only $55.00 Straits Dollars a month. During the Japanese occupation, however, the Japanese issued their own currency notes for the Malay States – popularly referred to as 'Banana Notes.'

Dad served as a clerk on timescale in the GCS for over twenty five years and was only promoted to Special Grade barely three years before his retirement. During Dad's entire working life, he served in the forestry service under the State Forest Officer, Selangor – most of whom were Brits. (M.L. Webber, C.L. Carrier and J.O Egerton to name a few). I can well imagine how very frustrating it must have been for a very intelligent and capable person like my Dad to work under his orang putih bosses for many years with little reward. Yet, I have never heard my Dad complain or vent his frustrations on his family. It was after all 'British' Malaya in the years prior to independence in 1957.

As an employee in the colonial service, (the term officer in the colonial service usually referred to the Brits) my Dad dressed in a shirt, tie, jacket and trousers. Starched collars were the order of the day while trousers were also starched. In numerous photographs in the family album, Dad is dressed in jacket and tie. In post independence years, attire for clerical service personnel became more casual – the jacket and tie were discarded. Only those higher up in the ranking dressed more formally. Needless to state, the colonial service was essentially a male preserve. This trend continued initially in post independence years but the gender balance has tipped since then. So has the ethnic imbalance, especially in the Public Service – which has virtually become a Malay preserve.

When my father passed away in 1982, I was most fortunate to have access to his collection of private documents that he had carefully preserved over the years. My perusal of these proved to be an eye opener. As far back as I can remember, the family had always celebrated Dad's birthday on 19th September. However, a certified copy of his birth records found among his papers revealed that his actual birthday was on the 21st September but the birth was only registered on 25th September 1905.

Picking up the threads of the story from the past once again, grandfather was possibly still celebrating the birth of his eldest son and may have contributed to the inaccurate recording – of names and dates. A further piece of information that may be of interest is that my father may have been born at home, in Railway Quarters, Seremban, (where my grandparents lived) rather than in a hospital. When I asked Mum whether she knew any of this, she said that she was as much in the dark as I was.

Another surprising document in the collection was a Statutory Declaration signed by my father before a Magistrate of the Sessions Court, which stated: "I, James Robert Solomon Wijasuriya, do solemnly and sincerely declare that the name SALIMAN appearing on my birth certificate, STANISLAUS KOSTKA JOSEPH WIJASURIYA appearing on my marriage certificate, SAMUEL WIJASURIYA appearing on the birth certificate of my daughter Irene, JOSEPH SHANISLAUS WIGASURIA appearing on the birth certificate of my son Donald Earlian Kingsley and J S WIJASURIA appearing on the birth certificate of my son Clarence Patrick refer to me and to one and the same person.

I further declare that my father's name appearing on my birth certificate should be James Peter Wijasuriya and not I R Wijasuing and my mother's name should be Mary Josephine Jayatilaka and not Mary Joskpene Jayatelaku."

Yet two years later, Dad signed another Statutory Declaration dated 26th March 1957 with virtually the same wording, except that the last paragraph states: "I further declare that my father's name appearing on my Marriage certificate is James Peter Wijesuriya and not I.R. Wijasuing which was entered on my Birth certificate in error." Surprisingly, I also came across an earlier Statutory Declaration made by my father dated 25th September 1939 with virtually the same wording, but also including the following statement : " I further declare that the name of my wife Dona Cecilia Mabel Florinda de Silva refer to one and the same person as Florence de Silva." Small wonder that there had to be three Statutory Declarations. I am the eldest son and I am confused!

Yet another curiosity that has come to light is my Dad's rather ornate Baptism Certificate dated 6th September 1906 – well over a hundred years ago. Although the certificate has torn in two, an attempt was made to repair it with cellophane tape (which has also worn out with age). Yet, despite the age of the document, the illustrations, colours and text as well as the hand-writing are quite distinct.

Dad's baptism certificate clearly shows that Dad was baptised in St. Mark's Church, Seremban, Negeri Sembilan, which was an Anglican Church. It was also signed by the 'Chaplain'. The term 'chaplain' or pastor was an Anglican or Protestant practice. Although Dad was baptised in the Anglican Church, he grew up as a Catholic, went to a Catholic School and remained Catholic all his life. When, where and why this Anglican/Catholic shift took place is not known. Yet, his mother (Nanny to us) remained staunchly Buddhist all her life. What exactly grandfather's religious affiliations were is open to conjecture – he may have been Anglican too.

Dad's baptism certificate is an original document (not a copy) written in English over 110 years ago. By way of contrast, my very own baptism certificate is a copy (not an original) and was translated into English from the original in Latin. It was dated 10th March 1951. It is further to be noted that my Dad was baptised on the 6th September, 1906 – nearly a year after he was born while I was baptised on 1st December 1934 – less than 2 weeks after I was born!

My father appears to have had what could best be described as an identity problem. He seems to have given himself different forenames at different stages in his life. Some names may have been given to him at Baptism or during the rite of Confirmation within the Catholic Church but other names used have been a complete mystery.

Even in my father's School Leaving Certificate issued in 1927, his name is cited as Stanislaus J. Wijasuriya. Yet, in the Certificate of Marriage, Diocese of Kandy, Mission of Matale, Dad's name is cited as Wijesundara Arachige Stanislaus Kostka Joseph, son of W.A. James Peter Wijesuriya. This is another variation of his name.

All of us in the family were so absolutely sure that Dad's name was Joseph Stanislaus Wijasuriya. On occasion, Dad used a rubber stamp in which his name was given as J.S. Wijasuriya. In fact, as I was gathering various documents to be incorporated in 'Footprints', I came across my very own Marriage Certificate (I got married on the 3rd April, 1961), in which I have, by my very own hand, given my Dad's name as Joseph Stanislaus Wijasuriya! How wrong we all were!

We never thought to question why everybody called him Sam, rather than Stan or any other name that appeared on various documents. My mother, my Dad's sisters and brother called him Sam. All my cousins called him Uncle Sam. Noting that Sam was usually a short form for Samuel, it is indeed most curious that my father himself used Samuel in only one of the documents I came across. I wonder what Dad called himself when he first introduced himself to Mum? If only I knew all this when my father was still alive – I would have loved to have found out, from the horse's mouth so to speak, how all of this came about.

Although Nanny lived in our house for many years, I have never heard her refer to her eldest son by name except once when I heard her call my Dad Sammy. It could well be that among the previous generation, it may not have been the convention to call your children by their first names. In fact, Nanny simply called each of us 'putha' meaning child.

When my parents got married

There is no doubt that it was Nanny who was the driving force in my father's youth and it was Nanny who decided that it was time my father got married. At that time, the prevailing norm within the Sinhalese community was for marriage to take place only within the community itself. Unfortunately, the Sinhalese community in the Malay States was woefully small – so, in 1931 Nanny made up her mind that it would be necessary to go to Ceylon to seek out a suitable wife for her oldest son but she did not take my Dad along. This may have been because my Dad was working and could not get the necessary leave. Instead, she took ship to Colombo accompanied by her eldest daughter (my Aunty Gladys). The journey would have been rather uncomfortable and would have taken several weeks.

As the story goes, Nanny and Aunty Gladys visited several families in Ceylon who had suitable daughters of 'marriageable age'. Nanny was obviously a woman of singular purpose and discernment. We were told that my father, then 25 years old, received a telegram back in Kuala Lumpur indicating that they had made contact with a de Silva family in Kandy. They had a daughter who could well become a suitable life partner for him. The telegram furthermore urged him to take ship to Colombo with all speed if he was interested. He was – and the rest is history.

Based on the Notice of Marriage posted at St Thomas' Church Matale dated 18th July 1931 (document still existing among my father's papers) it is likely that my father arrived in Colombo in early July and stayed at an address in Wellawatte, Colombo for a period of ten days during which he made a few trips to Kandy to meet members of the de Silva family and my mother in particular. According to my mother, the wedding took place three days after she met my Dad.

Looking at the matter in hindsight and appreciating the prevailing mode of public transportation at that time, the distance between Colombo and Kandy and the fact that my Dad possibly did not have extended leave from work, it is more than likely that my mother only met my Dad on three occasions – each visit, well chaperoned most likely! Brief though these visits were, Mum and Dad liked one another well enough and decided to get married. The Church Banns were posted on the 18th July and the marriage took place at St Thomas Church, Matale on 1st August 1931 – barely two weeks later.

In August 2013, on my third visit to Sri Lanka since 2009, largely to witness the Randoli Perahera in Kandy; to visit the Minneriya Wildlife park, the Wilpattu Game reserve and other places of interest, I took the opportunity to visit St. Thomas' Church in Matale where my parents got married. The old church has long gone but a large new Church has been built on the same site.

(**footnote**. In the world of to-day, the above scenario would have been unthinkable and unacceptable to most young people. It appears that my father may have been somewhat pliable and mild mannered to dissent or disagree with his mother. While I knew Nanny, I never had the impression that she was a domineering sort of person. She was physically rather diminutive, somewhat portly and she laughed easily. I simply cannot picture her cracking the whip in relation to my father!)

I called on the Rev. Fr. in charge and spoke of my parents getting married there in the thirties. To my great surprise, he confirmed that marriage registers had been maintained since the beginning of the 20th century. A search of the records for the 1st August 1931 revealed the relevant entry details of my parents' marriage. He personally copied out the relevant details and handed me a signed and stamped copy from the marriage register. This was an unexpected bonus from my most recent visit.

A somewhat fragile and brittle newspaper clipping from a Ceylon Newspaper dated 6th August 1931 (name of Newspaper not evident from the clipping), the Wijasuriya/de Silva marriage was duly reported. It is indeed irritating to note that even in our traditional homeland, the Wijasuriya surname was grossly misspelt in the news clipping.

It was a very Western style wedding – the celebrant was Rev. Fr. Marri OSB (Order of St Benedict) with High Mass (sung), followed by a reception at Barron Hall, Kandy. Western dress was the order of the day with the men in full suits while the ladies were sari-clad.

I recognise several members of the family in the photograph. Mum's step-brother Percy and brother Tiddy served as Best Man and Groomsman and Dad's sister Gladys and Mum's sisters Celine and Stella and step-sisters Trixie and Gladys served as bridesmaids and flower girls. I got to know all of them.

Interestingly, Mum's eldest step-brother Stanley and her youngest step-brother Gerry were 'persona non grata' and were not included in the wedding photograph. I doubt whether they were even invited for the wedding. This was

My parents' wedding photograph

apparently because they had gone against an injunction agreed to earlier within the family that none of the male members of the family were to get married until all the female members of the family had been given away in marriage. Stanley and Gerry defied this and married before their sisters as a result of which they were ostracised – not just at the wedding but for many years after so much so that I never really got to know these two uncles.

My step uncle Percy and my uncle Tiddy were regarded as the 'elders' within the family and all the sisters and even their husbands deferred (at least on the surface) to both of

(**footnote**. Percy on my Dad's right and Tiddy on my Mum's left. Seated far right are Mum's sister Sally and Dad's sister Gladys)

them. Nothing it seemed could be done without both brothers being informed or consulted. Not surprisingly, while these two brothers saw to it that all their sisters got married first, both of them never got married themselves and remained bachelors all their lives.

It is my impression that while these two brothers – really step-brothers – held sway over the family, they were not at all close to one another. I have never seen them in joyful conversation. Percy Uncle worked in the Drainage and Irrigation Department in Colombo, while Tiddy Uncle was a secondary school teacher in Kegalle.

For my parents, the beginning of their married life must have been rather hectic. This was not exactly the best of times to begin a life together coming as it did at the height of the great depression (1929-1932). During these difficult times Dad had to secure a steamship passage to Ceylon at short notice; he also had to have sufficient funds for an indefinite stay in Ceylon while looking for a prospective bride; if successful, he would have to secure passage for his bride as well back to the Malay States.

My Dad was only 25 then and he must have relied heavily on financial support from his mother. For my mother, the whole sequence of events leading up to the wedding and the departure to the Malay States soon after must have been stressful, but exciting perhaps too as it promised the prospect of a better life and the building up of her very own family. But it was possibly a rude awakening too.

Mum never talked about her trip coming by ship to the Malay States. I doubt that my father had the financial means or the time (leave from work) to have any kind of honeymoon. If at all, it would have been a shipboard 'honeymoon' – whatever that would have meant in those days. For my mother, it would have been her very first trip abroad – to the Malay States, a totally unknown and foreign wilderness, culturally dissimilar to what she had been used to. She did lament the fact that even the little jewellery she had when she arrived, had to be pawned and was never recovered.

Her new home (very modest government quarters, conforming to my father's General Clerical Service housing entitlement) which she expected to share with her new husband was also home to all my Dad's unmarried sisters and his mother. Imagine her great dismay and disappointment. Having cooked for her relatives in Ceylon for years, she was now cooking for his relatives in the Malay States. It seemed that nothing had really changed.

A photograph, taken in front of the Government Quarters Dad occupied in Cheras when he first got married, possibly about 1933 shows the Wijasuriya brood in full prominence (my aunties Gladys, Beta and Merley), my two sisters Jenny and Irene with Nanny in the middle and Mum somewhat in the background – indicative of the pecking order.

Uncle Roy (Dad's only brother) is not in the photograph as he was then a student in Technical College. Uncle Roy later went on to qualify as an engineer and carved out a successful career in Malayan Railways – in a way carrying on the tradition of his own father (my grandfather) who worked in the railways too. Uncle Roy owned a Meccano set which he may have used during his student days in Technical College.

He later gave this set to me and I got many years of enjoyment from this Meccano set, constructing bridges, cranes and railway carriages – but it failed to propel me into a career in engineering or the railways.

Aunty Mabel is also not in the photograph – perhaps she was already married and had moved out while Aunty Baby (Dad's youngest sister) who is also not in the photograph may have still been a student in the Bukit Nanas Convent.

Wijasuriya family at the house in Cheras

(**footnote**. From L toR - My aunts Gladys, Beta and Merley; Nanny and Mum; my sisters Jenny and Irene)

My Dad was a somewhat taciturn and uncommunicative sort of person. He was also far too mild-mannered a man to stand up to his sisters and so it was invariably my mother who lost out. Mum used to say that Dad would not even say "boo" to a goose. Mum also said that Dad's sister Mabel was not very nice but all the others were quite kind towards her. But fortune did smile upon my mother as one after the other my father's sisters got married and moved away to live elsewhere.

Most of the marriages of my Dad's sisters were "arranged" – how Nanny managed to dredge up Sinhalese men to marry her daughters (quite nice men too) one will never know. But then my aunts were quite nice too! Aunty Gladys married Uncle Henry and moved to Singapore. Aunty Beta married Uncle Alwin and also moved to Singapore. Aunty Mabel married Uncle Vincent and moved to Ipoh while Aunty Merley married Uncle Noel and moved to Port Swettenham and Klang. I hardly knew Uncle Henry and Uncle Alwin – I was too young and they were too far away.

Fortunately, the related practice of dowry paying (usually property or jewellery by the bride's family) was becoming a declining practice. Otherwise Nanny would have needed a fortune to marry off her daughters. One must make a distinction here between dowry and bride price – a practice prevalent in primitive societies – the idea of paying so many goats or cows to the father of the bride for the hand of his daughter in marriage.

Dowry paying is not necessarily more advanced but at least it is supposed to be paid to the newlyweds rather than to the father of the bride. During my parents' generation and that of my grand-parents, arranged marriages and dowry paying were an accepted social norm. In the case of my parents, their marriage was an arranged one but it was subject to both parties meeting and agreeing to get married. I seriously doubt that any dowry was paid by my mother's family to get their daughter married for the very simple reason that her family seemed to have little to give.

I also doubt that when my mother first met my father it was love at first sight. I suspect that my mother was quite fed-up with her lot in life and wholeheartedly grasped the first life-line (my father) that came her way to a better future for herself. I have to acknowledge however that it took very great courage for my mother not only to commit herself in marriage to a man she hardly knew, but also to leave her homeland and move to a foreign country, not knowing if she would ever return. As it turned out, I believe that it was my mother who gave a life-line to my father – my impression is that my father would not have managed as well without her.

While there is some merit in the payment of dowry to give a newlywed couple a stake or nest egg to begin their life journey together, the payment of dowry has been much abused. It has often impoverished families and has even led to physical and mental abuse on the person of the bride when dowry commitments fail to be met. In fact, the problem got so serious that in India, the Indian Dowry Prohibition Act was passed in 1961. In Sri Lanka or the Malay States however, there are no legislative provisions in place that prohibit the payment of dowry.

For the most part, arranged marriages seemed to last. As far as I am aware, very few broke down completely. To me, my parents seemed happy enough. They were devoted to each other and if there were deep seated grievances or disappointments, it never showed. But then, Asians are not overly demonstrative. The home I grew up in was harmonious – no violence, shouting and screaming or throwing of plates and cups!

Arranged marriages are still widely practised in Sri Lanka and other South Asian countries. For the most part, arranged marriages do not mean forced marriage – the parties to the marriage have the right of final consent. This was the case in respect of my parents – the marriage was arranged only to the extent that it brought two people together who met and made the final decision to marry without any coercion whatsoever.

But even in Europe and the developed world, arranged marriages were not uncommon especially among royalty and the wealthy – in order to safeguard family wealth and estates, to secure political alliances and the like or to secure business interests. It is interesting to note that in the Malay States in times gone by as well as in modern day Malaysia, arranged marriages among the Chinese, Malay and Eurasian communities are not as widespread. Within my circle of friends, I know of no examples.

But to come back to practices in Sri Lankan or Sinhalese society, there seems to be a growing tendency, as a result of widespread education and gender mingling in schools, tertiary institutions as well as the work place, where boy meets girl and personal choices are made leading to marriage. Both personal choices in choosing a marriage partner as well as the more traditional practice of arranged marriages have led to stable marriages with relatively low divorce rates – although this too is changing. In my parents' generation especially, the stigma of divorce was so abhorrent that couples simply stuck together, despite being in a totally unhappy marriage. Often, it was the children that kept the parents together.

In my own generation, several of my Malaysian Indian colleagues and friends in academia, in research establishments as well as the Public Service married young ladies from South India. Most of these marriages were arranged and I believe that a dowry was paid in each case – mostly in the form of jewellery or property while in some cases the dowry was negotiated by the parents of both parties.

All the men were academically and professionally qualified but nevertheless relied on their parents to arrange suitable partners for them. Two of the men were Catholics and two were Hindus. The ladies were educated too and some were professionally qualified. All these marriages have stood the test of time.

Today, the widely circulated newspapers as well as other communication technologies are exploited to the fullest in the search for a suitable life partner. A Sri Lankan Newspaper picked up on my last visit to Colombo in August 2013 is replete with marriage advertisements. For the most part, the advertisements are placed by the parents, seeking suitable partners for their sons or daughters. Religion and caste still appear to be of some importance and are mentioned in many of the advertisements. Although a dowry is not often mentioned, the prospective marriage partner's 'assets' (house and land, academic and professional qualifications, steady job etc.) are mentioned in order to attract or interest a prospective marriage partner.

In my own generation, the idea of an arranged marriage would have been totally unacceptable. Personally however, I would not have said no if a 'dowry' of house and land was gifted to Annette and me when we got married – but drat, no such largesse was available! We made our way entirely on our own from day one.

Growing Up

The second generation of Wijasuriya siblings began to make their appearance from 1932. My sisters, Janette Muriel Winifred was born on 14th June 1932 and Irene Beatrice on 8th June 1933. Yours truly – Donald Earlian Kingsley was born on 22nd November 1934 and my brother Clarence Patrick on 22nd March 1938.

I have reproduced in the Appendices two separate records of my birth – neither of them being my original Birth Certificate which I have never seen and which must have been lost a long time ago. The first is an 'Extract from Register of Births in the State of Selangor,' dated 22nd March 1955.

It is more than likely that this move to obtain a certified copy of my birth records was initiated by me, conscious of the fact that I did not even have such an essential document of identity, namely my Birth Certificate. It is propitious that I did so, as it facilitated my application for Citizenship, Federation of Malaya on 12th May 1959. Malaya obtained political Independence from Britain on 31st August 1957.

What is most surprising is that on 29th November 1960 I again applied for and obtained a certified true copy of my Certificate of Birth. The details on both copies are identical with the added detail in the later copy that I was born at 6 am. I greatly doubt that my mother arranged for a horoscope for her first born son (myself) from a reputed Sinhalese astrologer – which used to be a practice in Sinhalese families. I doubt she did so for my sisters or any of my other siblings either.

Unlike all the other houses I have lived in with my family in my growing up years, our house in Cheras (a suburb of Kuala Lumpur) was a two-storey brick and tile semi-detached construction with a common wall between two units. This was the house my Mum came back to when she first got married. Nanny and Dad's sisters also lived in this house.

Childhood home in Cheras

The baby on my mother's lap is me with my two sisters leaning beside Dad and Mum. I do recall some of the items of furniture in this house, especially Dad's writing table – I used to rummage through the drawers – which Dad used all his life and which was shifted from one house to another.

However sometime after the mid thirties, Dad who by then was working for the Forest Department was assigned a much larger house in Bukit Nanas (where the Kuala Lumpur Tower stands today). The house was made of wood with planks affixed horizontally, each plank marginally overlapping the other. The roof was made of slightly convex shaped clay tiles, brownish in colour and the floors were planked. A roofed open veranda with railings stretched right along the front of the house and partly on the side and the entire house was built on sturdy brick columns about three feet high and one foot square.

The house had a large living room which may have seemed huge in the perception of a child but in reality was quite small. The house also had two bedrooms and a single bathroom. Dad's mother and his youngest sister (then still unmarried) lived with us and occupied one of the rooms while Dad, Mum and the four of us occupied the other room.

A covered passage-way with cement rendered floors, led to the kitchen and storeroom, which doubled up as a room for the amah (Chinese maid in black trousers and white upper garment or blouse.). The house had electricity and piped water while in the kitchen, cooking was done over wood fires, using earthenware pots called 'chutty-pots.' The toilet was a free standing out-house about 20 metres away with a bucket system. Night soil was regularly collected by workers from the Conservancy Department.

Our Chinese amah only worked for the family for a few years but had to be discontinued as she was often falling ill – my mother had to attend to her from time to time. The amah's duties were largely confined to washing the clothes as well as sweeping the house. Mum did all the cooking – that was her preserve. Later, the cooking, washing and other household chores were done entirely by my mother and my two sisters.

In the garden of our Bukit Nanas home

Our home in Bukit Nanas was built on gently sloping land about 200 meters from Weld Road (now Jalan Raja Chulan). It was set in very generous grounds and did not have fencing of any kind. It was full of fruit trees, including mango, jack-fruit, rambutan (both sweet and sour varieties), pulosang, chiku and papaya. There were also several pineapple and sugar cane clumps as well as a single durian tree (which never bore any fruit). It was a great place to grow up in – so much room to run around in and trees to climb. Dad kept poultry as well as guinea pigs and rabbits as a hobby. We had no neighbours close by unlike housing estates at the present time.

Our home was also located adjacent to the Forest Reserve which constituted virgin jungle. It was fun to go into this jungle from time to time picking up seeds from specific trees which had 'wings' to carry them a considerable distance from the mother plant. The jungle was also frequented by chattering monkeys. We were careful not to leave bunches of bananas outside the house as they could disappear really quickly. The monkeys were rather bold and cheeky and thought nothing of entering your house and helping themselves to anything edible – if you were careless enough to leave a window or door open.

Although the Forest reserve at Bukit Nanas was pristine virgin jungle, we hardly ever encountered any other wildlife. This may partly be due to the fact that the jungle 'corridor' between Bukit Nanas and the foothills of the main range had been progressively eroded by human habitation – causing the wildlife to migrate into deeper jungle.

The football field of St. John's Institution (SJI) – the school I first went to, was no more than 100 metres from the rear of our home. The Convent of the Holy Infant Jesus my sisters went to was also located in Bukit Nanas adjacent to St John's. So we all walked to school and it did not even take us five minutes. Our lives revolved around home, school and church – all within walking distance of our house in Bukit Nanas.

(**footnote.** The Bukit Nanas Forest Reserve, covering an area of 9.3 hectares of virgin forest in the heart of Kual Lumpur was first gazetted as a forest reserve in 1906 and covered a land area of 17.5 hectares. The forest reserve has been greatly reduced in size because of logging and rapid urbanization and has been renamed the KL Forest Eco Park. SJI and the Convent, which were first established in Bukit Nanas at the beginning of the 20th century, have been designated as national heritage sites and remain among the leading schools in the country.)

Occasionally we went with Mum to the wet market which was quite messy and slippery. It would not have passed muster in the health checks of today. The building still stands today but has been renamed Pasar Seni (central market). It is no longer a wet market but has been refurbished and houses a wide collection of small boutiques, clothing stores, handicraft stalls and restaurants.

I do not recall that we ever travelled as a family outside Kuala Lumpur. I do however remember as a child being sent to Ipoh by train for some dental treatment. I am certain I was accompanied but not by my father or mother. We stayed at Aunty Mabel's place in Ipoh as Uncle Vincent (her husband) was a male nurse or 'dresser' at the Ipoh Hospital and had 'arranged' my treatment. Uncle Vincent was a devout Buddhist whereas Aunty Mabel was Catholic. On reflection, it seems that my grandfather and grandmother (Nanny) were in exactly the same situation – but this did not seem to bother them.

The Vincents' eldest son Lawrence or 'Lorrie' as he was called, was about my age. He had so many toys and I was so envious. Sadly, in later life Lorrie became mentally unstable and had to be discharged from government service on medical grounds. His youngest brother suffered the same fate and spent many years at the Tanjong Rambutan mental hospital in Ipoh, Perak. I believe over-indulgent parenting may have been a causative factor.

The second son extricated himself from the confines of his family, hitch-hiked his way to England and made a life for himself there. We never got to know how he achieved that. It must have been a very long and arduous trip, picking up work as he went along. In England, he worked as a stable hand for many years on a farming property, grooming horses. He later married an English girl and had one son.

While the 3 Vincent boys (Aunty Mabel's sons) were our first cousins, we did not interact much with them. This was because they lived in Ipoh and neither family owned a car at that time or travelled outside their home towns in Ipoh and Kuala Lumpur. We interacted far more with the Samarakkody family (Aunty Merley's children) who were our first cousins too and who lived in Port Swettenham and Klang where we lived too. We grew up with Cyril, Phyllis, Angeline, Roslin, Gordon, Bertie and Austin. Noel Samarakkody who married Aunty Merley was the only son of Jane Jayatilaka – Nanny's sister.

Taking up the family narrative once again, our family did not have a radio, a car or even a fridge during our stay in Bukit Nanas. All meals therefore had to be prepared fresh. I do recall that we did have a clock but relied on the main clock tower building which was visible from the house, to give us the correct time. The clock tower which is part of the Sultan Abdul Samad building still stands today and continues to keep good time – it is part of the national heritage buildings, among others that constitute the National Trust.

I also visited my old stomping grounds at Bukit Nanas on my last trip to Kuala Lumpur in August 2013. SJI still stands and continues to function as a school but our old house has been flattened in the march of progress. The old church still stands and continues to be used for services while a new cathedral has been constructed close to the old Telecommunications Headquarters building.

We had a really sumptuous lunch in the revolving restaurant at the top of the Kuala Lumpur Tower – courtesy of my affluent Malay friends who played hosts, complete with valet parking when we drove up in her posh limousine. Amazingly, the forest reserve, greatly reduced in size, has been preserved in the middle of bustling, cosmopolitan Kuala Lumpur.

It was also wonderful to get a panoramic view of the city skyline from the revolving restaurant. Spotting the new building of the National Library of Malaysia was a bit of a challenge as it had virtually been obliterated by other high-rise buildings which had been constructed after my retirement.

Picking up the threads from the past once again, it was a great joy to run freely on the SJI football field. I have a remembrance of playing football and often having to stop and lean on the goal post panting for breath as I suffered from asthma in those early years. I only attended primary school in SJI briefly in 1941, after I turned six.

By then I could read, write and count to some extent – thanks to my mother. I have no recollection of my father teaching us our 'abcs', reading any stories to us or changing diapers on my younger siblings. He seemed to have seen his role as the provider and left everything else to my mother.

It was my mother who assumed responsibility for disciplining the children. I do not recall my mother ever scolding my sisters but it was a different matter with the boys – especially Clarence and me and she was not averse to caning us, using a thin, pliable length of rattan which often left welts on our legs. Clarence and I did have serious disagreements at times which even got physical. But we remained quite close despite these growing - up skirmishes. I remember one occasion, after a fight had ended, my sister Irene spilled the beans and told my mother that we had been fighting and that "it was all Donny's fault." Needless to say my mother gave me some of the best – delivered in the usual way with the rattan cane. Clarence was smirking in the corner, but it was short-lived for he got a caning too. Both of us cried for a while, sitting on the settee (sofa). We stopped crying shortly after, looked at each other and started laughing.

Dad was a soft spoken and mild mannered sort of person. I do not recall that he ever raised his voice to my mother or to any of us – his children. Dad was not a drinker either and I have never seen him tipsy even once. In fact, beer, wine and spirits were never served at family gatherings during our growing up years. I recall after a game of badminton or tennis, Dad used to send me to buy a bottle of ginger beer – which he would drink all by himself. I vowed then, that when I grew up, I would have an unending supply of ginger beer for my personal consumption. Alas, this aspiration had to be nipped in the bud because of the onset of diabetes in my later life.

Was my Dad a ladies man? I very seriously doubt it. My Dad was in fact a complete contrast to his younger brother Roy. Uncle Roy was definitely a ladies man – he was good looking, slim, had wavy hair and was somewhat cheeky and daring. It is quite intriguing how the gene pool works – I sometimes recognise traits in me which are more akin to Uncle Roy than to my Dad!

Dad was however a smoker. It is quite possible that Dad started smoking when he was still a young man. This may have been his only vice and which may have led to his early demise. Still his life span exceeded that of his own father by over twenty five years. I wonder whether that means that my own life span would exceed that of my Dad by an equivalent number of years. Would that not be something? But I certainly do not want to live that long, if there is no longer any quality of life for me. I have had a good life and made the most of what life threw at me.

I have always admired Dad's handwriting – his penmanship was neat, small and readable. It is indeed quite remarkable that Dad was able to keep a steady hand in terms of his handwriting and signature well into his late seventies. I was always fascinated by Dad's signature. I tried to incorporate features of it in my own signature, which has changed and taken the distinct form that it has at the present time.

Above all, Dad was a devoted family man and he had simple tastes. He was never rich but he got by and whatever he had he gave to the family. I did manage in my early working life to make a modest financial contribution to my Dad to help out with household expenses. I was staying at my parents' home then, at No.4, Road 5/3 – off Jalan Gasing in Petaling Jaya. But I was not able to continue doing so when Annette and I got married in April 1961 and moved to our little rented terrace house in Jalan Carey, in the old part of Petaling Jaya. Fortunately both my sisters who were qualified teachers, stayed with my parents until they got married and were able to help out.

Recalling my early years in school, I remember an incident of extreme anguish when I lost my school bag containing my exercise book, ruler and pencil. To a six-year old, that was the ultimate disaster – the end of the world even! Apart from that, my experiences at SJI were quite unremarkable and I do not remember any of my teachers.

I had a few friends in those early years – they were my schoolmates at SJI. I remember in particular Cyril Gomez and Albert Trivino. Cyril and I used to go into the forest shooting birds with our catapults. We never hit anything although there were occasional near misses. On one occasion which I still remember, I was blissfully unaware that a red centipede about six inches long was about to crawl onto my bare foot. Cyril spotted it from about ten feet away and let fly with his catapult. The shot was spot on and sent the creature spinning and writhing – it was indeed a near thing. Centipede stings are poisonous and can be quite painful. Episodes such as this did not faze me at all – we still wandered into the jungle shooting birds or anything else that moved or flew.

The family were very isolated in our growing up years. We had very few visitors to our house. Dad's office colleagues – mostly Indians, Chinese and Eurasians – dropped by at Christmas to enjoy my Mum's cooking. I do not recall that we ever had Malay visitors. Some of our relatives also dropped by from time to time but mostly to help themselves to the fruits from our garden – chiku, jack fruit and rambutan in particular. My sister's Chinese school mates came to the house for tea from time to time. Apart from this, there was hardly any community interaction.

Aunty Baby's very good friends who were her teaching colleagues visited on occassion. I remember them well – Lin Yoke and San Cheok – they were both Chinese. Even as a little boy, I thought Lin Yoke, with her rimless glasses, was so beautiful. When Lin Yoke died in the late 1990s, Aunty Baby shared with me the eulogy Lin's son wrote about his mother. One line in particular I never forgot when he said "my mother brought us up to set us free"

My school days in Malaya

My primary school years were quite unremarkable. In the late nineteen thirties, there were no provisions whatsoever for pre-schools or kindergartens. Schooling began when one was six years of age. Schooling or education was never compulsory —- it was simply the done thing. Whether a child was sent to school or not was dependent mainly on family circumstances. In many poorer families, children had to help supplement the family income. This even happens today in many countries. But in our family, none of the children ever had to go out to work to supplement the family income. Dad's modest earnings as a clerical officer in the public service were sufficient to sustain the whole family.

Digressing somewhat and recalling my own experience in the mid eighties – nearly forty five years later – doing a bit of 'marketing' (shopping in the wet market) for my mother, I stopped by my regular vegetable stall to pick up a bunch of 'kang- kong' – a light green coloured leafy vegetable my mother liked to use when preparing her very tasty stir-fried 'mee-hoon'(very thin) rice noodles. But the older Chinese gentleman – the stall owner – was not at his usual place, selling his vegetables. Instead, I found a little Chinese girl sitting in a cramped bit of space doing her homework – she could not have been more than nine years old. She had a small kerosene lamp to illuminate her little work space. She appeared to be totally self absorbed and motivated. When she saw me, she smiled, set aside her homework, weighed the bunch of 'kang kong ' on hand held scales – measured the bunch I had picked in terms of 'katies and tiles' – (before the use of the metric system) – and gave me a price in "Ringgit and sen'. I was impressed and that image never left me. I thought how lucky I was growing up.

Coming back to my story line, my primary school years came and went by without any meaningful 'learning'. It is really my mother who taught me to read and write. I attended the primary 1 class at St. John's Institution (SJI) for just one year with English as the medium of instruction. This was followed by the Japanese Occupation when I continued schooling at SJI with Japanese as the medium of instruction. There was no real continuance in terms of education. My sister Irene and I then dropped out of school and went to live with my father in Kepong, where there was no school attendance whatsoever. We kept house for my father and looked after our four cows for the rest of the Japanese occupation of the Malay States. They were lean years but they were happy and carefree times as weil. We learned to fit in and get on with everybody. It was an ethnically mixed community and all the kids – both girls and boys – played football as it was the only affordable game.

At the end of the war, I had two further years of primary education at SJI. English was the medium of instruction once again and I regained lost ground by skipping several grade levels, but coped without any problems. I have no clear recollection of my transition from primary to secondary school. As far as I remember, the school system seemed to comprise of several grade levels referred to as Primary 1-4, followed by several years of secondary school, graded as Standard 5-8, although the term secondary school was not used. Standard 8 was the Junior School Certificate Year while Standard 9 was the Cambridge School Certificate Year.

In December 1947, the family moved to Klang and J had two further years of schooling at the High School Klang (HSK) on Meru Road. I did much better in school then and was invariably first or second boy in class exams. I took part in school plays and one of my water colour paintings was featured in the school magazine. When I left HSK in December 1949, I had not even sat for the Junior School Certificate Exam.

It is interesting that in my school going years in Malaya, the Malay language or Bahasa Melayu was never the medium of instruction, neither was it a compulsory subject at school certificate level. Dad however had the foresight and arranged for me to attend Malay language classes which came in very useful in my adult life.

Dad was himself quite fluent in Malay as he had a lot of work interaction with the forest rangers, most of whom were Malays. It is interesting to recall that there were never any Indian or Tamil forest rangers while Chinese involvement in forestry was mostly as timber merchants.

When I look back on my school going years in Malaya, I must admit that while I was friendly and interacted with my classmates, I only considered a few of them as my friends but never visited any of their homes, neither did they visit mine.

This apparent lack of communal or social interaction was partly brought about by the relative isolation of our home in Bukit Nanas, the scarcity of public transport at that time and the absence of any access road to our house – just a long pathway uphill. I was far too young to own or use a bicycle then.

This scenario changed somewhat when the family moved to Klang and Dad acquired his Austin 7 and later his Wolsley 8. I was given a brand new Raleigh bicycle for performing well at school. While the mobility of the family improved somewhat in physical terms, our interaction with the wider community was restricted to family friends and relatives. While in Klang the family now had Malay, Indian, Chinese and Eurasian neighbours, the social interaction was superficial —- we never visited any of them in their homes and neither did any of them visit our home.

My teachers at SJI never made any impression on me and neither did the teachers at HSK, although I remember their names better – T.K.Taylor (an Englishman) was our Headmaster, while Paul Chang, Thiagarajan, Razak Khan and Wong Ah Fat were my subject teachers. Arianayagam, the science teacher had a very negative effect on me which put me off the sciences completely. I do not recall that I ever came across any Malay teachers on the staff.

Throughout my growing up years in Malaya, I never had the experience of being taken to the cinema to see any film –

although there were cinemas in Kuala Lumpur and in Klang. Our family were not party goers either. When I was growing up in Malaya, the family never organised parties with invited guests – not even at Christmas – and we were never invited to parties either. As a result, there was no exposure whatsoever to any dancing – especially ballroom dancing – the foxtrot, the quick-step, the waltz or the rumba meant nothing to me. Small wonder that interaction with girls was never a part of my growing up experience.

But while living in Klang and attending HSK, my bicycle gave me access to the library – and books gave me my window on the world. I began to realise what lay beyond the little world I lived in. I never dreamed then how very far away from home I would travel on life's pathway.

Shophouse
Old Kuala Lumpur

Japanese Occupation

The Japs are coming

Primary school for me ended all too soon when the Japanese attacked Pearl Harbour in December 1941. It brought the theatre of war, hitherto largely fought in Europe, to the Far East, especially Southeast Asia. "The Japs are coming", "the Japs are coming" – the rumours flew thick and fast. "Kuala Lumpur is going to be bombed". And there we were in Bukit Nanas, right in the heart of the city!

Dad had built an air raid shelter or bunker in the grounds of our house in Bukit Nanas. A few of the adults who were around at that time dug a 6 ft. deep trench about 10ft long and 5ft.wide. It was covered with heavy logs across the top and camouflaged with leafy branches. Digging the trench was the easy part.

The more challenging tasks were sawing the logs to the required length and rolling them down the jungle clad hill-side to the compound of our house. The logs, uneven in girth, often rolled away from the desired direction and had to be laboriously corrected, with many irritated shouts of 'get out of the way you little buggers'. As kids, we simply wanted to be a part of everything.

(**Footnote** Japanese military forces landed in Kota Bharu, Kelantan in December 1941 and proceeded in a two pronged thrust southward towards Singapore. Despite stiff resistance by British and Colonial forces, the southward movement of Japanese troops could not be halted. Within a period of barely three months, the Japanese had routed all defence forces which progressively retreated south. With the fall of Singapore in February 1942, the Japanese had total control of the Malay Peninsula. The administration of occupied territories since then was carried out by the Malai Gunsei Kumbu <Malay Military Administration> of the Imperial Japanese Army until the Japanese surrender in September 1945.)

A small opening with a few steps was built into the bunker. The bunker however was only used once or twice when a few bombs were dropped on the railway yards in Sentul, about 5km away and on the railway yards in Brickfields, which were uncomfortably close to our home in Bukit Nanas. But the family were never in any danger.

When I call to mind the appearance of this bunker, I seem to remember that the opening to the bunker was rather narrow and it did take some doing to negotiate Nanny through the opening as Nanny was somewhat tubby. There was much giggling, pushing and tugging Nanny through the opening. Nanny was laughing too.

While there was some bombing of Kuala Lumpur, the family never experienced any of it. This was largely because the family moved into the 'ulu' (jungle) long before the Japanese forces landed in Malaya. This was quite unlike the experience of British civilians who gravitated to Singapore to secure passage on any steamer bound for England. Many never made it home. Those who remained were interred in detention camps in Singapore and few survived.

Dad decided it would be better to get out while the going was good. There was frenzied activity stockpiling foodstuffs – boxes and boxes of canned foods and bags of rice. My parents must have spent most of what they had but probably kept back something in reserve. We knew nothing of this but do recall that one day, all the kids were locked up in the house. Mum and Dad were in the garden doing something. We tried peeping through the cracks in the wall but could see very little. Long after the War ended Mum told us – they had buried biscuit tins of currency notes. This must have come in very handy when the war ended.

Initially, Dad was so very unsure, not only of where to go, but of how far to go to find refuge, remembering that we had to take Nanny along – and Nanny moved rather slowly. All of us kids knew little of this unfolding drama. To make matters even more worrying, several of Dad's sisters with their husbands in tow also descended on our Bukit Nanas home. The logistics of the whole operation must have been mind boggling. Fortunately, all of them made their own arrangements and only Aunty Baby and Nanny remained with us. While all my brothers were born while the family were still living at our Bukit Nanas home, I have no recollection of any of them as babies. They seemed to have 'just turned up'.

I remember Uncle Noel particularly. He was married to Aunty Merley (Grace Merline in the pecking order) – they had no children then. Uncle Noel liked to drink and remained a bit of a boozer all his life. There was one incident I recall vividly involving Uncle Noel. We had all turned in for the night. Mum and all the kids slept on the floor. To get to the bathroom, one had to pick one's way between several sleeping bodies. In the middle of the night, Uncle Noel needed to relieve himself and made his way to the bathroom. He was quite 'high' and had been drinking. In his befuddled mind he thought he had reached the bathroom and began to relieve himself. Mum got up with a start and I still remember her shouting "Noel, what on earth are you doing?"

Getting back to the story, each of us had to carry a little load – as I recall, a cloth bundle on a stick. In those days there was little in the way of public transport. Dad arranged for one of the forest department lorries (referred to as trucks in Australia) to take the family part of the way to the foot-hills, close to the Selangor/Pahang border.

Dad came part of the way and one of his trusted forest rangers guided us the rest of the way. Dad left us then as he had been called up – he served in the volunteer reserve forces and had to join his Unit. The rest of the trek on foot was laborious for the adults, especially those responsible for our safety but for us kids, it was great fun. We set out early in the morning and reached our destination the same day, late in the evening.

Nanny was a real problem. They tried to seat her sideways on the carrier of an old bicycle, but the front of the bicycle kept rearing up as Nanny was plump and over-weight. Needless to say, we kids were in stitches. Nanny was chuckling too. Fortunately, we came across a set of disused rail tracks and lo and behold, there was a flat cart on it with four wheels intact.

The obvious happened: they piled Nanny on it together with all the 'barang-barang' (goods) and simply pushed the cart along the track. Squeaking and grinding, the rusty wheels of the flat cart began to move. We kids kept a relatively slow and steady pace, taking turns to jump onto the cart when our legs got a little tired. The flat cart, long abandoned, was probably used to transport rubber sheets from the interior to central collection stations. It came in very handy.

Everything seemed to be progressing very nicely until we hit a slight downward gradient in the track. We could not hold on to the cart which seemed to have a mind of its own. We lost sight of Nanny – her grey hair streaming in the wind, as the flat cart took off. Fortunately, Nanny never attempted to get off the cart while it was in full flight – smart woman. Eventually, the flat cart ran out of gradient and slowed down to a stop. Nanny was none the worse for wear.

Mum however was not pleased. It must have been very difficult for my mother. Dad was away serving with his unit up North – we were not told where. Mum therefore shouldered the main responsibility of ensuring that everybody was safe. This was indeed a tall order as Mum herself was a relative newcomer to the Malay States.

The jungle hideout

Our destination was a thatched, wooden 'kampong' (village) house built on stilts (sturdy tree-trunks) about 6ft. high and largely hidden by thick 'lallang' (sharp edged tall grasses) undergrowth. Access to the house was by a step-ladder which could be pulled up. This was a safety measure as we were in the midst of tiger country. The floor of the house was made of bamboo strips with spaces in between. There was good ventilation and the house was quite airy.

All of us slept on mats – no basic comforts such as mattresses and pillows. There was no whining and moaning. A little stream meandered through the jungle from which we got our water for washing. I did not relish sitting on a rock by the side of the stream and having a bath – the water was quite cold despite the fact that we were in the tropics. There was also a small well for drinking water. From time to time, our forest ranger's village contacts from the nearby 'kampong,' brought us some vegetables and sweet potatoes.

For us kids, the carefree days went quickly by. My mother however was especially concerned that the kids kept as quiet as possible in order not to alert patrolling Japanese troops. Fortunately, only Aunty Baby (Dad's youngest sister) and Nanny came along with us to the jungle hideout. I have no recollection of where my Dad's other sisters and their families went to. I still have a remembrance of those plain but lovely meals of boiled rice and canned sardines – I still find them irresistible today! Aunty Baby helped a lot especially in preparing the meals, while Nanny fed us, mixing the soft rice and gravy into little balls or 'guli' and feeding us by hand.

Looking back in hindsight, it is quite logical to assume that Dad had very good relations with his Malay work colleagues, who made arrangements for the family to be led to the kampong house in the 'ulu' (jungle) and to live there until some semblance of normalcy returned to the country.

The British military machine, in all its wisdom, decided that the Japanese invasion would come by sea and so they concentrated their ground forces and heavy artillery in Singapore, leaving a token presence of Australian and other Colonial forces in the Malay Peninsula.

Months before the Japanese invasion, companies of Colonial forces – British, Australian, Indian, New Zealand and Gurkah (Nepali) kept marching southward. But the Japanese confounded them all by landing in Kota Bahru, Kelantan and then marching southward. There were pockets of resistance with heavy fighting – especially in Slim River, but these were all eventually over-run.

Emerging from the jungle

The family emerged from our jungle hideout and made our way to a pre-arranged house in Kapar, occupied by some distant relatives. The kids called him Uncle Arthur. Our stay at Uncle Arthur's place was relatively brief. All the while my mother waited anxiously for my Dad to turn up.

We had a bit of a scare at Uncle Arthur's house when a stray bomb from a low flying Jap Zero fell on a major pipe-line close by – the water kept gushing out for days before the waterworks people could stem the flow. People from the surrounding area rushed to the scene with large empty cans and buckets to collect as much water as they could.

We also observed one of the Brits. in disguise, attempting to flee from the Japs. He was dressed in a sarong, had a songkok (muslim cap) on his head and was struggling to crank-start a battered old motor car. He was pink, sweaty and stuck out like a sore thumb. He eventually took off but it is doubtful that he made it. How the mighty had fallen!

In the meantime, my father having been discharged from his Unit, was making his way back 'home' on his bicycle. Japanese troops passing by, took his bicycle and pushed him into a ditch. Dad gave no resistance, picked himself up and simply plodded on. Then one day, mud-splattered, unshaven, bleary-eyed and totally ragged, he walked in. Needless to say, my mother was overcome with joy and so were we.

While we were at Uncle Arthur's place, I still remember a little incident that took place there. There was a shallow ditch with brackish water in front of the house, in which the ducks loved to swim. A rickety wooden bridge spanned the ditch and one day, my little brother Clarence (about 3 years old) was attempting to feed the ducks and the clumsy little twit fell in. He must have gulped in quite a lot of that brackish water. We kids struggled to pull him out – he was none the worse for wear but Mum gave the three of us a hiding for not looking after our little brother properly.

Back to Bukit Nanas

Life soon returned to normal and Dad decided it was time to return to our house in Bukit Nanas. The house was intact – there was no looting whatsoever. The Malay States were now under Japanese Military Administration and people were told to return to their former jobs. How exactly this was communicated is unclear but gradually things fell into place. Dad resumed work in the Forestry Department in Kuala Lumpur.

There was an addition to the family at this stage – Basil Srisena was born on 22nd May 1942. I have absolutely no recollection of the birth of my brother Basil and can only conclude that it took place in Bukit Nanas long after my sister Irene and I were moved to live with our father in Kepong. Basil was a war baby and I really marvel at how my mother would have coped with the pregnancy and most likely the home delivery of the baby, not to mention keeping the home fires burning during a period of extreme privation – without my father's presence on a daily basis. My mother was truly a remarkable woman.

It is also most unusual that Basil was the only one of my siblings who was given a Sinhalese forename as well as an English one. I wonder what the circumstances were that brought this about. Yet when Norbert was born in 1947 – well after the war had ended, my parents seemed to have reverted back to form and Norbert was only given English forenames. I recently asked Basil whether he knew why he was also given a Sinhalese forename – but he acknowledged that he was completely in the dark.

It is interesting to point out that the first three boys in the family – Donald, Clarence and Basil were born on the 22nd day of the months of November, March and May in 1934, 1938 and 1942 respectively. Someone remarked a few years ago – I think it was Basil – who said that Dad appeared to be thinking in Olympic terms. Norbert, my youngest brother however was born five years later, on 8th July 1947 – well after the war.

The Japanese issued currency notes for the Malay States to replace the pre-war Straits Dollar. The new currency (Banana Notes) had little value but it was adequate for general trading purposes in the market place. Dad's salary was now paid in Banana Notes. Checking back on Museum displays of these currency notes, it is clear why they were called banana notes because an illustration of a clump of banana plants was depicted on the currency notes.

Japanese school

Jenny, Irene and I went back to school but it was school with a difference. Clarence and Basil were too young for school. Everything was now taught in Japanese and in a relatively short space of time we began to acquire an elementary level of proficiency in the language. We even got some exposure to the Japanese script called 'katakana', 'hiragana' and 'kanji' and were able to count in Japanese as well.

Even our former teachers had to learn Japanese if they wished to keep their jobs. I am not sure how my sisters coped as we never spoke in Japanese at home, only English;

while in the market place, we used colloquial Malay. Sinhalese was seldom spoken at home although sometimes my mother and Nanny did.

Our Brother Director (Christian Brothers) at SJI retained his position but served under the authority of a Japanese military officer who appeared at Assembly each morning in full military regalia complete with sword by his side. The morning routine at Assembly for the whole school started with disciplined physical exercises called 'taiso'.

The Assembly, on command, then turned and faced East (Japan: Land of the Rising Sun) and sang 'Kimigayo' (Japanese National Anthem) in honour of His Imperial Majesty the Emperor of Japan. There were several other songs with a march or military beat we learned to sing in Japanese. While in Japanese school we were each supplied with an exercise book made of very coarse yellowish paper. If you pressed the pencil point too hard when writing it simply went through the paper. But we coped well enough.

During the weekends, the Japanese Military Administration allowed the youth wing of the Indian National Army (INA) – a rag tag group of local Indian youth – to march and parade, singing in Hindi – which I remember as the 'jai Hind, jaya, jaya, jaya, jaya –ho' song. The Japanese tolerated them (but did not arm them) as they saw the INA as a means of destabilising the British in India.

Learning to survive

The Japanese authorities did manage to provide some food assistance to the students at SJI – it is likely that this was done in all schools. Each student was supplied with a loaf of bread each day which was yellowish in colour and about a foot long. It was probably made of tapioca flour (cassava) and was very rubbery. If you held both ends and pulled the loaf, it would elongate like elastic but would not break. The bread had to be cut. We took the loaf home to share with the family, but this was hardly enough.

We also grew a lot of tapioca plants in the fertile soil of our garden in Bukit Nanas. Tapioca was fairly quick growing and when uprooted, yielded a healthy cluster of tubers or yams. We survived largely on a diet of tapioca and sweet potato – which was also easy to grow. Tapioca or manioc, called 'ubikayu' in Malay, was usually peeled, boiled and eaten with grated coconut or sugar. We also grew some 'jagong' (maize or corn).

My mother was very resourceful and even prepared meals from the young tapioca and sweet potato shoots. Even young jack fruit was cooked with spices and was quite tasty. The purple coloured banana flower (at the bottom end of a comb of bananas) was also cooked as a 'mallun' – a Sri Lankan vegetable dish. Other vegetables were also grown while our fruit trees never failed us.

Rice, our staple food during the war years was in very short supply. Uncle Roy was however able to smuggle rice by rail from the Thai border, in several sturdy wooden crates with rope-loops for handles. Uncle Roy worked on the railways and was stationed in Gemas at that time. He took a great risk nevertheless. If caught, he would have lost his head. Japanese justice was swift – no trial, no prosecution, no defence, just execution!

Eventually the crates of rice ran out and we had to cultivate an alternative grain that needed less water. We could not grow rice as rice needs flooded fields during the planting and germination stages. We grew a kind of millet called ragi (Eleusine Coracana) which yielded clusters of brown grains that could be ground into flour and baked or simply cooked like rice. Mum sometimes made pittu (ragi flour mixed with grated coconut and steamed in a bamboo cylinder). Indians used ragi to make roti and idali as well. It was food but not nearly as tasty as rice.

The front lawn was levelled and hoed to create long parallel beds. The seeds were then planted and regularly watered. There were no hose pipes or spray nozzles. Two watering cans were placed at both ends of a pliable length of bamboo and the cans were tipped as you walked up and down the beds. Ragi was an annual crop. It was hardy, more drought resistant and far more nutritious than rice. Ragi is widely cultivated in India and with our close interaction with Tamil and other South Indian friends, the family got to know of ragi cultivation. It proved to be a life saver.

The interesting part was the fertilisation. You could not buy chemical fertiliser (it was probably not even known then) while cow dung or goat poo was hard to come by. Dried chook poo from the chicken coops was also used but was quantitatively quite insignificant. So our toilet bucket became valued property. We even took precautions to place barbed wire across the bottom flap of the toilet to guard against night soil robbers – the poo poo bandits so to speak!

Sheer survival drove the family to take steps, we would never otherwise have even considered. There was no room for the squeamish. I seem to remember that Irene and

I invariably ended up doing the unpleasant tasks. My other sister Jenny always seemed to get out of any involvement in the preparation of these obnoxious concoctions. The daily bucket output was upturned into a large tub, mixed with several buckets of water and stirred with a long stick. It was then delivered in individual cans to the rows of planted seeds. The front garden stank to high heaven and attracted droves of flies. Fortunately, being in the tropics it rained often and we all breathed fresh air again.

We rarely had any fish or meat to eat. We kept some chickens but that was mostly for the eggs. We also had two dogs, Topsy and Blackie by name. Topsy was a black and white shaggy dog while Blackie was as black as black can be. Neither of them were pedigrees and their parentage doubtful, but they were good dogs. Both dogs must have been vegetarians!

There was a large mess hall in the adjoining property next to our house in Bukit Nanas, occupied by Japanese military officers. It was located on the opposite side of a large monsoon drain, about 10ft below the level of both properties. The Japs lived well. They were well supplied with rice as well as sake or rice wine and they also kept a piggery. We often heard raucous laughter emanating from the mess hall.

And then one day, horror of horrors, we noticed that Topsy and Blackie had killed one of the little piglets and were dragging the carcass alongside the monsoon drain towards our house, leaving a trail of blood. In great trepidation, we kids sneaked into the monsoon trench, grabbed the piglet and brought it home to mum. The dogs did not resist. We tried to obliterate all traces of our 'crime', namely the telltale blood trail. Fortunately, it rained cats and dogs that afternoon and we felt safer. What glorious pork curry we had after such a long time!

My parents also kept a single goat for its milk but it was a most uncooperative goat. We kids waited for milking time – not so much for the milk but for a belly-full of laughs, for it took three grown adults to hold the goat and one to do the milking. The goat struggled and kicked so much that often the squirts missed the milking jug completely. The goat simply disliked having her udders tweaked.

From time to time Mum took me to the central market – our modern-day supermarkets were unknown then. The market was a central place that people came to regularly. One morning at the market place with Mum, I saw impaled on flag-poles the heads of several men who had been beheaded. Mum finished her marketing hurriedly and we went home. Thankfully, we did not witness the executions and never knew where and when it had taken place. But I never forgot.

It was a frightening experience and served as a dire warning to all and sundry. The Japanese were especially severe on the Chinese community – because of smouldering resentments over overseas Chinese support for China during the Sino-Japanese wars. By and large, the Japanese left the Malays and Indians well alone. I remember bowing to an armed Japanese soldier on general duty and even getting a half smile. The Japs seemed to love children.

At major roads there were sentry posts manned by an armed Japanese soldier. Anyone passing the sentry was expected to bow – failure to do so would invite a physical reprimand, usually a slap or a kick up one's backside. The family however never experienced any encounter with the dreaded Japanese 'Kempeitai' or military police.

It is most curious that Clarence is the only one among his siblings who acquired a Japanese nick-name, which stuck to him for many years after the end of the war. He was called 'Kiki Fato Yama'. Unfortunately, only the 'Fato' (Clarence was quite overweight at that time) stuck to him in those days and both of us were often referred to as 'Donny and Fato'. It took a very conscious effort within the family to drop the nickname "Fato' for my brother Clarence as well as the nickname 'Baba' for my sister Irene.

Prior to the outbreak of WW II, members of the family travelled almost entirely by foot – to school. work, church or market place. Public transport, such as was available at that time, was rarely used. The only luxury or indulgence was the occasional use of a rickshaw – this happened when Mum had too many 'barang-barangs' (packages) to carry from the market, she used to come home in a rickshaw. In post-war times, after the family moved to Klang, Nanny used to travel by rickshaw too – to her rubber estate in Kapar.

Rickshaw pulling seemed to be mostly associated with the Chinese – one rarely saw Indians or Malays pulling rickshaws. The Chinese rickshaw pullers were wizened and weather-beaten and ran in their open strapped sandals pulling their rickshaws behind them. They all stayed in a 'Kongsi' or clan house located at the bottom of Court Hill in Bukit Nanas. Many of them were opium addicts and smoked their way into oblivion in their dingy 'Kongsi', stretched out on rope-beds. We could catch glimpses of them from outside the kongsi. There must have been a similar 'Kongsi' in Klang too but we never knew where it was located.

The Kepong wilderness

My days in Japanese school did not last for much more than a year. The reason for this was that Dad was transferred to the Forest Research Institute (FRI) in Kepong, Selangor which at that time was considered a remote part of the State. How Dad's assignment or transfer to FRI came about is unclear. In Dad's Statement of Service, there is no entry whatsoever for the period 1941-1945 except for the statement "reported for duty after liberation in September 1945". This period without entry in Dad's service record coincides with the period Dad served in the FRI. I know, for I lived with Dad in Kepong too and remember it only too well. I can only infer that since British staff at FRI had been interred in work camps in Singapore, Dad was probably one of the locals sent to Kepong to fill the breach and keep some basic routines ongoing.

Several months after Dad's transfer, Irene and I were taken to Kepong to live with Dad. I guess our education was hardly a consideration – it was Japanese school anyway. So we simply dropped out of our respective schools. I doubt that the schools were even notified. Shortly after, my sister and I were taken, one at a time, on the back of Dad's bicycle to the house he occupied in Kepong and there we lived until the end of the war.

(**footnote**. The FRI was founded in 1929 as a research and conservation centre in Kepong. In 1986, the institute was made a statutory body and became the Forest Research Institute of Malaysia (FRIM). The original colonial building I used to wander about in as a lad still stands and continues to be used. FRIM has greatly expanded and covers an area of 1528 hectares of 'recreated' forest)..

When I reflect on those happenings so very long ago, it seems to be that there may have been other considerations that influenced the decisions my parents took. They were hard times indeed and with my father working elsewhere in Kepong, my mother had to hold the fort so to speak and take care of her five children all on her own.

It made sense to split the load – hence the decision to send Irene and myself to live with my father. During the years that Irene and I lived in Kepong, we were completely cut off from the rest of the family – not even a week-end visit once a year. One might well ask, what about contact by telephone – we never knew such devices even existed – certainly not in private homes.

This probably was my earliest experience of being cast adrift and thrown in at the deep end. But my elder sister Irene was with me. This greatly blunted the 'trauma' of separation. It seems that 'acceptance' of what life tends to throw one's way became part of my mental fabric from very early in my life.

I remember Dad's bicycle well. Like all bicycles at that time, the tyres were made of solid rubber and were fitted to the rims of the bicycles by stretching. Inflatable tubes to fit the tyres were unavailable. When one combines all three – solid rubber tyres, poorly maintained roads and gravel tracks – it all made for a tedious and uncomfortable ride, not only for the cyclist but also the passenger. We took a few tumbles but suffered no serious mishaps.

Dad's house was a small, semi-detached, two bedroom, brick and tile unit with plain cement floors and a separate kitchen and bathroom. Dad occupied one room while Irene and I shared the other. The jamban or out house (toilet) was about 10 metres away and was almost completely hidden by overgrown 'lallang'. When using the jamban at night we sometimes felt eyes on us – whether real or imagined we did not know. They could have been wild animals but in the innocence of childhood, we felt no fear – there was no one to comfort you anyway.

Life was tough but Irene and I were happy enough. There was no school there and no home tutoring either. Irene did the cooking and cleaning and I helped a little. She was ten and I was nine years old. These were care free days for Irene and me. There was not much to eat and we lived mostly on tapioca and sweet potatoes. The little rice we had was mainly for Dad as he suffered from a stomach ailment. There was no money to spend or buy even the basic necessities. How we even survived is altogether a miracle.

If you wanted to eat, you had to grow it yourself or catch it yourself. From time to time, we did get to eat a little meat and fish. On one occasion, a large ugly looking wild boar with a mean set of tusks wandered into one of the office rooms at the Forest Research Institute. It was trapped, killed and Dad brought home a good cut from the hind leg. We never had beef or lamb although we sometimes got goat meat – which was referred to as 'mutton.' It was probably an 'old nanny goat' as the meat was tough and stringy.

We did have a few fowls though (we never referred to them as 'chooks' in the Malay States) – a strutting rooster and his harem of speckled hens – we kept them for the eggs. Some eggs were separated for hatching. I disliked having to go into the chicken enclosure to collect the eggs – gingerly trying to avoid stepping barefoot on fresh poo.

Fish was also harvested from small lakes in the forest from time to time. The method used was rather primitive as an outlet was dug into the side of the lake and fish that swam through were soon floundering on the leaf covered ground. The lakes were only partially drained and were sealed up soon after. Irene and I helped to gather up the slithering fish – mostly talapia, which were relatively small but were tasty enough. A few catfish also came through. They were hard times but exciting times nevertheless.

Projecting a little into the future and at the same time sidetracking a little, a special bond between Irene and me was forged in those years we spent together as children. Those bonds remained strong all our lives. I still remember meeting Vernon Wickremasinghe at the Kuala Lumpur railway station when he first came down by train from Singapore to meet Irene for the first time. Irene was then a teacher at the La Salle School in Brickfields (suburb of Kuala Lumpur) and was staying with my parents at their house in Petaling Jaya. Irene and Vernon later got married and lived in Singapore.

We kept in touch by phone and I always stopped over in Singapore on my travels abroad – often staying with them. Irene always prepared some great meals whenever I stopped over – roti and fish curry was my favourite. I took Irene and Vernon out to dinner at restaurants from time to time to give Irene a bit of a break.

Irene was unfortunately not in the best of health and often suffered from severe attacks of asthma. I was present once or twice when she had these attacks and it was very disturbing as she became quite disoriented and irrational. She battled on nevertheless.

Returning to the main thread of the story, I recall that while we lived in Kepong, Irene and I looked after Dad's four cows – taking them out to a grazing area in the morning and herding them back at dusk to an enclosed corral built beside the house. Dad arranged for bales of grass to be supplied to the house. These were then transferred to wooden troughs using a rough wooden pitchfork in order to provide feed for the cows at night.

One of Dad's neighbours did the milking of the cows – he got a bottle of milk for his labours while we had the rest. I guess this is what kept us reasonably healthy. Irene and I also helped to light a fire at night to keep the mosquitoes at bay and this proved a real challenge. I do not recall that Irene and I ever got ill! Having put out the cows to graze, Irene and I often wandered through jungle streams catching little fish and prawns – the same streams often visited by tigers and other wild life. The Forest Rangers sometimes reported that tiger claw marks had been seen in areas we had recently been. Despite these reports, we never spotted any tigers or other wild life and both of us remained completely unfazed.

One evening when leading the cows homeward, one of the cows chased me. This was very unusual. The cows were normally quite docile and could easily be controlled and directed using a thin bamboo stick. Something must have spooked the stupid cow. I scampered and jumped over the low fence in front of the house, losing my sarong in the process. The neighbourhood kids saw me in my birthday suit and had a great laugh! I was mortified and did not show my face outside the house for several days!

Usually in the evenings when the day's chores were over, the neighbourhood kids got together on the open grass covered field for a game of football (soccer). The boys and the girls all played together. It was great fun and there was much laughter. Everyone got on well with one another – there were Malays, Chinese, Indians and Eurasians. There was no inter- ethnic friction whatsoever.

Our fathers were all associated with forestry, either as research assistants, forest rangers or as clerical and other support staff at the FRI. British officers who held various positions in FRI in pre-war years had all been interred in work camps and the bungalows they occupied remained empty and unkempt. FRI was now under Japanese administrative control.

One day, we were shocked when several gunmen (Three Star fighters) entered the home of our Chinese neighbour and shot him dead in front of his family. His children were our very good friends. The gunmen did not harm the family. It was a very traumatic experience for all of us, especially for the family, most of whom were about our age. We lost track of this lovely family when the war ended.

By 1944 it became evident that the war in the Pacific was going badly for the Japanese. The Japanese Newspapers, *Asahi Shimbun, Syonan Shimbun and Malai Shimbun* continued to paint a picture of Japanese victories. But we knew otherwise. We did not have a radio but there were those who had clandestine access to BBC broadcasts and the news spread. With the dropping of the atomic bomb on Hiroshima and Nagasaki, the Japanese folded.

But it was not a tame surrender. There were members of the Japanese War Cabinet who were still resistant. It finally required the intervention of the Emperor of Japan to direct the War Cabinet to accept the terms of surrender. On 2nd September 1945, the formal surrender of Japanese Imperial Forces was formalised on the USS Missouri in Tokyo Bay. The USS Missouri was chosen because Missouri was President Truman's home state.

The Japanese never anticipated that their homeland could be touched. In the Malay States and in Kepong where I lived, it was thrilling to see low flying Allied aircraft distributing thousands of leaflets and we kids scrambling around to get copies. There was great jubilation everywhere.

In researching the war years in Malaya, I am absolutely amazed at how well, we as children, were shielded from the horrors of the war. I knew nothing. If our parents knew anything at all, they kept it from us. Thousands died, many were executed and thousands were forced to work on the 'death railway' in Siam (Thailand). Very few ever came back. In the period 1943-45, when allied forces began to make a comeback, there were allied blockades, guerilla attacks on Japanese outposts, as well as bombings by B29 aircraft. We knew nothing at all. We did not even know of the many atrocities committed by Japanese commanders in Malaya.

Although the war years and the period of Japanese occupation was a traumatic experience for many, we were not aware of any within our circle of family and friends who were so affected. No member of our family ever experienced the brutality of the war. For us, food shortages were the most serious problem and staple foods like rice as well as other foods the family had got used to in pre-war years were no longer available. But Dad and Mum were very resourceful and I do not recall that any in the family ever experienced real hunger.

Dad was a respecter of authority. During the Japanese Occupation, Dad steered clear of any involvement in anti Japanese activity. Neither was he a collaborator for the Japanese either. Dad just went about doing his normal job – and that kept the family safe.

Although I attended Japanese school (at SJI) for only a year, I picked up enough Japanese to converse at an elementary level. I have long forgotten much of it but can still count in Japanese and sing a few Japanese songs. I do not know how all of this was ever accomplished as none of my former teachers at SJI were Japanese speakers and had to learn the language themselves.

Never did I dream then that years later in my working life I would visit Japan on more than one occasion as a guest of Japanese institutions, to serve on expert panels, deliver working papers or chair sessions at international conferences in Tokyo.

The Ending of Rule Britannia

The ending of the War saw the British back in control, with the setting up of the British Military Administration – but not for long. We were just glad that the war was over.

The Malay States were in dire straits with the shortage of food and medical facilities. The rubber plantations and tin mining activities had ground to a halt. A huge military victory parade was staged soon after the end of the war. This was a great morale booster. The military parade of tanks, troops and heavy artillery passed by along Weld Road (today called Jalan Raja Chulan) right opposite our house in Bukit Nanas. We had a grandstand view!

Rejoining the family

It was a wonderful feeling for the whole family to be together again in our Bukit Nanas house. There was no public transport that serviced the Kepong area at that time and so Irene was brought back to Bukit Nanas on the carrier of Dad's bicycle while I got a lift from one of the Forest Rangers.

Later, when Dad finally left Kepong, he brought with him a whole tub-full of live fish – mostly catfish. They must have drained the lake in Kepong. We transferred the fish to several containers but in the morning most of the fish had jumped out and had slithered into the monsoon drains that surrounded the house. Although there was no water in the drains, the fish were still alive. We recaptured all of them and had a diet of fish for days on end.

The Japanese occupation proved that the British could be beaten and this fuelled nascent movements striving for independence. While liberation ushered in a period of British Military Administration (BMA), other political developments also took place as progressive stages of self-government were put in place. Among them were the British Proposal of the Malayan Union which was rejected and short lived.

These developments have been well documented elsewhere and will not be touched upon unless it impacted in some way on the family story. But the British were not exactly bundled out. They held on to power one way or another for another 12 years. The Malay States only achieved political independence in 1957. British influence and particularly British interests in the mining and plantation industries remained virtually unaffected for decades.

Mum's family members in Ceylon sent over parcels of second hand clothes which came in very useful. Fresh fish and meat became available in the Central Market and things began to look up. For the first time, butter in large tins, became available.

It was roughly about this time that I fell seriously ill with typhus and nearly died. There was little in the way of medicines and medical facilities were seriously wanting. Typhus is an acute infectious disease characterised by high fever, total exhaustion and dark red skin eruptions and can be fatal. My mother refused to give up and nursed me through it all. In the process she was infected too and nearly lost all her hair. But we both recovered. I remember during the war years we were given quinine (made from the bark of the cinchona tree – to ward off attacks of malaria) but do not recall how it was administered.

All through our growing years our sleeping arrangements hardly changed. We kids always slept on thin woven mats which were rolled out on the wooden floor. They were rolled up and put away when we got up in the morning. Mum and Dad had a mattress and pillows but my recollection was that they were stuffed with coconut fibre and were somewhat lumpy. We never had the luxury of sleeping in individual beds or having our very own rooms.

Even our individual grooming was quite simple. We all used coconut oil for our hair and crushed charcoal applied with the index finger to clean our teeth! There was no such thing as tooth-paste or hair-gels, deodorants or scented soaps. We all used crude bars of washing soap for washing our clothes as well as our bodies.

Most important of all, we went back to school. English was the medium of instruction once again. On my first day at my old school (SJI) – I was already 12 – the pupils were told at Assembly to go back to the class they attended before the war started. Yours truly, being conscious of the fact that four years of schooling had already been lost because of the war, decided to stand with the kids in Standard three, rather than the kids in Standard one. Nobody questioned me. I felt I could cope and I did.

Dad went back to his job in the Forest Department Kuala Lumpur. His Office was on Weld Road, on the opposite side of Bukit Nanas and so he walked to work. My sisters went back to school too but I am not sure about the class they were placed in. Mum continued to manage the home and practically everything else.

Since cooking was done on wood fires, there was a need for a regular supply of firewood. Being in the Forestry Department, Dad knew which trees could be cut and from time to time we all went deep into the jungle clad hillside beside our house in Bukit Nanas where selected trees were felled. This was done entirely by the adults using a long two-handled saw drawn by two people. The kids kept well out of the way and took great delight in shouting 'timber' when the tree was on the verge of toppling over.

Only one or two trees were felled at any one time, but it gave us enough firewood to last us many months. The tree trunks were then sawn into convenient lengths. Only at this stage were the kids allowed to participate by rolling the sawn logs downhill. The logs rolled and tumbled, flattening the undergrowth as they thundered down the hill side, stopping only metres from the house. Later the adults chopped the logs into smaller pieces for firewood.

But times were still hard and from time to time the whole family went into the nearby jungle with small 'gunny-sacks' slung over our shoulders, to collect insect skins of a particular insect species which shed its skin casing on leaves and branches. These were then sold to the Chinese medicine shops.

At some stage Dad and his brother (Uncle Roy) and another cousin (Uncle Noel) decided to go into the salt-fish business and they came back one day with 'gunny sacks' of salt-fish. Unfortunately, the salt- fish were not properly salted and went bad. In an attempt to salvage something from the joint venture (besides their pride), they spread the salt fish on the roof of the house to dry out further. The whole venture was an utter disaster and they never went into the salt-fish business again.

L/R Roy, Noel Samarakody, Dad

I remember another incident, again involving my brother Clarence. The grass around our house in Bukit Nanas used to be cut from time to time using a scythe blade. When not in use, the scythe blade was kept in the store room adjoining the kitchen. One day when mum was in the kitchen cooking (we were all out), Clarence was amusing himself chasing the cat which darted into the store room. Clarence followed, ran straight into the scythe blade and was cut to the bone at the ankle. He was bleeding profusely. Mum stemmed the blood flow as best she could and carried him (he used to be a bit plump) nearly 2km to the Hospital in Pudu Road. Clarence got five stitches and carried the scar his whole life through.

Mum was always a very caring sort of person. I recall an occasion while accompanying her to the market, a motor cyclist took a corner around the back lane we were walking by, hit a lamp-post and was thrown off his bike. He was bleeding profusely. Mum immediately went to his aid and tried to stem the blood flow until neighbours close by came over and took the man to the hospital. We did not have ambulances then – I never knew they even existed.

The family's shopping needs were very modest – the Central Market and the towkey's provision shop supplied most of our needs. We never did any shopping at the up market stores – John Little, Robinsons or Whiteaways – which were frequented by the orang putih. We only looked from the outside but never walked in – all this the orang putih took for granted for it was British Malaya.

Other little incidents also come to mind. Dad kept a few rabbits and guinea pigs as a hobby. One day before leaving for work, he asked me to clean out the rabbit pen. When he came home during the lunch break, he was furious to note that the rabbit pen had not been cleaned. I could see that he was pulling out his belt to give me a few of the best but I was having none of that.

I knew I was faster than him and besides, I figured that if he removed his belt, he would have to use his other hand to hold up his trousers which meant that he would not be able to move very fast. I jumped out of the kitchen window and took off. Mum calmed him down – must have been a bad day at the office. I came back when the coast was clear and cleaned out the rabbit pen. No more was said about it.

In the last few years of our stay at our home in Bukit Nanas, we were fortunate to enjoy a durian 'fest' during the durian season when Dad's contacts in the Forestry Service would bring to the house a gunny sack full of ripe durians. It took a few days to eat all the durians – all of us, including Nanny sat on a mat on the covered passage way leading to the kitchen while Dad prised open the ripe fruit with the sharp point of a parang or machete. Durian eating was usually followed with mangosteens to counteract any negative effects of eating too many durians. The soft golden flesh of the durian pods and the sweet white pods of the mangosteens were an unbeatable combination.

During my last visit to Kuala Lumpur a month or two ago, my nephew Arjuna and a few friends took me out to a stall of durians, not too far from our old house in Section 17, Petaling Jaya – it brought back many memories. These days however, durian eating has become far more sophisticated – there are so many more durian varieties to choose from and fresh coconut water to drink using a straw dipped into the lopped off top of a green coconut.

Dad's abiding interest was in his poultry. I watched him when he made the chicken coops and small cages for the incubation of little chicks. There was ample room in our Bukit Nanas home for poultry keeping. Later when the family moved to Klang, Dad developed an interest in specific breeds such as the Rhode Island Reds, the White Leghorns, the Plymouth Rock, the Australorps and the Speckled Sussex – it all sounds so very British!

Dad also won some prizes for his birds at the Agricultural Shows. Dad was able to keep his chicken coops, not at the house in Camp Road, Port Swettenham or the Riverside Road house we lived in later, but the house the family moved to in Bukit Kuda Road, Klang. This house actually belonged to Encik Mydin – Dad's boss at the Forest Office, Klang.

Once the family moved to their new house in Petaling Jaya, the poultry had to go. This was when Dad began to cultivate his orchids and developed his interest in stamp collecting – these interests kept him going the rest of his life. When Dad retired in 1960, he worked as a volunteer in medical records at the Assunta Hospital until he died in 1982 – an exemplary record.

Dad kept in touch with a few of his friends after his retirement. There were two or three of them – who were also stamp collectors. Curiously, these friends were never identified by their first names. One was referred to as 'Petrol' Silva – simply because he operated a Shell Petrol Station in Bungsar – his surname was Silva. The other friend was called 'kata Perera.' I always thought that this friend was given this nick-name because he had a big mouth – a chatter-box or motor mouth so to speak, simply because 'kata' in Sinhalese meant mouth. It was only long after Dad died that I discovered that it was not 'kata' but 'cutter' – the bloke was simply a tailor and a good cutter of cloth and Perera was his surname. I wonder whether my Dad was identified by them in similar vein as 'kale' Wije or 'kale' Suriya – since 'kale' in Sinhalese meant forest. Dad was always identified with the forestry service.

Dad smoked all his life – it is probably what killed him at the end. During the Japanese Occupation Dad used to carry a little tobacco pouch with strips of wafer thin cigarette paper in a pack. A little tobacco was sprinkled on to a single strip of paper; it was licked at one end and rolled up to make the cigarette. He also carried two small pieces of flint which were struck to create a spark and held to a tuft of fluff – and this is how the cigarettes were lighted.

Later on in life he bought his cigarettes in tins or cartons and from time to time also smoked a pipe. Dad had a habit of smoking a cigarette until the ash curled to virtual dropping point and Mum would say "Sam, for God's sake, use the ashtray!" He invariably did when it was too late and my mother had to sweep up the ash. She was not pleased. Dad would just grin and say "Flo, cup of tea?"

The move to Klang

In 1947 there was an opening for the position of Chief Clerk in the Forest Office in Klang, which was on the coast about 30km south west of Kuala Lumpur. Dad was persuaded, mostly by Mum, to take up the post – which he did, and the family left Bukit Nanas for good. Dad could not find suitable housing in Klang to rent. Eventually though, we ended up in a semi-detached house built in the traditional style on columns on Camp Road, Port Swettenham (today called Port Klang). We only stayed there a year and travelled each day to school by taxi.

My two sisters attended the Convent of the Holy Infant Jesus in Klang while Clarence and I were admitted to the Klang High School, which was a secondary school on Meru Road.

Basil attended St Bernadette's school (which was close to Dad's office). My school leaving certificate signed by the Brother Director, St. John's Institution dated 30th December 1947 stated that I had passed Standard III and was promoted to Standard IV. Norbert was too young to be enrolled in school and stayed home with my mother. There were no kindergartens at that time.

Clarence and I attended the High School Klang for only two years. When we left for Ceylon at the end of the school year in November 1949 I had only passed Standard six and was already fifteen years old. My scholastic record in High School Klang (HSK) was always very good. I was invariably either 1st or 2nd in the class exams. Paul Chang, my English teacher, used to say that he would fail the entire class in English except Donald and he would tap my head with a ruler – I usually sat in the front row.

The Riverside Road house

In 1948, the family moved again from Camp Road in Port Swettenham to Riverside Road, Klang. As usual, Dad was able to have the use of the 3-ton Lorries (trucks) from the Forest Department motor-pool to move the furniture and other 'latta lottas' (household goods). There were no fridges, cookers or other appliances to move as we had none. But we did take with us a few traditional kitchen tools – in particular, the wangediya (a very heavy pounder, fashioned from a single block of Jak wood with a larger and smaller cavity for pounding ingredients) as well as the mol gaha (stone grinder) and the hiramanaya (coconut scraper).

Our move was to a semi-detached house on Riverside Road, about 5km from the school. The house was built in the traditional style on columns. This was a rather small two room house with a single bathroom, a small veranda in the front and a rear veranda where we had our meals. A covered passageway led to the kitchen and adjoining storeroom. An enclosed backyard with a high wooden fence provided some privacy as well as parking for the car while the wc (water closet), out-house or toilet was set against the back fence.

The whole family – Dad, Mum, the six children and Nanny lived in this little house. Mum cooked over a wood fire for everybody. She cooked daily as there was no fridge and she did all the washing too with a little help from my sisters. The house did have electricity as well as running water from a tap. Sunday was an off day for Mum as we attended mass and then bought some take-away from the Indian restaurant on Rembau Street – usually dhosai, sambah, pol sambol, sodhi and idali. The very wide range of take-away meals available today were unknown then.

We often got lifts to school; sometimes we walked. Later my parents bought me a brand new Raleigh bicycle and I sometimes gave Clarence a lift to school. I disliked doing so as Clarence was not a light-weight. The road to school traversed the muddy, crocodile infested Klang River. There was a single pontoon bridge for all traffic to cross the river, the level of which changed depending on whether the tide was coming in or going out. At low tide, most of the pontoons fell to the low level of the river making the ends very steep. At such times, one had to get off the bike and push it up the slope. Going down was naturally risky if you did not have good brakes.

It was about this time that Dad bought a small second-hand car. It was an Austin 7 and had a fold-down canvas hood. It was green in colour and was started manually by cranking up the motor. Uncle Roy used to visit us from time to time in his brand new Morris 8. Wow, the car even had very nice carpeting! Dad's Austin 7 was indeed the poor relative. Dad traded his Austin 7 about a year later and bought a brand new black Wolsley 8– most cars were black in those days. Since Basil's school was close to Dad's Office, he often got lifts from Dad to school.

One morning when cycling to school, I passed by one of the houses by the riverside which had a little garden enclosed by wire netting. During the night, a large crocodile – about two and a half metres long – had crept into the garden to get at the chickens and had got its snout firmly trapped in the netting. Quite a crowd had gathered. I stopped briefly as I did not wish to be late for school. The croc was an ugly looking creature and it kept thrashing its tail in trying to get free. I did not tarry to witness the drama unfold, but it was an unusual experience.

Nanny

Nanny stayed with us for one or two years. Nanny was a cheroot smoker and had the habit of tucking her half smoked cheroots on the side planks of our wooden house, no doubt intending to smoke them later, which she never did. We had the task of picking up all her cheroot butts and throwing them in the rubbish bin. A closer examination of Nanny's photo will reveal a drooping of her lips on one side – the result of her many years of cheroot smoking.

Nanny used to sit in the evening in her favourite recliner settee, her tubby legs extended on the low armrests which could be swivelled and extended. We kids used to lie on the wooden floor facing her, our chins cupped in our palms, just waiting in anticipation for what would surely happen and then, a cherubic smile would appear on Nanny's face and she would sway her tubby little body ever so slightly sideways and release a pent up explosion of wind. The kids were in fits of laughter and swore that when Nanny broke wind in Klang, she could be heard all the way in Port Swettenham. And then Nanny started laughing too, her droopy breasts resting on her tummy would jiggle with her laughter. How could we ever forget Nanny – she was quite a woman.

Family photo outside Riverside road house

Nanny's rubber plantation

I remember that Nanny owned a small rubber estate or plantation in Kapar, not far from Klang town. The plantation was relatively small. I have no idea of its acreage nor do I know whether she inherited it from grandfather or whether she bought it herself. It is probably the latter as grandfather died as far back as 1919. Simple logic seems to suggest that the plantation was an astute post war purchase but who really were the key players in all this is a matter of conjecture. It certainly was not my Dad but it could have been Uncle Roy who was somewhat more business minded. One may also wonder where exactly the money came from to purchase the plantation.

When I consider that in my Dad's generation and in my own, we did not dare go beyond the purchase of modest building blocks on which the family home was built. And here was Nanny having the gumption to purchase a whole plantation, employ 'coolies' or rubber tappers as well as mandores or kangkanis (foreman or overseer). But that was not all. Nanny obviously had an overall appreciation of managing a rubber smallholding.

I do remember as a lad going with Nanny to the rubber estate in a rickshaw drawn by a rickshaw puller, to pay the coolies their wages and attend to other matters, including inspecting the living quarters for the coolies and the building of a small kovil (Hindu Temple) on the plantation. Most of the coolies were Tamils and were Hindu by religion. I think Nanny could speak a little Tamil as she often had to deal with the mandore or kangkani. The kangkani – a somewhat lean and skinny Tamil man – was called Muthu. Nanny and Muthu got on very well.

The ride in the rickshaw was quite interesting too – especially when it came to crossing the Klang River on the pontoon bridge – the only bridge across the river at that time.

It was all very well if the bridge was crossed at high tide as the bridge kept level with both banks. But if the crossing was done at low tide, the rickshaw man's task pulling the rickshaw upslope with Nanny and me in it was an uphill task to say the least but even the downslope descent was difficult as rickshaws do not have any brakes – it had to be leg brakes all the way – the poor rickshaw man's, of course.

While on Nanny's plantation, I used to observe the rubber tappers cutting v-shaped grooves at the base of the rubber trees and watch the milky white latex trickle down into a cup. The cups were later emptied into containers and taken to the smokehouse where they were treated with a special acid in order to coagulate, after which they were manually hand rolled into sheets and hung out in the smoke house to be cured or dried. The smoked rubber sheets were then packed in bales and taken to the Chinese rubber traders for transport, shipping and export. Malaya was then the world's largest exporter of rubber and Nanny as a small-holder was part of this.

As a child, I remember collecting dried up strips of rubber from the base of the rubber trees which we wound into little balls which we could play with. We also collected the dried, shiny shelled rubber seeds to play with. On another occasion I went with Dad who was standing in for Nanny. We went in Dad's little Austin 7 and Clarence came along too. We were both making a nuisance of ourselves in the back seat and Dad was most annoyed with us.

Regrettably, the plantation was sold after Nanny died as neither my Dad nor Uncle Roy had the interest or the time to take on the management of the estate. They both had their full time jobs to cope with as well as their growing families. Exactly who handled the sale, how much was realised and who benefitted from the sale is unclear.

I gather that there were some frosty exchanges within the broader family when the proceeds of the sale were discussed. I was not there and never witnessed any of it. True to character Dad said nothing and did nothing – but not Mum. I very much doubt that Dad got anything but he never complained or said anything. I believe the proceeds went largely to Aunty Baby as Nanny stayed mostly with her and Uncle John in the last few years of her life. I was in Kuala Lumpur when Nanny died and went to her funeral at the Cheras Road Cemetery.

Diabetic strands

Nanny was a diabetic but as far as I know the condition was treated using traditional medicine as well as diet control. I do not recall that Nanny ever took pills of any kind and neither did my Dad, who later in life also became diabetic. I still recall that after dinner Dad drank a small glass of 'tairu.' This was home made yogurt mixed with water to which a pinch of salt was added. Whether this helped to contain the condition I do not know for he seemed to enjoy my mother's cooking. I do not recall that my mother ever cooked special food to accommodate Dad's diabetes.

I do recall however as a lad being sent on my bicycle to the abattoir – about 2km from our home in Riverside Road, Klang – to collect freshly slaughtered pig's pancreas which was boiled in water. This Nanny drank regularly to keep her diabetic condition under control. I disliked very much having to go to the abattoir and having to watch the pigs being killed. I tried to time it so that I arrived when it was all over.

Diabetes is hereditary as later in life both my sister Irene (now deceased) and I were deemed to be type 2 diabetics. A combination of diet control and medication helps to keep my type 2 diabetes under control. In more recent times, my diabetic condition has deteriorated and it has been necessary to have daily insulin jabs. Perhaps traditional remedies used by my father might be worth exploring.

In more recent times, it was brought to my attention that an insulin jab once a week was also available on the market. I thought this was wonderful and decided to ask my diabetic specialist what he thought about it. He categorically told me that he did not think it would suit me but said I could try it out if I wished. He said that he had a sample in his desk drawer and brought out this enormous syringe and needle. I was absolutely horrified and told the doctor I was fully convinced . No more was said on the matter.

Rekindling links with Ceylon

In 1948 my mother's elder brother Percy (Percy Uncle to us kids) came over from Ceylon for a visit. We later understood that there was an ulterior motive for that visit. Nanny was still alive then and may have played some part in trying to arrange a suitable match between him and her youngest daughter (our Aunty Baby). My mother told me years later (after Dad passed away) that Dad paid for Percy Uncle's visit. I have no recollection whether Percy Uncle came over by air or sea.

Percy Uncle's visit

Percy Uncle was very sociable and entertaining. He had a pleasant voice and entertained us with Baila singing and other popular numbers both in English and Sinhalese. His rendering of 'Goodnight Irene' went down rather well especially with my sister Irene. I also remember his rendering of a Sinhalese ditty called 'handha paney' (the moon is shining).

My parents also organised a visit to the sea side at Morib for Percy Uncle. Nanny came along too and Mum looked good in a one-piece swim suit. Dad arranged to use one of the Forest Department lorries(trucks) to cart the whole ranchuwa (group) to Morib. Percy Uncle's visit overall was quite pleasant and enjoyable. He left a few weeks later and life returned to normal.

(**footnote**. L to R standing: Irene, Percy Uncle, Jenny: seated: Uncle Stephen, Aunty Jenny, Nanny, Mum, Norbert, Dad, Aunty Baby: seated on floor: Clarence, Basil, Donnie)

Cultural footprint

I very much doubt that the Sinhalese in Malaya ever established a significant cultural footprint. In the 1930s, the Sinhalese community were numerically of little consequence. At the political level, they had little presence and were simply categorised as Ceylonese, while the socially more prominent and successful among them were the Ceylon Tamils – often referred to as Jaffna Tamils. The Malayan Ceylonese Congress which was established in 1958 supported the Alliance leadership but even within this group, it was the ethnic Tamils who were the more prominent.

Sinhalese culinary traditions however continued to be passed down from generation to generation. There were even short lived attempts to establish a Ceylon or Sri Lankan eatery or restaurant where one could get 'hoppers', 'seeni sambal', 'pol sambal', kiri hodi and a variety of authentic Sri Lankan curries. On festive occasions in Sinhalese homes, 'kiri bath' (rice cooked in coconut milk) and 'kaha bath' (yellow rice) were invariably served – this was very familiar fare in our own home.

Unfortunately, the community as a whole, failed to recognise that one of the most important features of cultural expression is language. This should have been fostered not only within individual families but it should also been institutionalised – most logically at the Buddhist Temple in Brickfields, which remained a focal point for many Sinhalese who were Buddhists.

Percy Uncle seems to have stirred up something within the family, for not long after his visit, my parents decided, for some reason unknown to us, that the children needed to learn Sinhalese. They engaged the services of a Sinhalese gentleman (not a qualified teacher) who turned up once or twice a week in a white sarong and sandals to conduct a Sinhalese language class for all of us at the same time. Unfortunately, none of us took the classes seriously and they proved to be a complete flop. Giggle, giggle, giggle! It might have helped if we (the children) had been told why it was necessary for us to learn Sinhalese.

It seems to me that during our growing up years, my mother could easily have taught us to speak and write in Sinhalese but she never did. I suspect that she probably deferred to my father who did not speak a word of the language and felt that it had little application in the Malay world – true enough but nevertheless short sighted. The Sinhalese language with its close association with Sanskrit and Pali is an ancient language and it should have been kept alive within the family, at the very least.

Years later, in the seventies, we all took Sinhala classes at the Buddhist Temple in Brickfields. The class included not only our own family but also a few of Annette's siblings including her sister Chitra and her brother Brian and wife Gwen. The hamuduruwo or Buddhist monk at the temple was our instructor. Unfortunately, teaching a varied group such as the lot of us, some of whom had no exposure to the language at all, was an uphill task. This valiant effort to keep the language alive within the family did not last very long.

My own visits to Sri Lanka in 2009, 2011 and 2013 has brought back to me some level of competence in the language. It is my hope that all my sons will make a special effort to visit Sri Lanka from time to time to get a real feel for their ancestral country, its history and its people. There are many second cousins the boys could reconnect with.

The communist insurgency

The insurgency in post war Malaya was a struggle largely played out while the country was still under British control. It was still British Malaya and hence the Colonial Office was able to draw, not only on its own resources but also that of the Commonwealth, particularly Australia to contain the armed struggle. The air base in Butterworth – now Seberang Prai – was built by the Australians where they maintained a strike squadron which was effectively deployed against the insurgents.

The insurgents – mostly Chinese youth – were earlier part of the Malayan Peoples Anti Japanese Army(Three Star Fighters), who were armed and supported by the British to destabilise the Japanese forces in the Malay Peninsula. They were however abandoned after the war and became the military wing of the Malayan Communist Party which sought to overthrow the British in Malaya. In the hostilities which followed, the Brits in management positions in the rubber estates and the tin mines were the main targets. It was not unusual to see these Brits fully armed, venturing into town on their normal day to day business. The locals, unless they were in the armed forces or the police were not caught up in the conflict to a great extent.

Political developments put in place in the aftermath of the war further increased communal tensions. Terrorist activities also escalated after 3 British plantation managers were ambushed and killed in Perak in 1948. In 1950, General Sir Harold Briggs was recalled to active duty and installed as Director of Operations in Malaya at the height of the emergency. Briggs recognised that the insurgents were able to sustain their operations especially in terms of food supply, because of support from rural Chinese communities. In addition, these rural communities were also potential sources for recruitment.

Briggs instituted what was referred to as the Briggs plan in which about 500,000 Chinese in the rural areas were resettled in about 450 'New Villages' which were surrounded by barbed wire with security patrols at exit points. Some Malays and Indians were also caught up in these enforced resettlement schemes. While this was initially resented, the resettlement programme proved very successful as the new villages were provided with electricity as well as educational and health support facilities which rural communities never had previously.

The Briggs plan to win the hearts and minds of the people and to progressively rid the states of the communist threat starting from Johore in the south was beginning to work. Despite this, it was unfortunate that the British High Commissioner Sir Henry Gurney was ambushed and killed on his way to Fraser's Hill in 1951. Briggs himself only served for a short period and went back into retirement in Cyprus but recommended that to sustain the progressive developments put in place, the Director of Operations should in future also have executive authority. Following this, Sir Gerald Templer was appointed High Commissioner and also Director of Operations in 1952. Under Templer's leadership, the tide bagan to turn as other measures were also put in place. Templer was somewhat authoritarian but he got the job done.

As a family of urban dwellers living in Kuala Lumpur and in Klang, we were never caught up in any facet of the insurgency. While the family were living in Klang, I remember as a boy being a part of the family's occasional trip to the seaside – usually during the school holidays. The seaside for us was a place called Morib, located on the coast not far south of Klang.

This was at the height of the insurgency. Seaside holiday makers were required to arrive at a designated assembly point to join a convoy of vehicles with an armed escort at the front and rear of the convoy. The same security precautions had to be adhered to for the return journey. We never stayed overnight and we never faced any problems in our seaside outings – largely because the relatively flat and open terrain and Malay 'kampongs ' (villages) we passed through afforded little cover for communist insurgents. Morib was the furthest we ever ventured from home so we were never in any real danger.

Morib was particularly memorable for us when we were growing up. We enjoyed frolicking in the shallow water and digging up clams or shell fish called 'kerang' in the muddy sea-shore when the tide receeded. The clams were somewhat bloody when shelled but quite delicious when fried with 'kwey theow' – a very popular flat noodle dish. Those halcyon days have been captured in photographs – one particularly memorable one is of Nanny in her Malay sarong sitting on a stool at low tide – surrounded by the water. It reminded me of Hemingway's 'Old man and the sea' except that Nanny was a very far cry from the character depicted in the novel!

While active forays by the armed forces and the police, including air support were conducted into areas where the insurgent jungle camps were located, we were unaware of it all. We did not even have a radio at that time to listen to the news broadcasts. I grew up completely in the dark about the evolving political landscape.

It is only in more recent times that I discovered that the period of armed conflict from 1948 -1960 was labelled the 'communist insurgency' and the 'emergency' rather than a 'war' because of insurance considerations regarding claims for damages by Lloyds in London. The stepping up of psychological tactics, the policy of winning the hearts and minds of the people, effective propaganda, the offering of substantial cash rewards for valuable intelligence supplied as well as amnesty without penalty for those who surrendered, progressively starved the insurgents and pushed them further and further north. By 1952, the insurgents – referred to more often as bandits or terrorists, had become a spent force. The 'new villages' of long ago – now without the barbed wire – have become vibrant, thriving communities.

Other measures put in place in 1948 and 1960 in regard to an identity card (IC) as well as The Internal Security Act have become a lasting feature of political control and has affected all of us. In fact, nothing can be done these days in Malaysia without the IC or smart card!

Our little world

In all our growing up years in pre-war and post-war Malaya, the family never received the daily or weekly newspapers in English. As kids we were quite unaware of happenings in the wider world around us. Information and news was largely communicated by word of mouth. We knew nothing of the evolving political situation in the country.

If Dad had any political leanings he never showed it within the family. For that matter there were never any meaningful discussions within the family – about anything. If more weighty matters were discussed at all, it was only between my parents and not for our ears. From time to time when Uncle Roy visited, he often touched on developments within the country – we kids strained to listen, but never got a sense of what was really happening in the country.

There was little music in our lives either at that time. My mother however loved to sing. I learned from her many popular songs from yesteryear – including 'Beautiful Dreamer', 'Let me call you sweetheart', 'I'll be loving you always', 'With someone like you,' 'I am a gay caballero', 'Constantinople', 'Me and Jane in a plane' and many others.

Dad was however not very musically minded. At our home in Bukit Nanas and later at Riverside Road, Klang, we did not even have a radio or a musical instrument of any kind. The musical environment at home changed, a few years later, with the addition of a piano as well as a radiogram. The reason for this was that both my sisters had qualified as teachers and were now able to contribute towards the household expenses. Jenny and Norbert subsequently took up piano playing under a private tutor and were able to make music a career line later in life.

While mum made regular trips to the market to buy the family's daily consumables like fish, meat, vegetables and fruit, she also made purchases, usually once a month, from her regular provision shop. This was for rice, salt, sugar, flour, coffee, tea, condensed milk. lentils,canned fish, sauces and other goods – which were purchased on credit. The Chinese 'towkay' (shop owner) kept tally of goods purchased, which were totalled and paid for at the end of each month.

Those were the days of the itinerant vendors or hawkers, who pedalled their bicycles with a full load of their 'trading 'goods. This included the cloth man – usually a turbaned Sikh or 'Bangaliman' as we used to refer to him with bales of various fabrics at the back of his bicycle. He would measure out and cut a piece of fabric my mum had chosen, on the front veranda of our house in Riverside road. This did not happen when the family lived in Bukit Nanas as it was far too tedious for these street vendors to push their heavily loaded bicycles up the hill to our house. Our Riverside Road house on the other hand, had a roadside location and was easily accessible.

The rotiman (bread man) and the milk man were regular callers and supplied us with fresh bread and milk. The dhoby (laundry-man) turned up once a month to collect the family's dirty clothes. Food hawkers also came by our street frequently.

It is most interesting that the various tradesmen and hawkers were invariably associated with a particular ethnic group –

the shopkeeper was Chinese; the dhoby was Chinese; the cloth-man was Sikh; the rotiman and the milkman were invariably Indian Muslim. The hawkers who came to our street regularly to offer their eating specialities – 'taufu-fa', 'mee-yoke', 'kwey theow goreng' and 'popiah' were always Chinese while the 'rojak' and the 'chendol' hawkers were always Indian Muslim. Malay hawkers were very rare. One may run into a Malay hawker on occasion – usually a satay seller who preferred to remain in a single vantage point.

Strangely, the only Malays who turned up were the gardeners – grass cutting was entirely manual, using scythe blades. Indians took on these roles at later stages, carrying their lawn mowers on the back of their motor-bikes. Mum's gardener Arumugam was Indian (Tamil).

Societal wedding

Not long after the family moved to Klang, there was much excitement over Uncle Roy's wedding which was to take place in Singapore and we had never even been to Singapore before. We gathered from my mother that Uncle Roy was to marry a young lady named Lennie de Silva (later to become our Aunty Lennie) who was the elder of two daughters from a well known Sinhalese family from Singapore.

Dad and Mum decided that the whole family would be going to Singapore for the wedding and arrangements were made for all of us to stay at Aunty Gladys' small terrace house in Geylang - how we all fitted in is quite amazing! The wedding reception was to be held at City Hall, Singapore and a further reception was to take place at Eastern Hotel in Kuala Lumpur for the homecoming celebrations.

There was even ball room dancing with the bride and groom leading off other couples on the dance floor. I remember that Uncle Roy attended dance classes for a while in preparation for the big event. All of us kids got new clothes not only for the wedding but also pyjamas for night time wear – in case we had to be billeted with our 'new' in-laws! We had to be appropriately dressed!

Prior to the wedding, Mum and Aunty Gladys went to 'Change Alley' in Singapore to do a bit of shopping. Both were dressed in sarees – voile and taffeta were the favoured fabrics then. Unfortunately it rained while they were out shopping and they were drenched. They came home in a rickshaw looking quite comical as their sarees had shrunk to just below their knees.

The trip to Singapore by train was exciting but uneventful. This was at the height of the emergency and we were warned that if there was any shooting directed at the train, we were to lie down flat for safety – but nothing happened. The night–mail (train) to Singapore was hooked-up to an armoured car equipped with a machine gun both at the front and the rear of the train. We travelled in a second class carriage and shared a couple of sleeping berths. There were no passport formalities whatsoever on entering Singapore. Malaya and Singapore were then still one country (or colony) under the British.

Although nothing was said about this at the time, this was another 'arranged' marriage - just like that of my parents, with no coercion of any kind. The parties concerned were introduced to one another but were completely free to make up their own minds whether they wished to marry or not. Who made the 'arrangements' and whether a dowry was paid or not is not known.

Neighbourhood games

Coming down to the realities of everyday life back home, we had the open spaces for our entertainment and we were inventive. We played games that entertained us but did not cost much. 'Court Marshal' only required a brick and a soft ball and was played by two teams – both boys and girls in two mixed teams; rounders was another softball game while 'kaunti kaunta' only required a firm stick or sapling of a branch about 18 inches long and a little piece about 3 inches.

Kite flying and top spinning added another dimension but it only came after the war. The collecting of various brands of cigarette packets also became very popular – Rough Rider, Capstan, Ardath, Players. These were used to play throwing games with. They were also bartered or exchanged and made into toys. Like most boys, we took to shooting birds with catapults – we rarely hit anything and only succeeded in putting the birds to flight.

In our growing years, I do not recall that we got toys as gifts at Christmas or on our birthdays. These only came in the post war years. I still recall one Christmas when the family lived in our Riverside Road house in Klang, I was looking forward very much to getting a train set as a Christmas present but got a one volume encyclopaedia instead – I was so very disappointed and cried. But looking back, it was a far better gift as it placed within my hands a world of knowledge and information – not that I used it much.

Dad used to play tennis at the Klang and Coast Club. I used to go along and served as ball picker. Dad also used to play tennis at the courts in the Hospital Grounds while I played in the Church grounds located almost opposite the Hospital.

On one occasion, while playing basketball, I accidentally fell on a bamboo fence beside the basketball court and a sharp spike entered my temple. I was bleeding profusely. Dad was informed and he came rushing down and carried me to the Hospital. It was indeed touch and go. There was a small scar on the side of my temple for some years which I wore like a badge. It has since disappeared.

Reading and story telling

Dad himself was a voracious reader. Apart from Dad's interests in his orchids, reading was a regular activity – usually before his regular afternoon nap. But Dad never bought any books or frequented any bookshops – he simply could not afford to. Instead, he became a regular user of libraries – such as were close enough and accessible at that time. The Klang Public Library and the Kuala Lumpur Book Club were his principal sources of reading material.

I picked up the reading habit only after the family moved to Klang. I frequently rode my bicycle to the Klang public library to borrow story books. Robert Louis Stevenson's Treasure Island was one of my favourites but I read widely – Victor Hugo, Charles Dickens, Joseph Conrad and many others but Shakespeare was never my cup of tea.

Dad had a bookcase of his personal collection of books by P.G.Wodehouse as well as an extensive collection of Westerns (Dad's cowboy books), tales of the buccaneers and the Spanish Main – Captain Blood and Blackbeard as well as tales of the Scarlet Pimpernel and the French Revolution. Dad also had a small collection of detective novels. I read everything in Dad's book collection.

Taking the story line far forward, I took up reading again only after my retirement. However by then, my reading interests had completely changed. Political thrillers, set against current day political realities are my main interest – books by Tom Clancy and Fredrick Forsythe are among my favourites. I might add that my late brother Basil was also an avid reader – but not other members of the family.

Coming back to my father, I have to admit that despite his extensive reading, Dad was no story teller. In fact, it was my mother who told us tales during my younger years from books she read. Some of this may have rubbed off on me as I used to relate stories from books I had read to my friends. But this only happened while the family were living in Klang. While I know I am a good story teller, I have little recollection of story telling to my own sons – something I regret very much. Perhaps I can make up for this a little by telling stories to my grandson.

Socialising

The family began to have more interaction with other families only after the family moved to Klang. However this socialising was within a very limited circle of family and friends. This was also because Dad had his own car which made the family more mobile.

Our favourite weekend visits were to the Perera family on Telok Pulai Road, a few miles away – the kilometre as a unit of distance measure was unknown then. The Pereras were a gregarious Sinhalese family. We addressed the older couple who were friends of Dad and Mum as Uncle Stephen and Aunty Jenny. Aunty Jenny was a fantastic cook. The older children – Cecil. Harold, Jenevieve, Monika and Pat – were much older and we did not interact with them as much as with their younger siblings – Joe, Eddie and Merril – with whom we got on famously.

The Pereras were a very musical family and there were many sing along sessions followed by pot luck dinners for everybody. While the adults usually played poker with some alcoholic libation, the younger crowd entertained themselves in yard games.

With my brothers and friends

From time to time Dad also drove all of us to visit the Stickney family in Sungai Way which was a fair distance from Klang on the way to Kuala Lumpur – this was usually a week-end stay at the home of Sam Stickney who had married Jenevieve – the Stickneys had no children then. It was a big gathering of both families but we all fitted in as Sam's Estate Bungalow was a two storey house with many rooms and was set in an extensive garden. It also had a clear flowing stream at the rear of the Estate where some of us – the younger crowd from both families – loved to get into to catch the little fish – which were very elusive, but we had a great time.

The family also spent an occassional weekend at Uncle Roy's place in Sentul, Kuala Lumpur. Uncle Roy worked at the Railway yards in Sentul at that time and had by then married Aunty Lennie. They had two little boys, Bernard and Lucien. Nanny was staying at that time with Uncle Roy too so it was a big gathering. We enjoyed those visits very much too.

Living within our means

Our family lived simply – there were no frills of any kind. Austerity and frugality in almost everything was something the family got used to in my growing up years. My mother was quite fantastic – she did all the work and managed practically everything without the help of maidservants. Later, my sisters helped with the housework especially with the washing. My mother even sewed the dresses for my sisters and 'jungies' (one piece sleeveless garment) for the boys. When we started going to school, our short pants and shirts were sourced from cheap retail outlets in Petaling Street. All of us had cheap rubber shoes from Fung Keong – a popular shoe shop in Kuala Lumpur. Pocket money before leaving for school was unheard of.

The homes the family lived in while we were growing up, were 'quarters' provided by the Forest Department in accordance with Dad's housing entitlement – they were modest two bedroom bungalows built on raised columns. There was no rental payment but utilities for water usage and electricity consumption had to be paid for. It was only in 1955, a few years before Dad retired that he was able to invest in a small property with the help of my sisters. This was a small brick and tile bungalow in the newly created housing suburb of Petaling Jaya. The three bedroom house was built on a modest plot of land with a 99 year lease and remained the family home until my mother died in 2000.

Dad had a green thumb and it was on this, our very own home, that Dad planted several fruit trees which yielded abundant fruit each season. I remember especially the chiku tree, the rambutan trees and the avocado trees. This was also the garden where Dad grew his beautiful orchids. We even had a murunga (drumstick) tree growing in the garden which was regularly harvested for murunga (long bulbous pods) which my mother cooked in a pale saffron (yellow) coconut gravy. The leaves were also plucked from time to time and used whenever crab (mud crabs) curry was cooked. Years later, one of my aunts told me that the murunga leaves were used when cooking crabs in order to remove toxins from the crabs – whether this was true or just an old wives tale, I do not know.

Going back to our life in Klang, Dad was very helpful to many he came in contact with in his work in the forest office in Klang. They never forgot and continued to show their appreciation in one way or another. Chin Hin, one of the timber merchants in Klang regularly made available his car and his driver – a very pleasant older Malay gentleman called Manan – to take Mum and a few of us to Kuala Lumpur for a bit of clothes shopping. We never ever shopped at the up-market stores like Robinsons or Whiteways – not even at Gian Singh's or Doshi's and other stores on Jalan (road) Mountbatten.

Even when Mum went to the pasar (wet market) to her regular fish monger to purchase some fish, we were most surprised when he stopped charging us for whatever fish Mum purchased – we never knew who our benefactor was. Ikan Kurau (threadfin) was our favourite but Mum also selected other types of fish like Bawal Hitam and Bawal Putih (black and white Pomphret) as well as ikan Tinggiri (tuna).

Finally, one last memory of our lives at our Riverside Road home – honey collecting. It so happened that although there were three blocks of semi-detached houses or 'quarters' in our neighborhood, housing six families, it was only in our house that the honey bees made their hives. These hives were in the protected outer eves of our home. For the most part, it was a harmonious co-existence – the bees left us alone and we left the bees alone. But the hives were becoming alarmingly large and Dad decided that we should try to collect some of the honey and at the same time reduce the size of the hive. A smoking rag was held under the hive which caused the bees to take off. A part of the hive was then dislodged which fell into a wide container positioned below. The hive was then wrapped in a porous linen cloth and twisted at both ends – and the thick golden honey was squeezed out. It was beautiful stuff. Some of us did get stung in the process but it was tolerable.

Sojourn in Ceylon

The holiday interlude

Sometime in 1949, following Percy Uncle's visit the previous year, we were told that the whole family would be going on a three month holiday to Ceylon in December 1950. Joy! Joy! – no school. We were all looking forward to the trip – Mum most of all, if only to catch up with her own family members, whom she had left nearly 20 years ago, after getting married.

There were many preparations to be made we knew nothing about. My Dad's collection of documents included Inoculation Certificates and Emergency Certificates (EC) issued by the Passport Officer, Kuala Lumpur in November 1950, which served as travel documents. As it turned out, there were separate ECs for Jenny and Irene and for Dad while the one for Mum included Basil and Norbert but there appeared to be no evidence of any ECs for Clarence and me. As the family travelled to Ceylon seven years before Independence – ECs were issued on the grounds that the applicants were 'British Subjects'.

Yet, inexplicably, Dad's collection of documents also included an Emergency Certificate Ceylon (issued by the Controller of Immigration and Emigration (Ceylon), dated 12th March 1951 for my mother where her nationality was stated to be 'citizen of Ceylon by descent'. On the same date, Identity Certificates Ceylon were issued for Dad, Jenny and Irene by Ceylon Immigration and Emigration where their nationality was specified as 'British' The ICC for Dad also included Basil and Norbert as 'children under 16 accompanying'. Again, there were no ICCs for Clarence or me. It did appear that Clarence and I had fallen between the cracks.

All the above documents were stamped 12th March 1951 – which was the date of departure from Ceylon. Considering that the whole family came from Malaya on holiday with Emergency Certificates issued by the passport officer, Kuala Lumpur, it is rather curious that Ceylon Immigration had now issued Identity Certificates for members of the family which were valid for two years, i.e. until 12th March 1953!

It does appear that after the family arrived in Ceylon, the suggestion was made that the family should consider returning to Ceylon and taking up permanent abode in the country. I have little doubt that Percy Uncle suggested to Dad to apply for Identity Certificates to facilitate this. As children we knew nothing about all this. Fortunately, when the family returned to Malaya, wiser councils prevailed.

When I reflect back on these happenings so very long ago, I am so thankful that the family decided against taking up permanent residence in Ceylon. I am inclined to think that my sisters probably tipped the balance. For starters, what on earth would Dad have done in Ceylon – he could not speak a word of the language. Dad was 45 years old and there was no provision at that time for any kind of service benefit if he left the Clerical Service in Malaya. It was altogether a very bad idea.

For Aunty Baby in particular, the Ceylon holiday was most propitious as she met Uncle John, who was then a teacher at St. Benedict's College in Colombo. They later got married in Kuala Lumpur. My sisters Jenny and Irene, and Annette (who I'd meet later and ultimately marry) were Bridesmaids at the wedding while Basil and Norbert were page boys.

Both Aunty Baby and Uncle John carved out successful careers for themselves in the educational field in Malaysia and served for many years as Principals of their respective schools. As such they were able to send their only daughter Dina to Boarding School in England where she grew up. Dina went on to do her Doctorate, married an Englishman and like her husband worked in academia. They have three daughters. Although Dina is my first cousin, I have not met her since she was a child.

Taking up the main threads of the story once again, there must have been much that was going on in the background which was taken for granted. It must have cost my Dad much more than he could afford. It is more than likely that Aunty Baby, being a qualified teacher at that time, paid for her own passage.

Anyway the day finally dawned for the family holiday in Ceylon. All of us went by train to Singapore. Travel by train to Singapore was now quite safe as the communist insurrection had virtually come to an end with Chin Peng and his supporters being pushed further and further north towards the Thai border.

While we still loved travelling to Singapore – it was our second trip – Singapore was not a foreign country then and was still a part of 'British' Malaya. But a trip to Ceylon was something else again – it was our very first trip abroad and our very first experience of travelling by steamship. There was much excitement and anticipation.

*The family with our first cousins and our Uncles.....
guess who's the mug in a tie*

The whole family stayed a day or two at Auntie Gladys' place in Geylang. How all of us managed to squeeze into Auntie Gladys' rather small trellis house – it had only two small bedrooms – is mind boggling. As I recall, some of us slept on the open veranda in front of the house – fortunately, it did not rain.

Finally, D-Day dawned on us. All of us were up early. We piled into 3 taxis with an assortment of suitcases and arrived at Collyer Quay (which is still in use today). We boarded a launch which took us to the ship, the SS Napoli which was at anchor in the outer harbour and got on board soon after. Our journey had begun and in a week we were in Colombo. The steamship journey was a real novelty but otherwise uneventful. The ship anchored outside the breakwater and we proceeded by launch to the jetty.

*Holiday home in Wattala, Ceylon
all six of us with Auntie Baby*

Percy Uncle was there to meet us and took us to a house he had rented for the family in a suburb North of Colombo called Wattala. We stayed there for the duration of our holiday. I very much doubt that Percy Uncle paid for the rental of the house. In all probability, Dad and Mum would have paid for the rental as well. Percy Uncle did not have a car and hence it is most likely that the family had to use taxis most of the time.

While the rented house in Wattala had electrical lighting, water was drawn from a well (located within the compound of the house) using a manually operated pump, which pumped the water to the kitchen, bathroom and toilet. From time to time, the family travelled by bus within Colombo, but for longer distances, the family travelled by train on CGR (Ceylon Government Railway) – to Galle in the South to see Mum's youngest sister Stella (Sister Mary Clementa) who was a nun in the Galle Convent; to Chilaw on the coast

North of Colombo to visit mum's sister Sally and her family and to Kandy in the hill country to visit step-grandma as well as Mum's step-sisters, Trixie and Girly. We did not get to meet our step-uncles Stanley and Gerry as they were out of favour with Percy Uncle.

We kids enjoyed our stay in Ceylon immensely. On our trip to Kandy by train, we passed through spectacular scenery and various land marks were pointed out to us. We stayed at Grandma's place in Kossinna and visited the Peradeniya Gardens with some of our relatives. We were a fair sized group and even had our 'kussi amma' (cook) and 'Punchi Banda' (house boy) to help with the packed lunches. We spent the whole morning and afternoon in the Gardens.

It was an un-forgettable experience. Several photographs in the family album recall those times and the faces of many who have long since faded away.

I also recall that we were taken to witness the Perahera – a spectacular Buddhist pageant with gaily decorated elephants in procession, followed by vigorous dancers, drummers, whip crackers and flag bearers. The Perahera made a lasting impression on all of us. Malaya had nothing comparable.

I was always under the impression that we had witnessed the Kandy Esala Perahera. The Esala Perahera however is only held in Kandy in August each year. Since the family visit to Ceylon was from January to March, 1950, the pageant we did witness was the Kelaniya Duruthu Perahera, held in January each year to commemorate the religious significance of the Buddha's visit to the island centuries ago.

Apart from meeting our relatives, we did little else from a touristic point of view. The family never got to visit Anuradhapura or Polonnaruwa – among the better known of the ancient capitals of the country. No doubt the logistics of moving the whole family around on public transport must have been a bit of a nightmare.

The bombshell anouncement

Then one day towards the end of our stay in Ceylon, my parents told Clarence and me that they had decided to put both of us in Boarding School in Kandy. It was more than a bombshell. Clarence and I were not even consulted – it did not appear that our opinion mattered at all. As I recall, there was not even the semblance of breaking in the news gently. We were children and were simply told what had been decided. I was 15 and Clarence was 11.

My initial reaction of complete disbelief soon changed at the prospect of flying free and unfettered – without close parental supervision. I never discussed with Clarence what he thought of it all. We were far too young anyway to think of all the possible consequences of separation.

The family were in Kandy at that time, so one morning, Percy Uncle, my parents and the two of us visited the Boarding School, St.Anthony's College in Katugastota Road, Kandy. St Anthony's was chosen perhaps because it was one of the best known boarding schools in the hill country. The School had a good scholastic record. It was Catholic and was run by priests of the OSB (Order of St. Benedict). Besides, the family property (Grandma's house) as well as the homes of two of Mum's step-sisters were not too far away.

We met the Principal, Rev. Fr. Rosati and all was arranged for both of us to be admitted to the Boarding School when Term began. Not then but years later after Dad died, Mum told me that Percy Uncle also wanted my sisters to be left behind in Ceylon but she put her foot down on that. I sometimes get the impression that it was my mother who made the major decisions in the family – I could be mistaken.

The trauma of parting

To continue the story, the family returned to Colombo after that and a few days later they boarded ship, the SS Corfu, a P&O (Peninsula & Orient) liner for the return journey to Malaya. Clarence and I too went on board, to look over the ship but soon, it was time to leave. We said our good-byes and there was a lot of smiling and waving. We walked down the gang plank and got into the launch. It was only when the launch began chugging back to the jetty, that the reality of what was happening dawned on me.

I broke down completely and the sobbing and crying went on for days. I wouldn't even eat. Clarence took it all stoically and did not shed a tear. This helped me enormously to come to terms with the situation and was no doubt the beginning of a lifelong habit of depending only on myself – which seemed to have coloured my entire life.

I never understood my parents' motivation in placing us both in boarding school in Ceylon but I never questioned them about this, either then or any time after and I never blamed them. They must have had good reason.

On reflection, it is more than likely that Percy Uncle planted the seeds of the idea in my parents' minds when he visited Malaya in 1948 – the idea of the family returning to the homeland and that this was more than likely to happen if their sons were educated in Ceylon and hopefully decided to live and work in Ceylon. I am quite sure that Percy Uncle would not have missed the opportunity to wax lyrical about 'free education' in Ceylon and that the boys could get quality education without the attendant cost. Percy Uncle could be quite persuasive.

My parents on the other hand may have had some additional concerns, in particular, the fear of youth conscription into the armed forces in view of the escalating communist insurgency – if the two older boys were in boarding school abroad, there was little likelihood that they would be conscripted. This fear may have been completely unfounded. British colonial authorities in pre-independent Malaya were unlikely to train and arm local youth to help cope with the emergency as these youth could become a liability and accelerate the nascent movements for independence.

Coming to terms with reality

When I was admitted to St. Anthony's College in Kandy, Ceylon in 1950, I was emplaced in the Junior School Certificate Class. This helped to reduce the age gap between me and most of my classmates who never lost any of their school years because of the War. Nevertheless, I was still older than most of my classmates and this did weigh heavily on me.

My scholastic record in St. Anthony's College was quite good – I was invariably 1st in class exams and carried away several prizes at the annual prize-giving day at College. I disliked Sinhalese class though – especially when I had to front up and speak in Sinhalese – a totally foreign language to me. All in all, I spent nearly ten years of my life away from my family.

I kept in touch by writing regularly to Dad and sometimes to Mum but I had little interaction with my brothers and sisters. Unfortunately, my correspondence with my father was largely confined to the mundane – I was never kept abreast of the changing political climate in the Malay States and the approach to independence. Perhaps my Dad thought it unwise to bother me with such details as that might detract from my focus on my studies.

My life had changed completely. In many ways it seemed that Clarence and I were thrown in at the deep end and we had to learn to survive. Clarence was not much of a writer – he was only 11 years old – and hardly wrote to Mum or Dad. I did most of the writing for both of us.

Clarence and I formed a deep bond in those years we spent together in Ceylon but unfortunately, our days in boarding school virtually split the family and I never really got to know my younger brothers Basil and Norbert while my links with my elder sisters grew somewhat distant. It took years to repair that damage and to restore the shredded ties.

It must have been difficult for my Dad too, to pay for our boarding fees for so many years and later for my undergraduate studies at the university. Fortunately, my sisters had qualified as teachers and they helped to contribute towards the overall expenses.

Long after Dad passed away in 1982, Mum told me that they even paid for Percy Uncle's trip to Malaya in 1948. I also doubt very much that for the duration of our stay in Ceylon in Boarding School, there was any financial support from Percy Uncle. Dad must have struggled to shoulder that burden too.

I doubt my parents ever realised how difficult it was to learn a new language from scratch, including its totally unfamiliar script (called akuru) and to do it all in such a short space of time. I am sure they were not told that Sinhalese was a compulsory subject which I had to pass at the impending Senior School Certificate Examination. Coping with colloquial or spoken Sinhalese – the everyday language of the market place – was difficult enough, but the written language – literary or classical Sinhalese – was another matter entirely.

Fortunately following my parents' departure back to Malaya, Clarence and I were taken to mum's sister Sally's place in Rajakadaluwa, on the way to Chilaw. Aunty Sally's husband, Uncle Francis was the Village Postmaster and they had several kids, – Sybil, Marion, Sextus, Christo, Noeline and Bede – our first cousins, who were a little younger than the two of us. We got on famously and that helped. I was well on the way to coping with whatever lay ahead.

Boarding school

Shortly before the beginning of the new school term, Clarence and I were taken back to Kandy and then to the Boarding School at St Anthony's College, Katugastota. We were both admitted to a Dormitory called 'The Mansion' and each of us was assigned a bed and a small cupboard – and so boarding school life began. I was moved a year later to the 'Villa' – a dormitory for more senior students.

Tiddy Uncle hired a battered old jalopy to bring Clarence and me from Grandma's house in Kossinna to the Boarding School at Katugastota Road, carrying our equally battered suitcases with us. Clarence and I vowed that we would travel to and from Boarding School in future without any chaperoning uncles – and we did just that.

Travel to and from St. Anthony's College Boarding School was tedious, hot and sweaty. We had to walk downhill from Grandma's place carrying our suitcase, cross the main road in front of the village provision shop and then descend a further 15 meters to the rail track to wait for the rail-car – there was no platform whatsoever. It took real effort to get on board the rail car. Later we got more adept at using the buses – though these were invariably crowded.

From our first week at St Anthony's, private tuition in Sinhalese was arranged for Clarence and me. Since I was placed in the JSC (Junior School Certificate) Class, I only had about two years of tuition to reach the required standard to pass in the Senior Cambridge examinations. It was an uphill task all the way.

Tuition class lasted for one hour every morning before school started. Our private tutor was a Mrs. Nanayakara – she was a primary school teacher at St. Anthony's College. For all other subjects, the medium of instruction was English so we coped fairly well and even carried away some of the prizes at the School's Annual Prize Giving. It was St. Anthonys' Centenary Year.

Clarence and I soon got used to the routine of boarding school life. On waking up in the morning we had our wash using our own wash-basin which had to be stored after use. Catholic boarders would then have to attend Mass in the Chapel while non Catholic boarders had to go to their respective study halls. All of us then gathered at the main refectory for a traditional breakfast – usually Iddiappom (string hoppers) or appom (hoppers), pittu (granular rice flour mixed with coconut), pol sambol (coconut sambal) with a dash of chilli and kirihodhi (coconut milk) with a touch of tumeric. Bread, butter and jam were also served but we never got bacon and eggs. Parippu (lentils cooked in coconut milk with a sprinkling of turmeric or saffron) was also often served.

Lunch and dinner were also served at the refectory and invariably included rice with some mus (meat) curry – chicken or beef – and assorted vegetables (elolu). All meals were quite agreeable and were always preceded by the blessing or saying of grace despite the fact that many boarders were non Catholic.

Boarders were 'free' after school hours to take part in sports or other extra curricular activities but were not allowed to leave the school grounds without permission. All boarders spent about 2 hours after dinner in their respective study halls doing their home work or assignments.

Football or soccer was always my favourite game. Having easy access to the football field behind our home in Bukit Nanas gave me ample opportunity to play with friends. I became quite good at dribbling and could kick the ball equally well with either foot. I was however somewhat slight of frame when I was growing up and was easily intimidated by rough and aggressive players.

However it was only after I joined St. Anthony's College in Kandy, Ceylon that I began to show some potential as a footballer. Mr. Kandayah, the soccer coach selected me to play the inside left position on the forward line in St. Anthony's First XI soccer team. I continued in this position until I left a few years later to join the University of Ceylon. My team mates in the forward line were outstanding players – T.M.Deen (centre forward), Sali Dorenagama (inside right), Donald Wijasuriya (inside left), A.C.M. Lafir (left wing) and Ray Fernando (right wing).

For the first few years, I played barefoot with ankle guard support. It was only in my final year in College that I was able to get a second hand pair of boots which I paid for out of my meagre pocket money. Apart from sprains and the occasional hair-line wrist fracture, I survived each soccer season without any major mishap.

A nostalgic memento of my years at St Anthony's College – at least in terms of my involvement in sports – is a photograph of myself as a team member of the 1954 and 1955 Soccer team. The team photograph has been reproduced from "150 Anniversary 1854 – 2004 St Anthony's College Kandy Sesquicentennial Publication" which was published in 2004. I came across this publication quite by chance in 2009 at the home of a fellow Boarder who

First XI soccer team 1954 yours truly circled

First XI soccer team 1955 yours truly circled

had migrated to Australia in the mid seventies and now lives in Brisbane.

Cricket was very popular at the School too but I rarely played the game largely because I did not relish facing those fast bowlers. Besides I did not have the funds to be properly kitted out. While playing in the outfield on one occasion, a late cut from the batsman had sent the ball spinning at full force in my direction. I met the ball full on with my hands cupped – but I misjudged the direction of the ball ever so slightly and took the force of the ball on the middle finger of my right hand. It hurt like hell – I had sustained a crack on the finger joint which has remained with me all my life. I never played cricket again.

Hockey was played too but I was not overly interested in the game. Besides, I was not as slick with my stick-work and getting the hockey ball on one's shin did not help. I did play basketball which was relatively 'new' to most of us. I do not recall that there was a school team in both games at that time.

The Boarding School at St. Anthony's had several dormitories, where the boarders were housed, according to age groups. There was the 'Rainbow', 'Mansion' and 'Villa' followed by 'Journey's End'. Each dormitory had a mixed group of boarders – mostly Sinhalese, some Burghers and also Tamils – all of whom got on well with one another. Clarence and I were the only 'foreigners'.

Each dormitory was supervised by a warden – usually one of the priests. Clarence and I were too old for the "Rainbow' and were placed in the 'Mansion'. Our warden was Fr. George. He was Tamil and sported a black bushy beard. The boarders referred to him as 'Gogia Pasha' – after a well known Indian fakir at that time. When you heard shouts of 'Gogia is coming', everybody behaved.

A mini zoo was maintained close to the 'Mansion' where a few animals were caged – including several mongooses. The mongoose were rather aggressive and readily engaged king cobras who were their mortal enemies. One evening, one of the mongoose got loose and valiant efforts to locate the missing ferret proved fruitless.

Anyway the boarders turned in for the night. I slipped into my pyjamas and was soon asleep. Several hours later, I got up with a start and realised that something was wriggling up my pyjama trousers. I immediately thought it's the bloody mongoose. In my mind I told myself, don't panic – just stifle the mongoose with your blanket and get him out of your pyjama pants – which I did quite successfully and then transferred the whole bundle – blanket, mongoose and all – into a large suitcase, closing the lid firmly.

I was the hero of the hour. Fr. George (Gogia Pasha), took me aside and told me very seriously that one had to be very careful as it was the mating season for the mongoose. I was trying hard not to laugh as I thought what a misguided mongoose if it was really trying to get some action crawling up my pyjama trousers.

The whole episode was quite hilarious as Gogia Pasha arrived with his cane (rattan) in hand. One of the boarders, nicknamed 'Datha' (who had a toothless gap in his teeth) was in the toilet when the whole drama unfolded and rushed back to his bed with his fly (zip) completely open and exposing his little 'willie' to all and sundry. Gogia Pasha kept flicking his cane at the offending object, while shouting 'put it away, put it away' We were all in hysterics.

Grandma's house in Kossinna

During the school holidays, Clarence and I spent our time at grandma's house in Kossinna, a small village not far from Kandy. In true British tradition, the house was named 'Glen Eira.' The house was set on a two acre plot of land on the hill-side, about a hundred metres above road level.

Grandma's 'estate' comprised of several mango trees of different varieties, tea and coffee bushes, two small paddy fields(at the bottom of the hill), a single bread fruit tree, jackfruit trees, a couple of coconut trees, a single soursup tree as well as a rose garden (in the front of the house).

The small area at the rear of the house which Grandma referred to as the 'midule,' was just a patch of garden with low level tea bushes on which the washing was put out to dry. There was no lawn of any kind. There were no garden seats to sit on either – just an old weather beaten log – to park ones carcass! The toilet or dunny was located about 10 metres away – just a rustic shack. Piped water, flush systems and electricity were simply not a part of the rural setting at 'Glen Eira'.

The 2 acre property had two wells – a drinking well further up the hill-side and a bathing well further downhill. The water was always cold. Drinking water was always kept in an earthenware jug – referred to as a 'gurulethuwa' to keep the water cold. I do not recall that the drinking water was ever boiled before being placed in the jug.

Grandma had a 'kussi-ammah' (cook woman) and a house-boy called Punchi Banda. The house boy's duties were to assist in the kitchen and light and place the numerous oil lamps called 'kuppi-lampuwa'. In the morning, he would put out a basin of clean water for us to have our morning wash before breakfast. During the day, he would bring us innumerable cups of tea.

Grandma's house was a wattle and daub structure – it looked like an English country cottage. Its outer walls were white-

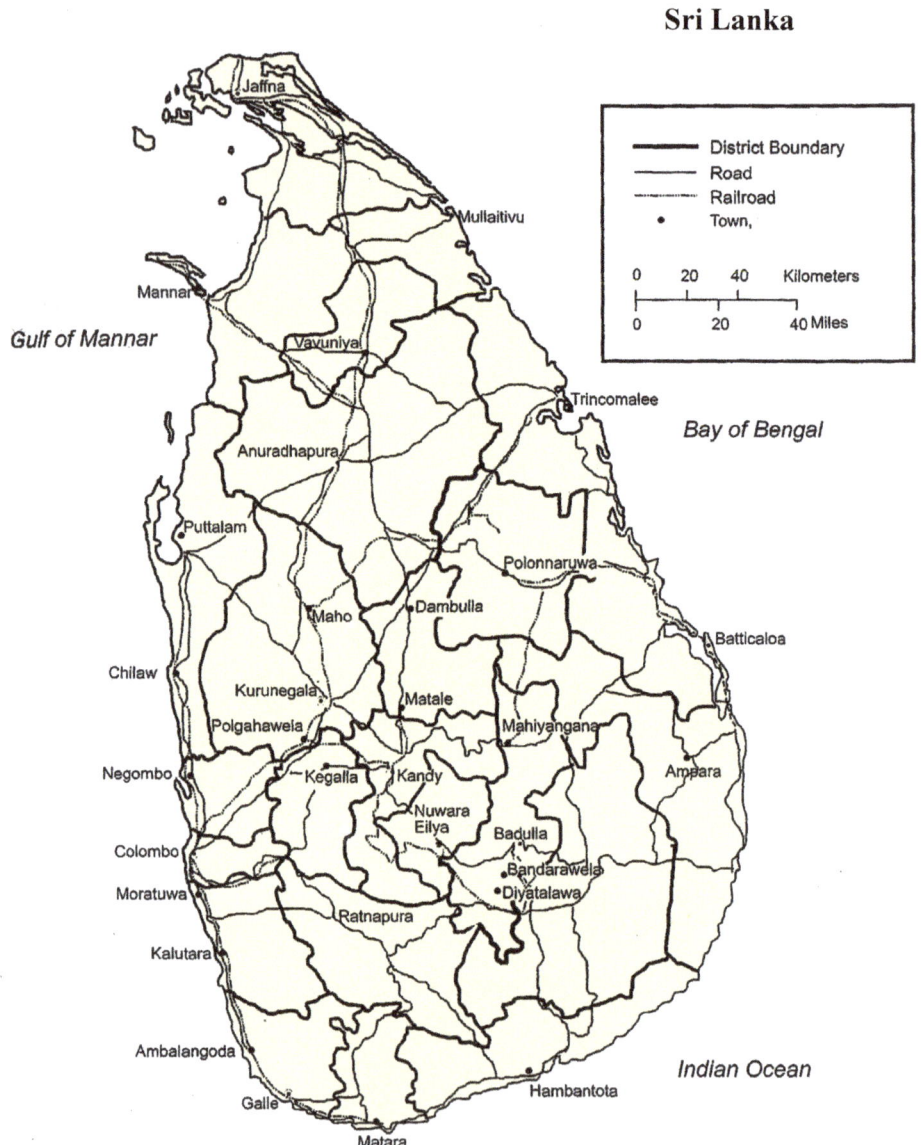

washed (not painted); the roof was tiled; it had two bedrooms, a lounge or family room, often called the hall, a veranda, a small store room as well as a dining room cum kitchen. There was an uneven path-way leading up-hill to the house from the roadway a hundred metres below.

While 'Glen Eira' had a certain rustic charm, there was very little to do. There were hardly any books to read; not even a radio, to listen to music or hear the news. But there was a carrom board with coloured 'dogs' (flat, circular chips about an inch in diameter) and a small flat disk to strike a pre-arranged setting of dogs to fall into corner pockets. Clarence and I played this game often and got quite good at it. The carrom board had a very smooth surface with marked lines; there were specific rules for carrom playing and the disc had to be flicked by finger action.

There were no daily newspapers delivered to the house. However on the weekends when Percy Uncle came over from Colombo, he had the weekend papers which we read from beginning to end. There was an old gramophone record player which had to be wound up in order to play the few records that were around the house.

Clarence and I found the whole experience of staying at Grandma's house to be truly boring – especially if you had to spend the whole of the school holidays at her place. Grandma's house was set in a very rural environment of undulating hills and green carpeted lowlands – mostly rice fields. There was also some rice cultivation on hillside terraces. There is no doubt that it was a beautiful countryside setting.

It was most interesting watching the farmers at work using water buffaloes to draw the ploughs. This was followed by the tedious back-breaking job of sowing rice-paddy shoots in flooded, muddy paddy fields. At harvest time, the cutting of ripened paddy stalks as well as the threshing and winnowing of the paddy grains was all done manually. The era of Japanese motorised ploughs had not arrived yet in rural Ceylon. Grandma's paddy fields were looked after by neighbouring farmers.

It is a wonder that we did not get into any real mischief – like sneaking behind the 'kakkussi' for a smoke. Kissing the local village damsels was also taboo although one or two did toss those long black tresses and blinked those long eye-lashes at me! It was a different culture entirely.

On Sunday morning, Clarence and I would catch the bus to Gampola – a small town about 15km away to attend mass. We were often asked to buy seer fish (tuna) as well as the weekend newspapers on our way home. We got off the bus about a mile from the house where the Mahaveli Ganga (Mahaveli River) cascaded over smooth rocks close to a bend in the road – we usually stripped to our jocks and plunged in for a nice swim. If Percy Uncle knew this he would have hit the roof.

Grandma's kitchen was initially located at the far end of the dining area which could get quite smoky at times. So it was decided to build a separate kitchen and store room. The piece of land beside the house was levelled and the bamboo framework for the extension was put up – the vertical and horizontal split bamboo poles were all tied together, creating a series of small squares which made up the walls – a sort of wattle and daub hut.

Provinces and Districts

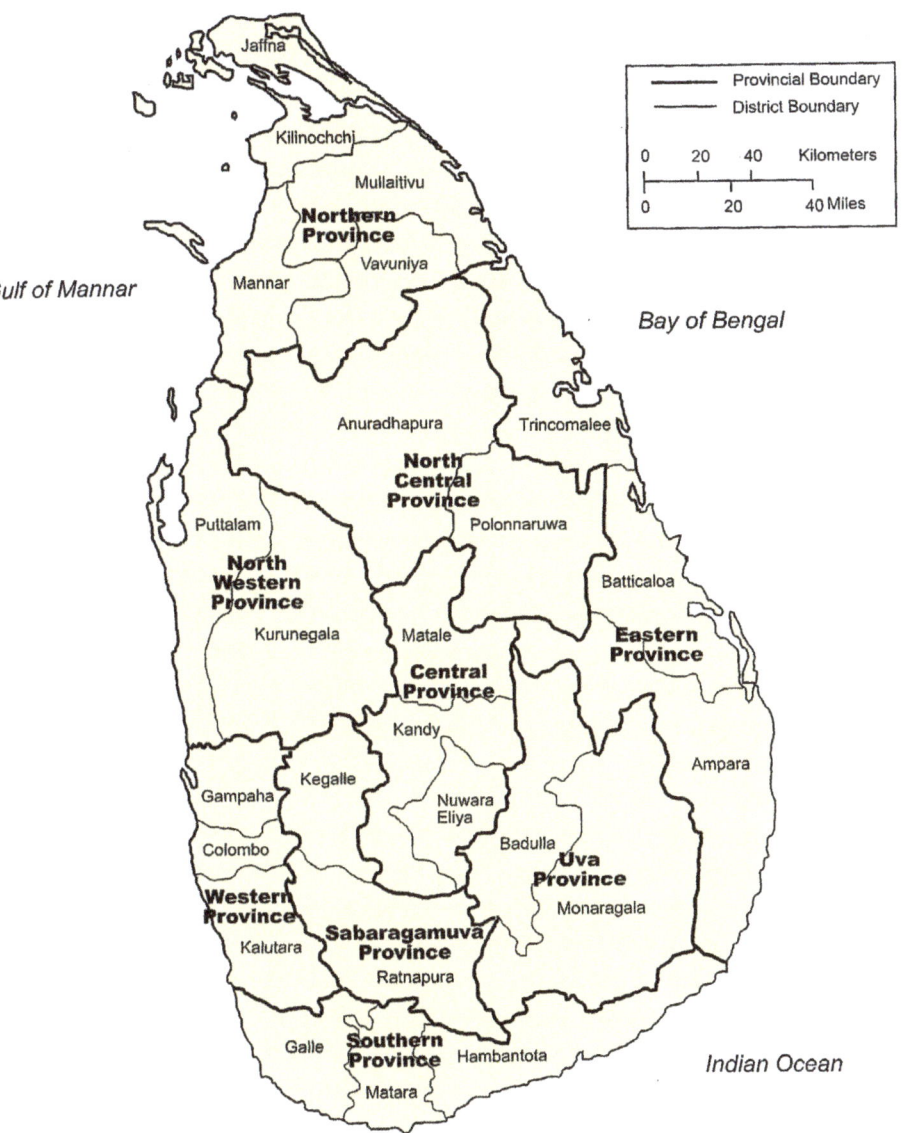

A pit was then dug beside the structure and with the help of the daily rainfall, lumpy mud balls were created and manually thrown into the bamboo squares – the mud balls splattered and clung to the squares and gradually the wall was built up. The walls were later smoothed with a mixture of fine sand and then white-washed or painted.

The door and window frames came later, followed by the roof thatching and finally came the raised fire place. The floors were created by spreading by hand, a watery mix of fresh cow-dung, which when dry made a very cool and durable floor. Clarence and I got stuck into all this and enjoyed the experience very much. We were however not allowed to thatch the roof as it was a riskier operation.

A few years later, Percy Uncle decided to put in a few renovations to the front of the house. The whole job was done on the cheap using some distant relative (we called him Uncle Pinto) who had some carpentry skills. One of the older mango trees on the property was felled and the trunk was placed over a deep pit – to facilitate the use of a two handed saw – to create the desired pieces of timber for door and window frames. I must admit that the end result looked quite professional.

The food at Grandma's was traditional; very tasty but somewhat frugal. But when Percy Uncle came up for the week-end, he brought lots of fresh food – including fish, meat and various vegetables and we had a bit of a feast. We did not have any dessert or a sweet after a meal. This was simply not part of the menu at a traditional meal. For the most part we had fresh fruit to eat.

Christmas time at Glen Eira, Kossinna was very different from what I had experienced at home with my parents. There was no tradition of Christmas trees, decorations, Christmas pudding or cakes, Christmas stockings or presents. The main event was attending midnight mass at a Catholic Church in Peradeniya or in Kandy. This was an absolute must and was unforgettable in some ways.

Descending the hill side from Grandma's house to the road far below walking on rough pathways downhill and meandering between flooded paddy fields – all in the darkness of night and dressed in our Sunday best, was truly an experience. Clarence and I each carried a little lighted candle held between two fingers with a coconut shell cupped in the palm of our hands to throw forward some light to guide our way in the darkness.

When we got to the bottom of the hill, it was necessary to find some clear flowing water to wash our muddy feet before wiping them dry and putting on our socks and shoes. We then hopped into Percy Uncle's little Bug-Fiat and were squashed at the back all the way to the Church.

I must digress a little here and mention Percy Uncle's Bug-Fiat which he must have purchased around 1952 or 1953. He had a mud-walled 'garage' built by the road-side beside the village provision shop at the bottom of the hill from Grandma's house . There he kept his precious car and used it mostly when he came up to Kossinna for the weekend.

He was very proud of his little car. Sometimes when we were squashed at the back of his car, he had to halt at a railway crossing along our route and he used to alight from his car and inspect it from one angle or another – despite the build-up of a long line of traffic behind us. It was rather embarrassing.

I remember the trip he took the two of us and Grandma to visit his friend Austin Perera in Bandarawela, up in the hill country in Uwa Province. We only stayed a few days there. But on the way back, Clarence and I were squashed in the very cramped space at the back of the car together with an assorted collection of fresh vegetables, cabbages, leeks and other leafy greens which could be purchased very cheaply in the Hill country. I do not recall any other long trips in his car – most of our travel was by train.

However on one of my last visits to Sri Lanka in 2009, on my return trip to Colombo from Galle on the South coast, we passed a toddy tapper along the road side in Hikkaduwa, climbing up the trunk of a coconut tree, using a rope loop around his feet to grip the trunk as he ascended.

We stopped to watch. He was tapping the sap of the coconut flower. The tapper only climbed the trunk of one tree and then moved from one tree to another, using sturdy ropes which linked the tree tops at two levels to facilitate easy movement.

Each tree yielded about 2 litres of toddy per day. When freshly tapped, the toddy was sweet and milky coloured but it soon fermented and had a high alcoholic content. We purchased a bottle of fresh toddy but it was not as sweet as I remembered it. Various stages of distillation turned toddy into arrack. Black label arrack was a popular drink on festive occasions. Percy Uncle loved his Black label arrack.

We hardly received any Christmas cards but there was some carol singing while we were in Boarding School. We never had visitors on Christmas day and there was no such thing as 'open house' for people from the neighbourhood. When one experiences nearly ten years of Christmas days such as this, it begins to look like the norm and Christmas day became 'just another day'.

The Rajakadaluwa' walauwa'

Some of our holidays were spent at Aunty Sally's home in Rajakadaluwa. It was a coconut estate, about 12 acres in extent. Harvest time was more interesting – driving a bullock cart and picking up the coconuts which had been plucked. The huge bull belonged to Uncle Ben (Uncle Francis's brother) who owned the adjoining property. The bull was a stud used mainly for breeding purposes. But it was docile enough and did not protest against being hitched to the cart.

The Navaratne brothers – Uncle Francis and Uncle Ben – owned fairly large coconut estates or plantations in Rajakadaluwa, adjoining one another. In the late fifties, the Government passed legislation to limit the acreage of these plantations. Uncle Ben lived in Colombo where he had his regular job. He was better known as a cricketer and was wicket keeper for the All-Ceylon cricket team. Uncle Francis however, lived on the estate and also served as the village post master.

There was an occasion when Clarence and I were in the back of Uncle Ben's car, returning from Chilaw after attending midnight mass. Uncle Ben was driving with Aunty Rose beside him. Uncle Ben was in a jovial mood and sang Danny

Boy in his rich baritone voice – it was the very first time I heard Danny Boy and it has remained one of my favourites ever since.

Life in Rajakadaluwa was most pleasant. Sometimes in mid-morning, Clarence and I and our cousins, walked to the shallow Deduru Oya (stream) for a dip in the cool flowing water. It was more of a river than a stream. In the cool of the evenings Clarence and I joined our cousins for chatty, fun-filled strolls in the countryside – which was essentially coconut country.

On Sundays we walked to Church and mass was conducted in Sinhalese. The sermon was also in Sinhalese – my Sinhalese was far too elementary to benefit from it. There were no chairs or pews. The congregation stood or knelt on the sandy floors. We sometimes took the bus to Chilaw – the main coastal town, to do a bit of shopping or see a film at the cinema. We never ate at a restaurant – we just could not afford to.

We often played cricket on the sandy soil. All the kids joined in. We fashioned our bats from pieces of wood. The wicket was made from the bottom end of a coconut frond (where it is attached to the tree-trunk) and propped up to serve as a wicket. We used a rubber ball or anything else which was suitable. We also scaled the coconut trees using a rope loop over our feet and brought down young coconuts called 'kurumba'. We split the nuts, drank the coconut water and scooped out the tender flesh which we ate with hakuru, referred to in English as jaggery or coconut sugar.

During the wet season, it rained quite heavily and water collected in various low-lying areas on the estate. From time to time little tortoises could be found in these pools – but we never attempted to catch them. I used to fashion little boats with sails – using palm frond casings from the coconut trees– to amuse myself in these little pools.

Aunty Sally's home was truly rustic. Nevertheless, in true British tradition, the house had a name for its postal address and was called 'Chesny '. The house had a thatched roof, crooked wooden upright posts, rough floors, rooms with door openings but no doors – just a curtain – as well as an open veranda in front. We felt very much at home at Aunty Sally's. There was no tap water and no flush toilet. The kakkusi or dunny (toilet) was a little enclosed outhouse with a circular opening over a deep pit. One had to draw water from a well for all bathing and washing. There was no electricity either.

We always enjoyed our stay at Aunty Sally's place, except when Tiddy Uncle (Mum and Aunty Sally's brother) also decided to turn up. He was a bit of a pain – especially with his insistence on after dinner prayers, kneeling on the rough floors and reciting the rosary. He put a real damper on everything but everyone deferred to him out of respect.

Tiddy Uncle was a somewhat pompous and holier than thou sort of person. He was also a bit of an enigma as he believed in mediums and had one of them deposit various talismans around Aunty Sally's house after Uncle Francis died. This was done ostensibly to ward off evil spirits. Clarence and I tried hard not to giggle.

Tiddy Uncle was also a bit of a punter – horse racing was his passion. He seemed to have a 'system' of his own to pick the winning horse at a race. This 'system' was based on the maintenance of detailed records of races and horses as well as the jockeys and their weights. As far as I knew, he never won anything worth bragging about.

When Uncle Francis died in 1954 – he was relatively young – Bede, the youngest son was a little baby. Tiddy Uncle came over to the Boarding School to fetch Clarence and me and take us by bus, across country, to attend the funeral. Aunty Sally was very distraught. She had been a housewife all her life and was untrained. But she picked herself up, went for training and took over her late husband's position as Village Postmaster.

Uncle Francis was a great story teller – his ghost stories were especially creepy. He had us mesmerised. He really had us believe that a spirit moved across the estate using a certain path and every time a shack or hut was built across the spirit's pathway, the hut came apart and simply collapsed. He had other stories too – about riding home on his bicycle in the darkness when he noticed a large figure in the gloom waving both arms to him – bidding him to come. And then, as he came closer and closer and more and more afraid, he realised it was a big banana trunk with its droopy fronds, waving in the breeze. I remember we screamed with delight!

The village post office – the 'thapal kantho:ruva' – as the local villagers used to refer to it, was housed in a brick and tile structure, located on the family property, beside the main road which ran past the estate. It was a quaint people-friendly place. There were lots of betel chewing villagers who called over for one reason or another. It was quite normal to see dried up reddish betel stains on bushes as well as white finger marks where excess 'chunam' (lime paste) were wiped away on columns and walls.

Several years after Uncle Francis died, Aunty Sally married Jacky Perera – one of Uncle Francis's long-time friends. Uncle Jacky worked in Colombo and came to Rajakadaluwa on the weekends. The Post Office by the roadside was extended with additional rooms and other facilities. I was proud to be asked to suggest some of the facilities to be put in. I do not think that Tiddy Uncle was overly impressed.

Some years later, I met Uncle Jacky and Sextus in Colombo en-route to London and Uncle Jacky said he was disappointed that I had not kept in touch since I left in 1959. I did apologise for that and promised to keep in touch. Apart from sending greeting cards at Christmas, I did visit Aunty Sally and family in Rajakadaluwa every time I had a stop over in Colombo. My university hall mates, Trevor Roosmalee-cocq and Cecil Amerasinghe drove me to Rajakadaluwa more than once to visit them. By then, Uncle Jacky had also passed away. My close relatives in Sri Lanka enriched my life and I never forgot any of my first cousins. I am looking forward to catching up with some of them later in the year.

I still remember the 'siyambala' (tamarind) tree on the Rajakadaluwa estate. It was a mature tree, quite old and gnarled but easy to climb. I used to perch on the branches with my cousin Sextus, plucking the ripened brown pods and squeezing out the brownish pulp which had a sweet-sour taste. When in full bloom, the tree had a blaze of crimson flowers. I never had a camera then but I can still visualize it in my mind.

In my culinary efforts these days, I use tamarind 'siyambala' from time to time (it is marketed in small rectangular slabs) especially when cooking a fish curry and this often takes me back to Aunty Sally's 'siyambala' tree. The older generation have long passed away but I would not be surprised if the siyambala tree still stands majestic where it always stood.

Journey's end at boarding school

My final year in boarding school was spent in a dormitory called 'Journey's End' which was located on the first floor above the Infirmary where Boarders were treated for minor ailments or sports injuries. Mrs. Mulholland – who had some nursing experience – was in charge of the infirmary. I did occupy a bed in the infirmary with severe tummy pains on one occasion following which I was taken by ambulance to the Kandy General Hospital for an appendectomy.

In 1954, (The Centenary of St. Anthony's College) I sat for my Senior Cambridge School Certificate Examination. I was expecting a Grade I Certificate with a few distinctions in specific subjects. Imagine my disappointment, despite getting distinctions in a few subjects, to be given a provisional pass as I had failed a compulsory subject, namely Sinhalese.

(**footnote**: Free education (primary to tertiary level) in Ceylon has been a policy provision enshrined in the Constitution. I benefitted from it, both during my Boarding School days at SACK and undergraduate studies at the University of Ceylon. Fees were paid only for boarding school residence but I have no recollection of ever paying fees at university.)

Fortunately, I was allowed to take a repeat Examination in Lower Sinhalese (as I was a foreign student) which I passed at the next sitting. This earned me a grade II Certificate. I was however allowed to continue in the University Entrance class (equivalent to the Higher School Certificate) and prepare for the University Entrance Examination conducted by the University of Ceylon and held on campus.

While attending University Entrance classes, I had to take one of the internal exams conducted at St. Anthony's College. I sat for the paper, answered just two questions (expecting full marks) and left the exam hall well ahead of time in order to attend a performance being held elsewhere. This was sheer cheek on my part which I apologised for later. My Form Master, George Denlow was furious with me and later said he did his level best to fail me but was unable to do so as I had secured the maximum marks required to pass even by answering only two questions.

In my final year in College I won the prize in geography (George Denlow's subject area) for my research study on Ancient Irrigation Systems in Ceylon. I also won the award for the most outstanding painting of the year. The painting hung prominently in the main corridor of the College for many years and was the first of other paintings that followed mine.

My nostalgic visit to the College in 2009, with friends from Boarding School days, failed to find any of these early paintings. My visit took place during the first term vacation. I called on the young priest who was in charge. He was also the choir master (choir practice was in session) and he came out to greet us. The Rev. Fr. invited us to hear the choir perform and invited us to request any specific number.

The choir boys were standing quietly in a semi circle – tall, short, tubby and lean. They were dressed in white, but all were bare-footed. I asked them if they could sing for us 'Nessun Dorma' They did and we were absolutely blown away. I recall my own days in the choir – it was more of a 'church' choir then which only sang during mass at the college chapel– a far cry indeed.

Cyril Brown was our music teacher and choir master. For a brief spell, while at 'Journey's End', I attempted to learn to play the piano under Cyril Brown's tutelage. I used to go to Cyril Brown's house for piano practice twice a week but did not have access to a piano on a daily basis for piano practice. Besides, I lacked the discipline required and gave it up before too long – something I have always regretted. Even today, I am a little envious of those who can play the piano.

When I look back on my school going years – my entire experience was in a same sex educational environment, both in Malaya and in Ceylon. The females of the species were never a part of our educational or social experience. This had its advantages and disadvantages. I do recall that some of my friends in College (SACK) had real or imagined relationships with girls in Kandy Convent – a few of them, however, did end up at the altar!

Uncle Noel's visit

Going back a little in time, I recall that in 1954 Mum and Dad bought two wrist watches for Clarence and me and sent them to us through Uncle Noel, who happened to be visiting Ceylon.

Uncle Noel was a bit of a boozer – as I have mentioned earlier – and when he arrived in Ceylon, he was a bit 'high'. Anyway, he managed to make it to the College to see us and handed us our new watches. I still remember the brand name of my watch – it was 'Ogival', not a very well known brand, but I treasured it and used it for many years.

Since Uncle Noel was a visitor from Malaya from Dad's side of the family, Percy Uncle invited him for lunch at Grandma's house in Kossinna. Clarence and I came over from College for the lunch too. Uncle Noel turned up and he had obviously been drinking before he arrived. He was literally 'high as a kite' and quite jovial.

In a typical meal at home – kaha bath (yellow rice) and kukul mus (chicken) curry, kiri hodhi, (light yellow coloured coconut gravy) seeni sambal (sambal made with shallots, maldive fish, spices and slightly sweetened), pol sambal (coconut sambal) and elolu (vegetables) – all eaten with our fingers with finger bowls of water for washing our hands after the meal.

The meal went down very well. Uncle Noel however mistook the finger bowl for soup, drank some of it and offered the rest to Percy Uncle saying: "drink, brother, drink." Uncle Noel also had a speech impediment – he stammered. Taken all together, it was really hilarious!

Visit home

In 1955, after years of scrimping and scraping, my parents arranged for Clarence and me to fly back to Malaya for a short holiday. Percy Uncle saw us off at the airport which was then at Ratmalana. I had the impression that Percy

Uncle was not too happy about our trip. He probably felt that this would undermine his efforts to bring the whole family back to Ceylon in the long run – I was far too naïve at that time to perceive any of this. This was our very first experience of flight on a BOAC (British Overseas Airways Corporation) constellation.

It was great to be back with the family again and to catch up not only on all the happenings within the family but also to share with them our life in Ceylon. It was wonderful to be the centre of attention and to enjoy Mum's fantastic cooking. While on holiday, I took the opportunity to visit Uncle John in KL and he took me over to meet the Jayatilaka family who lived nearby. It is there that I met Annette. We hit it off from the start and even managed to take in a matinee at a cinema in Brickfields, with her youngest brother Rodney in tow.

At the end of our short holiday, Clarence flatly refused to go back to Ceylon. He went back to school at SJI (St John's Institution) and I was sorely tempted to do likewise. I even attended school for a day but thought better of it and decided to go back to Ceylon and complete my studies as I had less than a year to go to complete my University Entrance. I had no clear idea of where I would go from there.

Mum and Dad joined me on the train to Singapore for my flight back to Colombo. We all stayed a few days at Aunty Glady's place in Geylang and did a bit of shopping – mostly some clothes and shoes for me. Mum told me years later that they had barely enough funds to get back to their home in Bukit Kuda Road, Klang. Mum and Dad subsisted on bananas on the train journey back to Kuala Lumpur.

A taste of campus life

I went back to College but it was only for a few months more. The University Entrance Exam was held at the University campus in Peradeniya. I and several of my fellow Boarders were sitting the Exam and the College arranged our transport to the campus. During a break between papers, we were sitting in one of the gazebos or summer houses built on the gentle slopes overlooking the campus. We were eating our packed lunches and feasting our eyes on the general ambiance of the campus – its beautiful buildings, manicured lawns, tree lined avenues, tennis courts and sports facilities – and wondered whether we stood any chance at all of being admitted to the university.

As it turned out, I passed with distinction and got a Direct Entry to the University of Ceylon. Having passed the University Entrance Examinations, students are either given a Direct Entry or are required to present themselves for a Viva (interview). Of the seven of us from College who gained entry to the University in 1956, only Rajaguru (who later became Inspector General of Police in Sri Lanka) and I were given Direct Entry – the rest were admitted only after passing the Viva.

Birthdays

I was born on my mother's twenty fourth birthday. Since we always celebrated Mum's birthday, mine was celebrated too but I have very few recollections of any of them. Quite often my birthday was remembered almost as an afterthought. But once I entered boarding school in Ceylon, my birthdays came and went by quietly. I received a birthday card from my parents with a money order for 25 Rupees. But that was all. My 21st birthday came and went by just as quietly. I got a greeting card from my parents and a small bank draft in rupees. From my uncles in Ceylon I got nothing, not even a greeting card. My birthday was just another day, with little cause to celebrate.

Not long after the university entrance results were announced, I happened to meet Tiddy Uncle at the Kandy Bus Depot quite by chance and mentioned to him the exciting news of my admission to University. His reaction was deadpan and totally deflating – and I was, after all the very first in the family to embark on university studies. I saw little point in mentioning my 21st Birthday either. But I did not let it get me down. I simply concluded that recognition was important only from those who mattered – and my uncle was certainly someone who mattered not at all.

Because of my own birthday experiences, I made sure that in my later life I never forgot the birthdays of members of my own family – Annette and the boys. I also remembered the birthdays of my parents and sisters but was not as conscientious about my brothers' birthdays. I wonder why.

Kandy bus depot

The Kandy Bus Depot brings to mind the experience of bus travel in Ceylon. The Bus Depot was a sea of humanity, hustle and bustle – steamy and sweaty. This was my primary mode of travel. There were taxis but I could never afford to travel in them. Today, Sri Lanka is chock-a-block with 'tuk-tuks' – three wheeled motorised vehicles. In my student days in Ceylon, there were none.

Queues were virtually unknown. Everybody rushed for everything – including boarding an already overcrowded bus. Digressing a little and moving to more recent times when Karen and I were in the departure lounge waiting to board an Air Lanka flight to Colombo, the departure hall was full of Sri Lankans. When the announcement was made to board the aircraft – there was an almighty rush to get on board. I smiled for it reminded me of the mad rush to board the bus in the Kandy Bus Depot.

Beetle chewing and spitting were the norm – the trick was not to get caught in the slipstream – especially when the bus was in motion. I got caught once, and I was not even on the bus – my cream trousers were ruined as I was unable to remove the reddish stain. The Kandy Bus Depot bears ample evidence not only of beetle chewing but of white lime or 'chunam' finger marks or daubs on walls and columns left there by betel chewers. Anything vertical, conveniently located such as lamp posts and even tree trunks were used to wipe away excess chunam.

Even when the bus was full – with seated and standing passengers, vendors were allowed to climb aboard, selling their trinkets, sweets or other goodies. There were even budding poets and authors who read our excerpts of their literary creations in Sinhala and attempted to sell copies of their 'works' which they carried with them. There were even the vendors who climbed on the mud-guards over the rear wheels of the bus and attempted to sell you their wares through the side windows of the bus. Nobody got angry or irritated – it was all part of life and of earning a living! For me it was truly an experience.

Career choices

In our day, there was little in the way of career guidance in school. In my school going years in Malaya, career guidance would have been somewhat premature. But when I entered Boarding School in Ceylon and was in the Upper Sixth or University entrance class, there should have been proper career guidance in order to enable one to make the right subject choices as a prelude to embarking on University studies. But none of this happened as St Anthony's College only had limited teaching resources and could only stream students into an 'arts' stream or a 'science' stream.

I got little from my family in this regard. and nothing at all from my uncles in Ceylon who were ostensibly my guardians – and one of them was a teacher. So at university level I chose subjects I was interested in and had done well at in school – history became my main subject with economics as a subsidiary. Several of my friends from Boarding School who were admitted at the same time had chosen this subject combination and I followed suit – safety in numbers perhaps? How very foolish!. Where this was going to take me career–wise I hadn't a clue.

College friends

While at College I had a number of very good friends. I still remember Clement Samuel, Winston Perera, Ivan Boteju and Percival de Silvie. Percy later was ordained to the priesthood. I lost track of all of them after I left College except for Ivan Boteju who became an Inspector of Police. In the late sixties, the last weeks of my Sabbatical were spent in Sri Lanka and I took the opportunity to visit Ivan in Hikkaduwa where he was stationed. It was a joyous reunion after a lapse of almost fourteen years.

Tragically, during the period of civil strife in Sri Lanka in the eighties, Ivan Boteju, while serving within the conflict zone, was mowed down by machine gun fire – every single officer in the station was killed. I never got to know of this until my visit to Sri Lanka in the nineties.

Winston Perera was a bit of an athlete – especially in field events, rather than in track. I remember particularly in one of the College sports events, Winston, in brand new track shoes, turned up to participate in the discus throw. I must say his twirling around was quite impressive but when he threw the discus, he released it, not down the field where the markers were placed but right into the crowd. Everybody howled with laughter. Fortunately, no one was seriously injured. I do not recall that Winston ever took to discus throwing again.

This brings to mind my own misadventures in track events. I had no running shoes – just could not afford them and so I ran barefooted. There I was in the line up for the 440. I heard the starter gun go off and took off like a bat out of hell! I was well ahead of the pack but failed to allow for the fact that I had to go around the track twice. True enough, the ignominious happened – I ran out of steam and there ended my notions of ever making it in track events.

My good friend Ivan Boteju was a real athlete. He was a sprinter – tall, dark skinned, good looking and with a brilliant set of white teeth, he was like a black panther. It was thrilling to see him run – with that graceful loping gait – the 220 was his speciality. I was proud to have him as my friend. Yes, my friends enriched my life and helped to give a balance to my life and perhaps make up in a way for my absent family.

Bullying at St Anthony's was never a part of my experience. I had many good friends with whom I enjoyed spending time with. I never entertained the idea of having a 'best friend' as such —- they were all my friends. Some were even very protective and would lean heavily on anyone who bothered me or attempted to bully me.

My stay at Kossinna, however was coming to an end as I had a serious falling out with Percy Uncle during term break. Percy Uncle was a bit of a control freak who earlier even objected to my getting into long pants without his prior permission – and I was well over nineteen! The latest altercation proved to be the last straw. I simply packed my bag and left – with little money in my pocket and nowhere to go.

I turned up at the home of one of my friends close by and his mother simply took me in, no questions asked. It was a life saver and I never forgot the kindness shown. Every term break after that was spent in rooms near Campus which I jointly rented with my friends.

The University of Ceylon

The University of Ceylon in my day was unique as it was totally residential unlike most universities today. Several of my school mates from St Anthonys' gained admission to the

University at the same time and were placed in various Halls of Residence. Three of us from Boarding School became residents at Arunachalam Hall.

Arunachalam Hall was fairly centrally located in relation to the whole campus and was close to the Great Hall, the Lecture Theatres, the University Library, the tennis courts, the basketball court, the soccer and hockey fields and running tracks. It took me a while to digest and take it all in and to realize that I (little ole me) had been given admission to the country's most prestigious and sole Centre of Higher Education. Our Vice-Chancellor in my first year at University was Sir. Ivor Jennings who subsequently became Vice-Chancellor at Cambridge University.

There were no mixed-gender Halls of Residence at the university. There was gender separation, conforming to societal norms. Each room was shared by two students and was fairly well equipped – two single beds, cupboards for clothes as well as a wash-basin and mirror. There was a nice little balcony too. Common showers and toilets were provided on each floor. Each Hall of Residence had its own kitchen as well as its own cooks and we had all our meals in the Dining Hall. Once a month the dhobi turned up to collect our dirty laundry – I do not recall that I ever paid any fee for food, board, or laundry services at Arunachalam Hall. This was the case at all other halls of residence. Each hall of residence was supervised by a Warden, who was usually a member of the teaching staff.

My interaction with Hall mates and other students on campus was most agreeable. I made many friends: some have remained my friends ever since. My years at the

With fellow hall mates - 1958

With my roommate Ray Forbes – 1958

University were a wonderful experience. In the mid fifties, the University of Ceylon only had two campuses – one in Colombo for science and medical studies and the other in Peradeniya for a wide range of other fields of study. The campus at Peradeniya was well laid out and set in gently undulating terrain. The campus in Colombo, set in a bustling city, was somewhat spread-out and seemed to lack a distinct physical identity as a premier seat of learning.

As a student I barely had enough money to cope with the basic necessities of life on campus. I rarely joined my

Hall-mates for a booze-up at Hantane – their favourite watering-hole. But once when I finally was persuaded to join them, a single bottle of beer proved too much and it seems I was walking rather unsteadily back to A-Hall. (Arunachalam Hall).

My hall-mates very kindly decided to carry me back to my room. I was really not that far gone and it was pleasant enough being carried back. My friends dutifully deposited me on my own bed and left. I then felt my room-mate fumbling with my belt. I got up with a start and said "Cyril, what the bloody hell are you doing?" The poor guy was only trying to make me more comfortable. In 2013, on my last visit to Sri Lanka, I visited my first year room-mate – Cyril Mendis – after nearly 55 years – and recalled the incident. We both had a good laugh.

I did not socialise much with the ladies on campus. I had very little money and did not come from a wealthy family. I figured I was not much of a catch anyway so why bother. I did however have a few lady friends both on and off campus. I must however confess that they were more interested in me than I was in them. One of them – her name was Doreen – used to cook tasty little dishes which she used to send to my room through her brother. We went out a few times and spent some pleasant evenings at the Peradeniya Gardens – but it got no further than that.

The other was an off campus interest which was somewhat short lived. We met from time to time. I used to disappear into the night, mostly disguised in high collar raincoat and hat – a far cry from cloak and dagger escapades – and came back to my room in the early hours – my room-mate was never the wiser.

Communication was rather difficult – no telephones were available at either end and so a system of flower pot placement was worked out to indicate the 'all clear' – the lady did have a rather formidable mother I was not too keen to meet. There were other serious obstacles too. The entire system of communication was seriously flawed and did not even amount to a bush telegraph! It was a real hoot. Some ventures into the night were complete non starters!

When I reflect upon it all, it seems that there were far too many variables. The buses did not function that late at night so I had to walk. There were no street lights. I did not have a torch and so I had to wait for partial moon lit nights. There was also the weather to contend with – it rained often in the hill country and when it rained it came down in buckets!

I had about five miles to walk and I invariably followed the rail track which was somewhat dicey especially when the track crossed a major river – stepping on railway sleepers in dim light with nothing else underfoot was not for the faint hearted. Had I missed a step, I would have dropped about ten metres to the flowing Mahaveli ganga (river) below – I could not swim! But I was young and foolish.

I had a real fright once as I walked in the pitch dark night – little natural light of any kind. And then while walking in the eerie silence of night, there was a sudden flapping of wings all around me. I stood stock still, hair on end until my rational mind took over – it had to be the fruit bats who were disturbed during their nocturnal binge as I passed under the mango tree laden with ripe fruit! It was the flapping of their collective wings that I had heard.

Major Rivers and Peaks

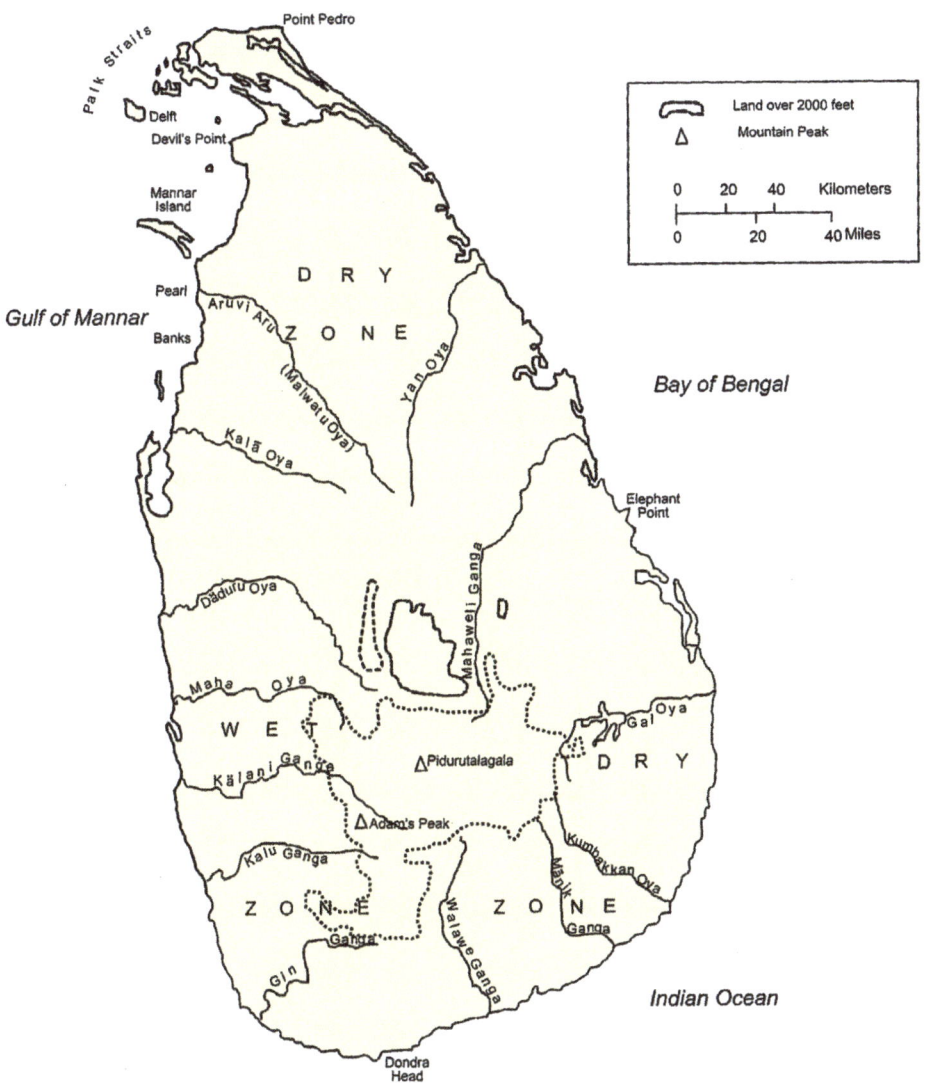

The Newman Society used to hold social evenings on Campus from time to time and I attended a few of them. We entertained ourselves with music and some dancing. There was no booze whatsoever. I remember Anne Cook (everybody's heart-throb) on the piano. I also recall singing a few numbers myself and my rendering of the Platters' version of 'Only You' went down rather well.

For a while there on Campus, I was called 'only you'. My friend Ray Forbes may remember. One of the girls – Moreen – got a little too interested in me after my rendering of 'only you', much to the displeasure of one of my Hall mates who considered Moreen to be his preserve. Moreen was nice enough but I was not interested. I just laughed it off and peace was restored.

But distractions aside, I soon knuckled down to my studies and spent my leisure hours in sport rather than in social activities – tennis, basketball, football and hockey. I was on the Varsity Football, Hockey and Basketball teams and earned my 'Colours' in all of them.

From time to time, four or five of us caught a bus just outside the campus and went up to Kandy to one of the cinemas to see a film. On one occasion, when we alighted from the bus on our return to campus, we passed the Peradeniya Rest House (situated at the entrance to the campus – it still stands there today and I had lunch there on my visit in 2009).

One of us – I recall it was Guy Motha – invited all of us for a beer. We readily agreed, took a table and were served our cold beers. It was a light hearted, fun filled gathering. After about half an hour, we had finished our beers and we looked to Guy to pay the bill. Guy said he had no money. We looked at each other and realised that none of us had any money to pay the bill either. There's only one thing to do said Guy – on the count of three, he counted, jumped over the balcony and sprinted away. We hastily did likewise and got back to our rooms without the campus marshal on our tails. We never showed our faces at the Rest House again.

In 1994, when Annette and I and our son Rohan visited Sri Lanka, we stopped by the Peradeniya Rest House for a meal. It was the very first time I was back on the premises, after nearly thirty seven years. I looked around and it seemed that nothing had changed. It was of course highly improbable that I would be recognised and that a waiter would come up to me and ask me to settle the long outstanding bill!! The visit brought back many memories – my undergraduate days on campus and my life in times gone by.

Irony of ironies, Guy later in his working life skipped the country with the tax office hot on his trail and ended up in the U.S. where he held a top-level post in the World Bank. One wonders what Guy really did there.

An up-country holiday

In 1956, my very first year as an undergraduate student at the University of Ceylon, I took the opportunity to visit my old boarding school at St. Anthony's College at Katugastota to catch up with old friends. It was there that I met up with Victor and Winston Bayley – they were a few years junior to me in College, but were nevertheless my friends. As it was close to end of term break, Victor and Winston invited me to spend the holidays at their family home on Keenakale

Estate – high up in the hill country – where their father was the PD (Peria Dorai) or Big Boss.

My friends subsequently picked me up at Kossinna and we took off for Keenakele, which was located in prime tea-country, between Nuwara Eliya and Badulla. It was a very pleasant holiday at their place. During the course of the holiday, some of the priests from the Boarding School also turned up (to our great dismay) – which brought in its wake the attendance at Mass each morning and prayers in the evening.

I was given an overview of the tea planting industry. It was interesting to see the operations of a large tea plantation – from tea picking on the steep hill sides and bags of plucked tea leaves transported on wire shoots moving far above the valley floor below to the buffer point at the tea factory.

From then on, the tea leaves went through a series of processes at the large tea factory located on the Estate. This included curing, sorting, grading before being transported to Colombo for packaging, labelling and shipping for the export market. Tea planting was in its heyday in Ceylon then and tea planters were a privileged lot.

While at Keenakele, I joined up with Winston and Stephen Joseph to climb Pidurutalagala, with an elevation of 2524 m – the highest peak in the country. The climb was not overly demanding. Though it was the highest elevation, there was no spectacular peak to reach – just pale green patna (grass) with stunted and gnarled trees near the top. We captured the moment with a photograph taken at the summit. It was cold and rather windy.

*At the summit of Pidurutalagala, 1958
with Winston and Stephen*

Pidurutalagala is no comparison to Gunung (Mount) Kinabalu in Sabah, Malaysia (elevation 4095m) which is far higher and spectacular and whose summit is not as easily reached. Although I have been to Kota Kinabalu, Sabah many times, I have never attempted to climb Gunung Kinabalu.

The PD's bungalow in Keenakele was a pleasantly designed residence set in landscaped gardens and with a small swimming pool to boot! We did jump in once or twice when it was not too cold. When Victor's mother discovered that I was a bit of an artist, she got me to paint a picture of the house and garden, which was later framed and hung up.

I lost track of the Bayleys after I left Ceylon. However, in the early seventies when Victor migrated to Australia with his young family, they made a brief stop over in Kuala Lumpur and stayed with us. The rest of their family including their parents migrated to Australia soon after.

Sri Lanka was no longer the idyllic comfortable haven for the Burgher (Eurasian) community it used to be in the mid fifties. Because of currency restrictions, most of the Burghers left the country with very little. Over the years, black market currency transactions enabled the more enterprising to transfer some of their liquid assets overseas.

In 2003, on my return to Perth from a consultant mission to Papua New Guinea sponsored by UNESCO I stopped over in Brisbane and spent some time with the Bayleys. It was very pleasant to catch up with them after such a long while.

Then in 2009 after Annette died, I spent a few very restful weeks at Victor's home in Brisbane and later at Winston's place on Wilson beach – north of Brisbane. My stay at the Bayleys helped me to come to terms with Annette's passing.

Soccer tournament in India

Picking up the threads from the past once again, in 1957 the combined soccer team of the University of Ceylon, with players selected from both campuses, participated in the Inter-University Soccer Tournament which was held in India. I was one of those selected to play for the combined team. It was a unique opportunity for me to travel abroad. Imagine my horror to discover that I had no passport or any ID whatsoever – and I was in a foreign country! How I got over this problem I do not recall but I did go to India with the team. Unfortunately, we were no match for the Indian teams and were roundly trounced.

Pilgrimage to Thalawila

That same year a few of us – all Catholics and fellow hall-mates – decided to attend the 'pilgrimage' at St. Anne's Church, Thalawila on the west coast of the island near Chilaw. Cecil Amerasinghe, Ray Forbes, Philip Fernando and myself did the trip together – entirely by bus. We had to change buses a few times. The trip took up the better part of the day – we reached sometime in the evening and roughed it out in make shift shacks, which had earlier been built for the use of devotees. The shacks were quite basic – sandy floors and a thatched roof to keep out the rain. Cecil was given the task of looking after the collective purse to meet transport, food and incidental expenses. Horror of horrors – Cecil lost the purse and we were virtually stranded.

At the Festival of St. Anne's, Thalawila, Ceylon, 1957 with Philip Fernando, Ray Forbes and Cecil Amerasinghe

Fortunately, we had some reserves and scrounged our meals from my Aunty Sally and her children who were also at the festival. All of us enjoyed the trip very much and we made it back to the Campus in one piece. I still keep in touch with Cecil and Ray and visit them both whenever I am in Sri Lanka. I completely lost track of Philip but received an e-mail from him recently. He is now a journalist and lives in the U.S.

Health concerns

When I look back on the many years I lived in Ceylon, I do not have even a single recollection of having to see a doctor. I never had any serious ailment, apart from the occasional cold and cough. These were invariably treated with traditional medicines. The 'kothamalee' treatment for colds and flu was very well known. It was the standard treatment, not only when we were growing up in Malaya but also during the years I spent in Sri Lanka. Coriander seeds (kothamalee) were boiled along with ginger and other spices and then the vapours had to be breathed in with our heads completely covered, over a steaming pot of 'kothamalee'. It was quite an effective treatment.

From time to time the wedha-mahathir (medicine man) was consulted. The man grandma consulted was named Bodhya. He knew all about medicinal herbs and roots – all part of an ancient tradition of ayurvedic medicine. It was most interesting observing grandma and Bodhya talking. Bodhya was a betel chewer and often punctuated his remarks by spitting red coloured spittle and betel juice on to the nearby hibiscus bush – he never missed. Grandma joined him in a 'chew' from time to time. I have tried it too, but it made no impression on me.

Bodhya usually greeted me with his beetle-stained near toothless grin. He called me 'punchi mahatir' – little master. 'Kohoma the' – how are you? It does appear that the overall change of climate from the Malay States to Sri Lanka helped greatly as I completely got over the asthma attacks I used to suffer from in my younger years.

Gampola Floods

I was on holiday at my Aunt's home in Gampola, when their house and surrounding township as well as paddy-fields and railway station were inundated by rushing flood waters, following several days of heavy rains. The Church and the school were on elevated land and became the relief centre for those affected by the floods.

Flood levels rose rapidly to over four metres in the Mahaveli Ganga (Mahaveli River). The water level in the Geli Oya, a tributary of the main river, also overflowed its banks, which resulted in a large area between Peradeniya and Gampola to be flooded. My aunt's house was flooded to a level of almost two metres. It was a real mess. The bathing well too, at the rear of the house was completely ruined.

Uncle Norbert was the Station Master at the Gampola Railway Station and had to be at the Station to cope with the problems arising there. Fortunately, the locomotives and rolling stock were heavy and did not float away with the rushing flood waters.

My Aunt and the kids were evacuated in the first available row boat to the relief centre at the school. I stayed behind, which left me virtually in charge of the family home. My main concern was the furniture in the open veranda which was not tied down and could have floated away. We foolishly thought that the railings of the veranda would be sufficient to keep the furniture safe.

But the waters kept rising and I knew that it was not only the furniture that was at risk. I had to leave too or I would be in big trouble. I remember wading through rushing, swirling flood waters, with floating debris, boxes and uprooted trees, barely able to keep my head above water to get to a rescue row boat about five metres away.

I remember being submerged a few times but I did not panic. I did not know how to swim then. I reached the boat eventually and had to be helped aboard. My rescuers took me and a few others to the relief centre at the school. It was a real challenge helping to clean up the mess in the house after the waters subsided. It was truly an unforgettable experience.

Trincomalee

My only opportunity to visit Trincomalee on the east coast of Ceylon came about when Uncle Norbert was transferred to Trincomalee and served as Station Master there for a few years. Trinco, as it used to be called then was at the end of the line in the northeast of the country.

During the school holidays shortly after, which coincided with semester break at the University of Ceylon, I was asked to accompany my Aunt and the children to Trinco. Since Uncle Norbert was an employee of the Railways, the family was assigned a first class compartment for the entire trip. The trip by train was most interesting and very comfortable and I enjoyed my stay in Trincomalee very much. All of us spent several days by the beach – I still remember the white sandy beaches and the crystal blue waters.

Looking back

Looking back on my years as an undergraduate student at the University of Ceylon, I have come to realise, that my reminiscences of the past which I have written about, have touched, in somewhat desultory fashion, on holiday trips up-country, the trip to India for the soccer tournament, the excursion to Thalawila, the train journey to Trincomalee, the Gampola floods as well as life on campus. Strangely, I never mentioned anything about the dreaded ragging on campus. I suppose it was because I experienced little of it. Ragging had in fact been banned although milder expressions of ragging did take place.

I never mentioned my studies either at the university. Yet this was the whole purpose of my admission to the University – to undertake a course of study – which hopefully, would give me my academic credentials. Admittedly at that time, we did not have a wide range of choice in terms of subjects and once chosen, there was little flexibility.

The euphoria of securing a Direct Entry to the university and the perceptions of several of my varsity mates that I would surely end up with a 'First' (first class honours) massaged my ego but failed to strengthen my resolve or my application to serious study. The result was that I coursed through my undergraduate years, without putting in too much effort, fully confident that I would pass – and I did. I saw my degree as a stepping stone – but where exactly it would take me, I had not the remotest idea.

While I dutifully attended all my lectures, I sometimes skipped the tutorials. I did however attend most of the talks by guest speakers but my attendance was quite passive unlike that of some of my batch mates, who were knowledgeable, articulate and confident. They gave a few of the speakers a hard time.

The University Library, one of the best resourced libraries in the country and just a stone's throw from my room in Arunachalam Hall, was not used as often or as well as I should have. My few visits to the main reading room were useful enough and I did lay my hands on a few key titles, but this was mostly a hit and miss method as I tended to pick up relevant material mostly by browsing at the book shelves. I rarely used the author or subject catalogues or consulted the professional staff of the library for assistance – what a waste!

The University of Ceylon campus at Peradeniya gave us students a very comfortable and pleasant living and learning environment. I never found any of it stressful in any way, not even at exam time. There were no doubt the student protests and demonstrations with singing, chanting and waving of banners – about the quality of food, the inefficiency of the laundry services (the 'dhoby') and the boring and conservative courses we were trapped into. I did not participate in any of these protests. Like many of my fellow residents at Arunachalam Hall, we watched from the side-lines and found it all somewhat amusing. There was never any aggression, violence or wanton damage of property. Mostly, it was the exuhuberance of youth, the expression of high spirits and the good humoured tolerance of diversity.

Underlying ethnic tensions

I am ashamed to admit that during my ten year stay in Ceylon, I was woefully ignorant of the undercurrents that were slowly building up within the country between the Sinhalese and the Tamils. Part of the reason for this may have been the fact that as a foreign student I was not overly interested in political or socio-economic developments taking place in the country. English was the lingua franca and the medium of instruction during my years at St. Anthony's College and at the University of Ceylon and my fellow students – whether Sinhalese, Tamil, Burgher or Moor (Indian Muslim) – were very comfortable with one another.

But it is tragic to see what has happened in Sri Lanka in terms of communal disharmony since then. I never realised at that time that the discrimination against the Tamils in Sri Lanka began with the passing of the Sinhala only Act in 1956 – my first year as an undergraduate at the University of Ceylon. The Act, put in place by the Prime Minister, S.W.R.D. Bandaranayake, appealed to the Sinhalese majority but disadvantaged the minority Tamil population. This discrimination has continued under successive Sinhalese dominated Governments, irrespective of the political parties in power. In 1959, the year I graduated, the Prime Minister SWRDB was assassinated by a member of the Buddhist clergy. In 1972, the country was renamed Sri Lanka.

As the fissures deepened and mired, peaceful attempts to effect political solutions for greater self government in areas of Tamil concentration in the north and east of the country failed to make any progress. Eventually these fissures escalated into armed conflict, the object of the dissidents being to bring about an independent Tamil homeland covering the north and east of the island. The bloody armed conflict between the Government and disgruntled groups – virtually a civil war – became the longest lasting civil war in Asia and dragged on for nearly thirty years The most prominent Tamil protagonist group was the LTTE (Liberation Tigers of Tamil Eelam) which was finally only defeated in 2009.

Over 100,000 people lost their lives during the period of armed conflict and thousands within the conflict zone were displaced from their homes. Atrocities were committed both by Government armed forces and also by the LTTE and thousands are still missing and are presumed to have died. Happily, my relatives in Sri Lanka lived far from the conflict zones and did not experience any loss of life or displacement from their homes. But I did loose some of my very close friends in the security forces who served within the conflict zone

It is time to rebuild and heal the wounds of the past. The Tamils (the Sinhalese refer to them as Demalu minissu <Tamil people>) have made the island their home since the 2nd century BC. Since then, there have been several invasions from south India – the Pandyas, the Pallavas and the Colas, not to mention people incursions as well as royal linkages in past history. One needs to acknowledge that that both the Sinhalese and the Tamils originated from different parts of the Indian subcontinent. They are brothers and are legitimate heirs to the country.

But the Sinhalese/Buddhist and the Dravidian/Tamil/Hindu divide runs deep. Restoring a harmonious balance and creating a level playing field for all – Sinhalese, Tamil, Moors and Burghers – will take great statesmanship and goodwill on the part of all concerned. There is a very long way to go in reintegrating the Tamils into the political and socio-economic life of the nation.

In visits to Sri Lanka after 2009, I have also visited areas inhabited largely by Tamils and Moors in Batticaloa and Trincomalee on the east coast of the island where a semblance of normalcy is slowly returning to the country. I have also visited Negombo, Chilaw and Puttalam on the west coast where there is a significant concentration of Tamils. The atmosphere in this part of the country seems somewhat different as many Tamils are bi-lingual and speak both Sinhala and Tamil and many are Catholic unlike their east coast brothers who profess the Islamic faith. I have however never visited Jaffna and Mannar in the north of the island where the majority of the Tamil population is concentrated. This is something I hope to correct within the next few years.

(**footnote**. According to Sri Lanka Government Census 2001, the population distribution in Sri Lanka consisted of 82% Sinhalese, 9.4% Tamil, 7.9 % Moors (Tamil speaking) and .7% others. From a religious perspective, most Sinhalese were Buddhist with a much smaller proportion who were Catholic or Protestant Christian while the majority of Tamils were Hindu with a smaller proportion who were also Christian. The Moors, who are a distinct group of Tamil speakers, profess the Islamic faith and are concentrated mostly in Batticola and Trincomalee in the eastern part of the island, while the northern Tamils, often referred to as Jaffna Tamils are the dominant Tamil group. The population demographic also includes the Indian Tamils who are the descendants of the labour force brought in from south India by the British to work on the tea plantations.)

I am conscious that I have drifted and have taken the story very far forward. I need to return to my story line and my life in the country at that time.

Farewell Ceylon

My time in Ceylon was coming to an end. I had mixed feelings about leaving a country I had got used to and was quite uncertain about the future. My final exams at the University were held in March 1959. I was confident I would get through and immediately booked passage on a P&O (Peninsula and Orient) liner without even waiting for the results. This was ill-advised. Had I failed, my Dad would have had to pay for me to go back – fortunately, when the results were posted later, I had passed.

It was time to say my farewells especially to family members in Ceylon who had helped me over the years. I thanked Grandma and other members of the family in and around Kandy. I also paid a courtesy call on Percy Uncle in Colombo, to thank him and say my farewells. Aunty Sally, Uncle Jacky and all my cousins came to Colombo to see me off on the ship. All my close Varsity batch mates were also there to see me off. I remember especially Ray Forbes, Cecil Amerasinghe, Milroy Ratwatte, Stanley Tenuwera, Trevor Rosemale-cocq and Stanley Harvey.

When I was a young man in my mid twenties, my ten year sojourn in Ceylon was something I accepted as part of the twists and turns of life. It is how life is. Nobody was to blame – certainly not my parents. They made choices with the best interests of the family in mind. But there is no doubt that my sojourn in Ceylon split the family.

It seems appropriate at this stage to stress the importance of maintaining family ties and relationships – especially with the immediate family. During my years as a student in Ceylon, I wrote regularly to my father, rarely to my mother and never to my brothers and sisters. It took years to restore the frayed ties. It never occurred to me then how very important this was. In this respect, I need to make mention of Mum's sisters and their families in Ceylon too – they were all such lovely people. While I did visit them in subsequent visits to Sri Lanka (most of their children were unmarried then), the ties grew distant over the years, but never really faded. It is so very important to keep one's friends close and one's family even closer. I very much regret that I got caught up with my own life and fell far short. When Mum died in 2000, I was so touched when Uncle Norbert sent a beautifully worded sympathy card to me, starting with the words "My Dear Donny".

*Dehiwela, Ceylon, March 1959
at the home of Ray Forbes*

There is little doubt that my sojourn in Ceylon derailed my career line and deprived me of the opportunity of getting to know and interacting with fellow Malaysians as I pursued tertiary studies. The friends I made as an undergraduate at the University of Ceylon have remained my lifelong friends. By way of contrast, the 'friends' I made in my working life in Malaysia were largely work colleagues – very few have remained my friends. And now that I have moved to Australia, my circle of 'friends' has shrunk even further. It is a truism, sometimes pointed out to me, that while I am friendly, I do not make friends easily.

Looking back on my ten year sojourn in Ceylon and comparing my experience with that of several of my Malaysian first cousins who spent several years abroad as students, it is most interesting to note how different the motivations appeared to be for each of us.

It is only when I started writing 'Footprints' and gaining access to basic documents that my father had carefully preserved that I realised that Clarence and I may have been placed in boarding school in Ceylon – not so much to further our education but rather to set up an anchor or base to facilitate the family's return to the motherland within the next two years.

Fortunately, later down the track, wiser councils prevailed and this plan was abandoned. But Clarence and I were already abroad and were virtually 'marooned' – the dye had been cast and had to be played out. My father could ill afford the expenditure of keeping us in boarding school but my sisters helped to lessen the burden.

Contrasting my experience with that of my cousins Bernard and Lucien (Uncle Roy's only two sons), they were sent to India to further their education. Uncle Roy wanted his sons to become medical doctors and Bernard did while Lucien ended up with a degree in microbiology. The difference was that Uncle Roy only had two sons and he was more than able to support his sons financially while they were students abroad. Both my cousins returned to live and work in Malaysia — Bernard still does while Lucien has retired. All their children live and work in Malaysia in the private sector.

Compare again the experience of my cousin Dina – Uncle John and Aunty Baby's only daughter who was sent to England for her studies when she was still a little girl. I never saw Dina again. I wonder what the experience would have been for a little girl growing up in a foreign country without her parents on hand on a daily basis. Dina went on from school to University and ended up with a Doctorate. Dina married an English academic, has three daughters and lives in England. It would have been an expensive proposition to keep Dina in boarding school followed by her years in tertiary studies. But my aunt and uncle were Principals of their respectiw schools and were relatively well off. Besides, they only had one daughter.

The prospect of securing government scholarships for any of us was quite remote and we never bothered to apply. We made our way on our own steam but we came back to serve in one capacity or another. But since the affirmative policies were put in place in the seventies, many Malaysians who left for study overseas, never came back to the country to join the workforce.

Coming back to my main trend of thought, following the final exams at the University and prior to my departure back to Malaya, I did give some thought to the possibility of sitting for the CCS (Ceylon Civil Service) exams and taking up positions in the Ceylon administrative and diplomatic service. There was one serious impediment however – I felt my level of competence in Sinhalese was woefully inadequate to enable me to reach my full potential within the service.

It seemed to me that my options were strictly limited. I needed to get back to Malaya post haste and start earning my keep; I was nearly 25. I was also hopeful of making a regular monthly contribution to my parents from my wages for the selfless support they gave to me throughout my studies abroad. My two sisters helped too, for which I am truly grateful.

I am no longer in Sri Lanka and apart from brief visits over the years, I have long severed my ties with the country but have maintained personal ties with my Sinhalese and Burgher friends from days of long ago.

While I acknowledge my heritage, my Sri Lankan ethnicity has not been especially important to me. Interestingly, my friends in Malaysia are mostly Malaysian Indians (Tamils) rather than ethnic Sinhalese.

Sibling Pathways

Whether my stint at university and the fact that I had obtained an academic degree influenced my brothers in any way I am unable to say. Both Clarence and Basil subsequently entered Teacher's College in Gelugor, Penang and qualified as teachers. Clarence subsequently taught in a secondary school in Kuala Selangor and there met up with a young teacher who later became his wife. Her name was Gurdev but she preferred to be called Anne after she converted and became a Catholic. Gurdev's conversion was a matter of deep personal conviction and not because she married Clarence.

The marriage of Clarence and Gurdev however began rather bumpily. It was a church wedding and after it was solemnised and the marriage register signed, the father of the bride – a bearded Sikh gentleman in traditional turban, turned up and caused a real commotion, with the intent of preventing the marriage from taking place. But he was too late – the newly married couple had to be smuggled out of a side entrance of the church and they took off on their honeymoon to parts unknown. It was left to yours truly to front up at the bridal reception and inform all and sundry that the bridal party would not be able to grace the occasion!

Clarence later obtained an Honours degree from the University of Malaya and went on to become Headmaster of the Methodist Boy's School in Sentul, Kuala Lumpur. Years later, they had two children, both girls – Desiree and Denise. In the late eighties, the girls attended Santa Maria secondary school in Perth and later graduated from Murdoch University and Notre Dame University. Both girls work in the private sector in Perth.

The family's attempt to obtain Permanent Residence in Australia dragged on for many years. Clarence died in 1992 following a heart attack which left him paralysed and bed ridden for several years. The remainder of the family only obtained Permanent Residence after 2010 – long after Clarence's death.

Basil too taught in school for some years and later graduated with an Honours degree from the University of Malaya. He went on from there to post graduate studies in England where he obtained his Master's Degree and then to Georgetown University in the U.S. for his Doctorate in linguistics. Basil spent the rest of his working career as a lecturer at the Universiti Kebangsaan Malaysia (National University) and later was appointed as Associate Professor.

Basil married Elaine de Fonseka who also graduated with an Honours degree from the University of Malaya and later went on to post graduate studies in England where she obtained her Masters. Their only son Arjuna went on scholarship to England and qualified as a pilot. He pilots those huge jumbo jets these days for major international airlines. Arjuna later married Sharmila. They have two children – Ayanna and Shamindra.

My sisters Janette and Irene enrolled in Normal Class, which was a teacher training course organised within the country prior to the setting up of Teacher Training Colleges. They both qualified as teachers and spent their working lives in various schools in Kuala Lumpur.

Following her marriage to Vernon and her move to Singapore, Irene taught school in Mandai, Johore and

Arjuna, flying for Malaysian Airlines

travelled daily across the Causeway (between Singapore and Johore). This proved to be physically very tedious for her. Irene and Vernon never had any children. Sadly, Irene passed away in Singapore in 2007. Vernon later sold their apartment in Woodlands, married a lady from the Phillipines and lived there for a few years but passed away in 2017.

In the early seventies, Janette (all of us called her Jenny) migrated to Australia with her family and set up house in Adelaide. Janette was the very first one from the family to migrate to Australia and has lived there with her family ever since. Jenny began her working life in Australia as a secondary school teacher but she also taught music. Her sons, Bradley, Bayley and Shenton graduated from Adelaide University – two as medical doctors and one as an engineer. Her only daughter Sharon became a school teacher and lives and works in Queensland. Jenny's husband Wence died several years ago.

The Family in 1972

We virtually lost contact with Jenny and her family after she migrated to Australia. I did however manage to visit them in 1978 and subsequently arranged for Mum and Dad to visit them as well. Irene and Vernon also visited them but long after Wence died. Jenny and Sharon visited Malaysia and Singapore a few years later and met up with Basil and Irene. I have not seen Jenny since 1978 but keep in touch by phone.

Norbert was the last of the second generation of Wijasuriya siblings. Norbert's own life journey seems to reflect grandfather's own predilection to wandering far from home.

Norbert was the youngest and for that reason, Dad and Mum may have been inclined to be more indulgent in his case. Norbert seems to have coursed through his school years at St. Johns's Institution with somewhat unremarkable grades after which he got involved with his neighbourhood music playing buddies. I remember Norbert in his growing up years as a cheeky little bugger. As a young man, he was a fun person.

Norbert had an abiding interest in music and took piano lessons along with my sister Jenny under a qualified piano teacher named Ms. Tivitdale. Dad paid for this tuition. Both Jenny and Norbert sat for the Examinations conducted by The Associated Board of the Royal Schools of Music in pianoforte playing and successfully passed several grade levels. Music became career lines for both of them.

Norbert was one of those guys with a natural sense of music and rhythm in him. He really surprised all of us at a dinner party at Dad's place in PJ when he belted out a catchy number called 'One night with you'.

Norbert however moved to Bangkok in his early twenties and became a night-club entertainer, playing mostly in some of the leading Hotels in Bangkok. Norbert came back for a visit a few years later and contacted me by phone. We met for a 'kopi tarek' (frothy coffee) at an Indian eatery in Petaling Jaya (PJ). Norbert then told me that he had got married and did not know how to break the news to Mum and Dad.

I advised him to just let them know and accompanied him when he called on Mum and Dad – who were simply delighted to see Norbert and took the news of his marriage to Juliellen very well. Norbert visited a few years later with Juliellen and the whole family were able to meet her and get to know her. Juliellen was a really lovely person.

I subsequently visited Norbert and Juliellen in Bangkok on one or two of my trips abroad and stayed briefly at their home. They had no children but had a rather big dog at home. They had a Thai maid who did all the cooking and cleaning.

I saw a bit of Bangkok with them whenever I visited. Norbert also took me to an elephant corral where he had a partnership in a troop of performing elephants. It was most interesting. Norbert later arranged for Dad and Mum to visit and stay with them. On another occasion, Irene and Annette went together to Bangkok for a holiday and stayed with them. We lost track of Norbert after that. He dropped below the radar and failed to communicate with any of us, including Dad and Mum for many years after.

From time to time we heard rumours that Norbert had been 'sighted' in Norway and Sweden. Communication was finally restored in the early eighties and we discovered that Norbert had been living in Germany. We finally had an address and a phone number and could keep in touch once again. He was no longer with Juliellen but had married a German girl named Edith and had three children – Brendan, Pascal (boys) and a daughter Sarina.

In the early eighties, I used to serve on one of UNESCO's (United Nations Educational Science and Cultural Organization) Expert Panels and flew to Paris several times for meetings. On one such visit I contacted Norbert by phone and told him that I could break journey in Frankfurt in order to meet him and the family.

Norbert was delighted and drove all the way from his home in Riederich (near Stuttgart) with his family in tow to pick me up at the airport. It was a joyous reunion. When we met, after so many years, he just put his arms around me and said "Hello Donny – it's so good to see you". I stayed several days with them at their home.

It was most interesting to note that while the family conversed amongst themselves in German, they spoke in English to me. It was also interesting to note certain speech peculiarities that Norbert had picked up where he tended to link his English sentences with the German 'und'.

Norbert visited Malaysia again in 1987 with his family and stayed with Mum. I was living with Mum then as Dad had died in 1982 and Annette and the boys had migrated to Australia in 1983. Norbert wanted to take his family to our old haunts by the beach in Port Dickson. He hired a car and we drove to PD as he was unfamiliar with the roads. We found a unit for them to stay by the beach. Norbert then dropped me off at the Railway Station in Seremban for my train journey back to Kuala Lumpur.

The train journey back to KL was pleasant enough. However about 10km before reaching the Railway Station in KL, there was a nation-wide breakdown of the electricity network. The entire country was practically paralysed for the rest of the day. I was in the middle of nowhere on a train that could not move.

The passengers stewed in the humid heat for one or two hours. Some of the younger ones jumped off the train, crossed a stream and scaled a somewhat high roadside fence to catch one of the busses to KL. I was seriously considering doing likewise but was unsure about scaling the high fence.

Finally, the railway authorities managed to despatch a steam locomotive which coupled up and towed the electric train back to KL. It was quite dark by then. All taxis refused to run because of impassable jams at all traffic lights which were not working. There was little choice and I had to walk all the way home to Petaling Jaya, several kms away.

I did meet up with Norbert one more time when he visited Annette and me at our home in Rockingham in 2002. He stayed with us for about two weeks and met up with some of his old school and music friends who now live in Perth. His marriage to Edith had broken down but his kids had all grown up. We kept in touch by phone on a few occasions after that but never got to meet again.

In 2011, Norbert phoned to inform me that he had been diagnosed with a form of aggressive cancer and that western medicine could no longer offer any hope of curing or even alleviating his condition. He was keen to try alternative medical treatment, in particular ayurvedic treatment in Sri Lanka. I contacted Uncle John in Kuala Lumpur who was able to tap into his wide network of contacts in Sri Lanka. A centre was identified and the information was conveyed to Norbert.

Norbert then made plans to spend a few months in Kuala Lumpur. He stayed with his friend Stu Marks and caught up with his brother Basil. I was on my way to Sri Lanka and on my stopover in Kuala Lumpur I had planned for a reunion with both Basil and Norbert. Sadly, this did not happen as Norbert's condition deteriorated very rapidly and he died before I arrived. Norbert's body was flown back to Germany for burial by his family.

Cultural norms and ethnic considerations that influenced relationships for earlier generations no longer seemed to hold sway. Except for Norbert who married Caucasians from

New Zealand and Germany, the rest of us married Malaysians from the Sinhalese, Tamil and Sikh community.

None of the marriages however were 'arranged' and I am certain no dowry was ever paid! None of us were fortunate to marry wealthy spouses but we got by. Career paths for most of us were determined by expediency and opportunity rather than by choice.

Four of my siblings have passed away. Clarence passed away in 1992 at the age of 54. Irene was 74 when she passed away in 2007 while Norbert died in 2011 at the age of 64. Basil died in 2019 at the age of 77 – the same age as my father who also died at 77.

I do not intend to expand any further on the lives of my brothers and sisters as it is their story to tell – and hopefully, may be taken up by their children should they be so inclined. It is unfortunate that each of us got caught up in our own lives over the years, and tended to drift apart. We shared so little – our joys, achievements and struggles – when there was so much to share.

The Federation of Malaya

By the mid-fifties, it was becoming increasingly clear that the sun was setting on the British Empire. Britannia no longer ruled the waves. Despite this, residual levels of arrogance among the orang putih (white man) were still to be seen. The white man's prejudice against race and colour were long standing.

It is unfortunately also true that there were those among the 'natives' or local population who tended to conduct themselves in a subservient manner when dealing with the 'orang putih'. This not only encouraged further white snobbery but also reinforced the white man's perception that he was still Tuan Besar – the big boss.

The 'orang putih' had long been adroit at manipulation and political manoeuvring. They were however careful to keep on the good side of the Sultans to secure British interests especially in the mining and plantation industries. Some of them, the descendants of well heeled families in colonial times, have been able to consolidate their gains and have made Malaysia their permanent home.

In the first half of the 20th Century – most of my Dad's working life – the British openly and blatantly advocated their belief that they were an infinitely superior class of people and any social intercourse with the locals irrevocably damaged that image. This attitude changed particularly after Independence with some even marrying local Malays, converting to Islam and immersing themselves in the Malay literary, artistic and cultural world. Very few of them married local Chinese or Indians – except perhaps in academia.

During colonial times, most expatriates were British and they enjoyed superior salary scales and terms and conditions of service including what was then known as "Furlough" – a three month fully paid vacation for themselves and their spouses and children. This entitlement was available to them after three years of completed service. Most of them regarded this as home leave and went back to England. When they returned, they got a new posting and the whole process started all over again.

In the first half of the 20th Century, while there was no 'apartheid' in Malaya in the South African mode, many British colonials refused to attend parties where Asians were present; they refused to work for Asians who possessed better qualifications and objected to addressing Asian Magistrates as "Your Honour". They even demanded private rooms when dining in Asian restaurants and always wanted British Doctors and nurses to attend to them. Our colonial masters also tended to keep apart from the locals socially – Dad's 'orang putih' bosses never visited our home even once – not even on festive occasions.

Even at the Lake Club in Kuala Lumpur – one of the last bastions of British exclusivity in the Malay States – Asians were not accepted as members. In fact, the non-whites (often categorised as natives or 'orientals' in a derogatory sense) were only allowed in Lake Club as servants, waiters, gardeners, chefs and drivers. Inviting Asian guests to the Orchid Room or the Batik Bar was one thing but admitting them as ordinary voting members was another – it came much later. It was only in 1958 – the year after Independence, that Club Rules were changed to permit Asian membership!

In post war and pre-independence Malaya, the 'orang putih', specifically the British, held key positions in most fields. The locals, no matter how able or qualified, only played supporting roles. The Brits. in the Colonial Service as well as in the plantation and mining sectors grew rich from the bounties of the land. Their children invariably attended leading boarding schools in England and were accustomed to come back to Malaya for their holidays.

We were glad to see the British go and to usher in the era of self determination and political independence. It has been a bumpy ride to date and we still have a very long way to go in order to achieve a more equitable society. This is a challenge that faces many countries. But on the flip side, one must acknowledge that the Brits did leave behind the English language, a framework of law and governance as well as a public service.

My own personal interaction with my English colleagues in academia and in the library world both within the country and abroad has always been most cordial. While the sun may have set on the British Empire – the way ahead, at least in the former Malay States and in Malaysia today, continues to be cloudy – in more ways than one.

The decade I was away from the country was a period of political change. With Independence or 'Merdeka' in 1957, the FMS or Federated Malay States became the Federation of Malaya. The Federation covered all the States in the Malay Peninsula and included the former Straits Settlements of Penang and Malacca but excluded Singapore which remained under the British Crown.

By way of contrast, Ceylon obtained its independence in 1948, the same year that India and Pakistan obtained their independence. In Ceylon, I was part of the ethnic majority but in the Federation of Malaya, I was part of the ethnic minority. Independence for the Federation came as a result of a united front by the three main ethnic communities – the Malays, Chinese and Indians. The thrust for independence however was led by Tunku Abdul Rahman, an aristocratic Malay.

Any disharmony or underlying mistrust between the three main ethnic groups was not apparent then. This balance weakened over the years as the Malays progressively became politically more dominant. It is into this cauldron of inter-racial interaction that I was now attempting to fit into and make my way.

In the early sixties, I was so utterly naïve in terms of the political realities within the country. In academia I had little exposure to the politics of race or of ethnic dominance and supremacy. I thought I would be entering a level playing field and that intelligence, ability and qualifications was all that would be required. How very wrong I was.

Joining the Workforce

I hesitated giving this chapter the heading Career. I finally decided that Joining the Workforce was a more suitable chapter heading. I just needed work – any kind of work. I had absolutely no idea what I could do work-wise or what I would like to do. A career? What was that? A direction I wished to go? A skilled trade? A profession even? At that time all of this seemed a pie in the sky!

Picking up the threads of the family story again, the P & O liner docked in Penang. Dad and Clarence drove up to Penang to pick me up. It was good to see them both after nearly four years and I was looking forward to catching up with the rest of the family. Dad was now driving a brand new Ford Consul. En-route, we stopped at Aunty Mabel's place in Ipoh for lunch.

We arrived in the evening at the family home in the newly created suburb of Petaling Jaya. It was my very first visit to No. 4, Jalan 5/3 – an unpretentious house on a quiet street. The house – one of three standard patterns – was built on relatively modest sized plots on a 99 year lease. This remained the family home until my mother died in 2000.

I stayed with my parents for the next two years. It was a difficult time as I had no job and no income for the first few months. My Dad gave me some spending money while I scoured the advertisements for job openings – I was not choosy. I was uncertain whether a foreign degree would be recognised in the Federation of Malaya and was literally flying blind!

But I was determined to be self supporting as soon as possible, not only to earn my keep but also to try and give back something to my parents. My natural inclination was to pursue a career in law – which would have meant a further period of study in England. But I knew my father did not have the financial resources to support me while abroad. This was an aspiration I had to put to rest and I never breathed a word of it to my parents or even to my very own family.

In the Federation of Malaya, there was no such thing as a safety net or the dole to tide you over. For that matter, there was nothing similar in Ceylon either. Simply put, if you don't work, you don't eat.

In Ceylon I was handicapped by the fact that my language ability in Sinhalese was rudimentary while in the Federation of Malaya, my level of competence in the Malay language was colloquial – suitable for the market place but nothing more.

So long as business was conducted in English, I would be able to cope quite well but should ability in the Malay language become a requirement to function effectively in a work environment, I realised that I would need to upgrade my level of competence in the language.

The Methodist Girls' Afternoon School

By this time Annette and I had been seeing each other for some time and it was in fact Annette's Dad who got me my first job at the Methodist Girls' Afternoon School in Kuala Lumpur. Mrs. Evelyn Woltz, the Headmistress appointed me as one of the teachers, purely on the recommendation of Annette's Dad, despite the fact that while I had completed my undergraduate studies at the University of Ceylon, the exam results had not been posted yet. As it turned out, I passed and was conferred my Bachelor's degree in absentia at the convocation in November 1959.

Teaching in English in a girls' secondary school was pleasant enough and the work load was moderate. I taught English and Geography. My students were mostly Chinese, a few Indians and Eurasians but hardly any Malays.

Staff Photograph, Methodist Girl's Afternoon School, September 1959

I got on very well with all my teaching colleagues although with my students – this was a girls' school – I was strict and maintained a no-nonsense demeanour. While I took part in some extracurricular activities in sports and assisted the

Hockey coach, for me, teaching in school was just a job – a stop-gap measure, until something better came up.

The University of Malaya in Kuala Lumpur

While staying with my parents in Petaling Jaya, I met one of their neighbours who worked at the newly established library of the University of Malaya in Kuala Lumpur. The University of Malaya was originally established in Singapore but in 1958, a decision was made to set up the Kuala Lumpur campus of the University in Pantai Valley, which was not too far away from our home in Petaling Jaya. The main campus of the University remained in Singapore.

Hedwig Anuar, who lived a few doors from our home, was a Chartered Librarian, having been trained in the UK. She told me that the University Library was looking for new graduate assistants for the library and asked me whether I would be interested in meeting her boss, the University Librarian. Since I was relatively free the next day, I visited the University Library and met up with him – an Englishman by the name of Wilfred Plumbe.

It was a very pleasant encounter – we talked for about an hour and I was shown around. He must have made up his mind pretty fast because at the end of my visit he said "so will you take the job Donald?" I meekly said "yes". After all, the job paid more than double what I was getting as a school teacher and all I was really looking for was a reasonably paid job. I had no real interest in libraries whatsoever and never dreamed of where this would eventually take me. Mrs Voltz, the School Principal reluctantly accepted my resignation.

My early working life

In September 1959 I was appointed as a Graduate Library Assistant at the University of Malaya Library. I was the very first graduate assistant to be appointed. Several other graduate assistants were appointed over the next two years.

During the first six months of my work life at the University of Malaya Library, I got to experience the mundane routines of working in a Library at a fairly junior level. This involved evening shift duties, work at the Circulation Counter, charging books out to borrowers and discharging the books on their return. There was also the very boring task of filing catalogue cards, the shelving of books and checking shelf arrangement order. While I realised that these tasks were the normal routines for unqualified staff, my observation of the tasks undertaken by my professionally qualified colleagues in the library did not excite me either. I despaired and wondered what I had got myself into.

I began to have serious misgivings about working in libraries. At the same time, I could not see myself going back to work as a school teacher either. But what else could I do? Job opportunities in the work place were quite limited. So I decided to stick it out – after all, the pay was quite good and I needed the money.

In 1960, Wilfred Plumbe secured scholarships for two staff members to undertake professional studies abroad. My colleague Edward Lim and I were selected for study abroad. Edward Lim was sent to Australia in March 1961 on a Colombo Plan Scholarship and I was sent to the United Kingdom in August 1961 on a British Council Scholarship.

It would seem that a career path was being opened up for me and I decided to go with the flow.

Fortunately, the British Council scholarship, the experience of study abroad in England and the opportunity for travel in the UK and Europe, seemed not only like a lifeline but also opened-up exciting vistas for the future. Although the scholarship was for a two-year period, it was not overly generous, but was sufficient to pay for the air fares for Annette and me (we had got married in April 1961) as well as for our accommodation and other everyday expenses in London. The University granted me no-pay leave for the duration of my studies abroad. This was an opportunity not to be lightly dismissed.

Annette and I were excited at the prospect of being in London over the next two years and started making the necessary arrangements. Annette decided to resign from her teaching position at the Bukit Bintang Girl's Secondary School in order to accompany me to London. In hindsight, this proved to be a mistake as she could have simply applied for the necessary leave to accompany me to London and thereby preserved her service benefits.

It seemed that too much was happening too soon for us, but we coped well enough. The British Council facilitated our Visa and travel arrangements. We also notified our landlord that we would be moving out of the small terrace house we were renting on Jalan Carey, Petaling Jaya. It was so sad to part with my brand new, emerald green VW Karmann Ghia – my very first car. Apart from that, we owned very little.

Post graduate studies in London

Annette and I discussed the logistics of our move to London and decided that I should go on ahead to London on my own in order to make arrangements for our accommodation prior to Annette's arrival. My flight to London was pleasant enough. A British Council representative met me on arrival and accompanied me to a British Council hostel in London.

I began flat hunting in earnest the day after and came across this advertisement for a bed-sitter at 28 Lisburne Road in Hampstead, London. Annette's brother Basil who had earlier enrolled as an undergraduate student at Durham University accompanied me in my search for suitable accommodation for Annette and me.

When we turned up at 28 Lisburne Road, a barrel-chested gentleman let us in. He looked us over and said "if you are good boys, no problem. Otherwise…" and he rolled up his sleeves and showed us his knotted hairy arms. We were impressed. It did not take me long to move in and get the place reasonably spruced up for Annette's arrival.

Annette flew over shortly after and we settled in to life in London. Our cramped bedsitter on the first floor had a kitchenette and a sink where we did the washing up – not only of the pots and pans, but also our clothes. Unsightly washing lines across the window completed the 'home decor'. We shared toilet and bathroom facilities with the adjoining tenant. Everything was very basic but we still managed to put in those little touches to make the place cosy. It was our home – at least for the time being. However a year later, we moved to a larger room on the second floor.

Annette and I got on famously with our Landlady – Mrs. Nossa Theophilou, a Greek Cypriot from Limasol, in Cyprus. Mrs. Theo – as we used to call her – had three young children – Stanley, Poppy and Dorothy. As Annette and I did not have a TV, we often watched TV with the Theophilou family in their living room and got to know all of them well. Mr Theophilou was a merchant seaman and we hardly saw him at all.

My monthly stipend from the British Council was rather modest and hence it was necessary for Annette to go out to work. Annette got a job soon after at the Camden Town Cooperative as a sales person and became very popular with the other staff. A year later, she joined Mullards electronics and was soon running the Stock Department. Those were the days before the advent of computers and Annette became quite indispensible because of her stock knowledge of components and parts.

Annette and I depended on public transport to get around – we mostly used the red double decker buses to get to college or to work. But we also got used to the London Underground. We never had enough money to eat out at fancy restaurants. Take away food at that time were called 'Wimpies' – which were the equivalent of today's hamburgers and Big Macs. We did however see films from time to time at the Palladiam in Hampsted as well as at other cinemas across London.

Professional studies for me was a breeze. As I had already passed some of the papers of the professional examinations prior to my arrival in London, I was placed in the advanced class at College and was able to complete all sections for conferment as an Associate. I then proceeded on to

Fellowship studies, which I completed partly in London and partly after my return to the University of Malaya. I was among the very first of the coveted Fellowship holders and joined the ranks of other Fellows, including Wilfred Plumbe and Hedwig Anuar. A period of practical experience at University College, University of London and at Reading University completed my professional induction. A few of my male colleagues from Malaysia and Singapore who were placed in the introductory class qualified as Associates a few years later and took up positions in special libraries. All of them passed away decades ago.

From time to time Annette and I took advantage of term breaks to visit places of interest in England, Scotland, Wales and Northern Ireland. We also joined a few small group tours sponsored by the British Council.

Annette and I were able to afford only a single trip at Christmas in 1962 to Rome, Venice and the Italian Alps. Armed with a cheap Agfa camera, we took off by train and caught the ferry to Calais. From there we went across the Alps by train through the Brenner Pass where reputedly Hitler met Mussolini. Christmas Eve and Christmas day was spent in Colle Isarco in the Italian Alps. We drank some beautiful wines there, one of which was called Vino Santo and the other Lacryma Christi – we were both partial to the sweeter wines. These wines did not appear to be widely marketed as we never came across them again anywhere else.

Annette took advantage of our stay in London to attend concerts at Covent Garden. Since both of us used to play tennis, we attended the Wimbledon Tennis Final and got good seats at Centre Court. However, we never got to play tennis while we were abroad.

On one occasion, I did go away on a pony tracking tour in the Black Mountains in Wales. It was my first experience of riding on a horse. Although the mount chosen for me was an old nag, it was not unduly uncomfortable. For the most part the guide on the lead horse kept to a sedate pace. However once the pace picked up to a gentle canter, I was hanging on for dear life. It takes real skill to stay astride your mount, especially in full flight. We stopped at a number of quaint pubs along the way for a beer. Thankfully, after the first two days, the group continued the rest of the tour canoeing down the River Wye. I never went on this kind of holiday again.

Life in Malaysia

Getting to know you

For my life with Annette, I need to go back a little in time – to 1955, when I met her briefly at her home in Jalan Inai, where she lived with her parents and her siblings. When I returned to Malaya in 1959, Annette and I began going out and getting to know each other. We were not exactly strangers as we had regularly corresponded with each other during my undergraduate days at the University of Ceylon and discovered that we shared many common interests. Usually in the evenings, I would catch the bus to Kuala Lumpur and make my way to her Dad's place in Jalan Inai which was just off Jalan Imbi. We would take another bus to the Lake Gardens where we usually spent our evenings.

Sometimes Annette would borrow her Dad's car for our evening outing. We usually had our dinner at one of the stalls within the Lake Gardens itself. All I had in my pocket was enough money to pay for my bus fare back to PJ. Annette always footed the bill and she seemed to have an unending supply of ten Ringgit notes. But the truth of the matter was that Annette was just a good money manager. I was as poor as a church mouse then and wonder what she saw in me – I surely could not have seemed like a good prospect – I did not even have a job at that time! But Annette probably saw a potential in me I did not see in myself.

Annette in her mid-twenties

One of our favourite stops while taking Annette home late in the evenings was a roadside kway teow seller on Jalan Imbi, who made the most delicious kway teow, which we ate by the roadside sitting on low stools. He gave us water to wash it all down which we drank from an old tin can, never failing to give us his toothless grin when we paid him. Those were unforgettable days.

Annette's eyesight

Annette had known for years that her eyesight was deteriorating. It was a problem she had been coming to terms with for many years. She was finally told by an eye specialist that little could be done and that quite possibly she would lose her sight completely. I was fully apprised of Annette's deteriorating eyesight but it did not put me off. Fortunately, a second opinion from the medical fraternity in Kuala Lumpur drew attention to the possibility of contact lenses to correct her peculiar eye condition – a conical cornea, in layman's terms.

Annette took it all very courageously and initially made plans to enrol at the School for the Blind in Penang. She also informed the Headmistress, Ms. Eleanor Cook of her intention to submit her resignation but Ms. Cook simply refused to accept Annette's resignation. She also drew attention to the progress being made with contact lenses and urged Annette to apply for leave and go to London for the purpose of being fitted-out with contact lenses.

Annette duly applied for the necessary leave and flew to London in January 1960. Annette spent several months in London and was treated by a specialist in Harley Street, a Mr Hudson who had her fitted out with a custom-made pair of contact lenses to suit her eyes, specifically to partially correct her 'conical cornea'. The plastic cup-shaped lenses to fit her individual eyes had to be inserted under the eyelid with the aid of a lubricant.

This was a daily operation – the insertion of lenses in the morning and their removal at night. Sometimes a change in mid-day was also necessary. Despite the fact that the use of contact lenses was awkward, Annette learned to cope with it as it did enhance her eyesight considerably and enabled her to continue working.

Annette paid for her airfare to London while her medical costs were subsidised. I sent my first pay-check to Annette to defray some of her expenses. Annette's stay in London was arranged by Ms Cook through the Imbi Chapel (Brethren) network. Annette was 'billeted' in London with the Patterson family where she received free board including meals in return for doing the washing and cleaning. Annette told me later that it certainly was not the Ritz.

Annette returned by ship which docked at Singapore. I drove down to Singapore in my new VW Karmann Ghia to pick her up. I stayed at Aunty Gladys's place in Geylang while Annette stayed with Mrs Assen and Erin – old friends of hers. We spent a few pleasant days in Singapore before driving back to Kuala Lumpur.

Getting hitched

Annette and I kind of drifted towards marriage. There was no engagement party and no special occasion when I 'popped the question.' We felt confident that we had met our partner for life – there was no one else on the horizon we were even remotely interested in. My parents liked Annette well enough but her mother would rather that Annette took up with someone of her mother's choosing who was hovering in the wings. His name was Jothi but Annette would not have a bar of him and this did not overly please her mother. But none of this stopped us.

Although Annette and I had Christian backgrounds, our varied traditions proved a great stumbling block. We did try to sort out our differences through correspondence, during my undergraduate days in Ceylon but it seemed quite futile. Nevertheless, neither of us was willing to end the 'relationship' – which was more imagined than real anyway. I guess we just drifted on hoping that our differences would sort themselves out over time.

However, getting married in the Catholic Church at that time proved quite problematic, as the non-Catholic partner was required to sign a bond confirming that all off-spring from that marriage would be baptised and brought up as Catholics. Neither Annette nor I were prepared to accept this requirement.

Getting married in her Church – the Brethren from the Venning Road Chapel – proved equally difficult as they wanted me to get baptised again in their church before we could proceed any further. That was the last straw. I backed away completely. Annette's father intervened at this stage and spoke to the Rev. Dr. Ho Seng Onn, Pastor of the Methodist Church, Kuala Lumpur, who agreed to marry us.

So, a date was set, the invitations sent out and other preparations were set in motion. I was not greatly involved in much of the arrangements – my relative newness in the country did not help one little bit. There was hardly anybody I could talk to, not even my family. I had no real friends, only work colleagues while most of my friends were far away in Ceylon.

Although I did not say anything, Annette sensed my underlying unhappiness. Unknown to me and completely on her own initiative she called off the wedding even though it was just a few weeks away. Her father was furious. He blamed me entirely and favoured me with a few choice expletives. The whole situation was very upsetting and I was relatively young – I could have exploded but I said nothing and took it all very calmly.

But I was devastated. Annette disappeared to parts unknown and stayed away from home for quite a while. I felt I had let her down. I wasn't too concerned with her father or her family but was especially concerned that nothing untoward had happened to Annette. Junie Lim was Annette's very close friend and if anybody knew anything at all it would be her and true enough, after some persuading, she told me.

I met up with Annette shortly after. She had been staying with friends in Port Dickson. We were both very upset and finally decided to make a go of it, blow the Church and blow the family and we did exactly that. A new date was set and we got married on 3rd April 1961.

I sometimes wonder what is it in the older generation in our community – both in Ceylon and Malaya – who seemed compelled to give away their daughters or female siblings in marriage, almost as if they were a drag or a burden on the family. My own perceptions were (I am sure Annette's siblings would agree) Annette was anything but a drag on the family. She was rock solid and totally dependable. In fact, Annette was often left in charge whenever her parents went on holiday to Ceylon or were away from home. To her younger siblings especially, she was a role model and a bit of a fashion plate as well! Rodney recently confided in me that the three youngest in the family were quite 'scared' of Akka – they called her Akka (elder sister).

Annette & Me

Picking up the story line again, prior to the wedding, my parents had told me quite clearly that they would not be attending the wedding and that they were only acting on the advice and directive of the Catholic Church. I recall that it was my mother who informed me of this. There was simply nothing for me to say. I was quite disappointed but I took it all very calmly. What was to be would be.

The Bridal Party

I did not feel aggrieved at my family in any way and although I never forgot, I never ever brought up the matter with my parents or any of my siblings. It seemed to me that what was most important in a marriage is the commitment two individuals make to one another. It mattered little who came to the wedding. At our wedding, there were no high-powered persona who turned up – no Ministers, 'Yang Berhormats' (members of Parliament) Tan Sris or Datuks – just ordinary folk – Annette's family and friends and some of our work colleagues.

At the reception

The fact that I was the eldest son and the first in the family to get married did not seem to weigh heavily enough on my family – the injunction from the Catholic Church had overriding sway and seemed to apply to the whole family for none of them attended the Church Service at all. For some time, I was not too partial towards some of the priests who I suspected were responsible for my parent's decision not to attend my wedding. I have always been independent in my thinking and would never have allowed the Church to dictate my conduct, even if my son was getting married outside the church. But the older generation was far more pliant and seemed to accept without question, directives from the Church.

Our wedding was a very low-key affair. It was held at the Methodist Church, Kuala Lumpur, followed by a reception at the Eastern Hotel. Chan Kai Meng as mentioned previously, was best man and Annette's only sister Bridget, was the bridesmaid. Following the reception, Annette's father hosted a dinner for a small group of family and friends. I am sure my parents were invited too but none of them turned up. There was no honeymoon whatsoever as we had little money. We simply went home to a little terrace house we had rented in Jalan Carey, Petaling Jaya. And so began our life together as a married couple.

That day, when I left my parents' home all dressed up for my wedding, my mother was at the door and I just said "so I'll be off then mum" – and I left home for good. My father stayed in the background. He disliked confrontation and was perhaps uncertain how I would react. When I reflect upon it, I think I really left home a long time ago! I figured that if I could leave home as a teenager and survive then I certainly could leave home as an adult and flourish.

I have attended the weddings of my brothers Clarence and Basil and of my sister Irene but not Jenny's wedding as I was a student in London at that time. Norbert's wedding – if there ever was one – was held somewhere abroad – we were never told when or where, nor were we invited.

Back to the salt mines

On completing professional studies in London, I returned to Kuala Lumpur and resumed work at the University of Malaya Library. I was placed in the Reference Department and worked under Joe Howard – a Peace Corps volunteer who was head of the Department at that time. Some months later, I took over as Head of Reference and Joe was moved to special duties within the Library.

In the University Library, the local staff were multi-racial and we all got on well with one another. There were a few expatriates as well, apart from Joe Howard and included John Linford, Alice Lage and John Harris. As more and more local staff acquired professional qualifications, our expatriate colleagues left to take up positions in their own countries. Beda Lim became University Librarian after Plumbe left while Hedwig Anuar became the Director of the National Library of Singapore. John Linford ended up at the British Library while Joe Howard became the Librarian of the National Agricultural Library in the U.S. I have met most of them since then at international conferences.

In our early days at the University of Malaya, there was a great sense of camaraderie among the library staff and the staff even went on trips to the seaside together. I remember one such trip to Port Dickson – a popular seaside destination, where a staff member dropped his dentures in the water and several of us groped in the sand for it without any success. It is quite possible that these dentures have provided safe refuge for successive crustaceans ever since! The same seaside outing saw the blossoming of a romance between John Harris and Silvia Stephens. Silvia worked in my section. John later married Silvia and took her back to England with him.

I rented a house on Jalan Putri in Petaling Jaya which had a small garden. Annette joined me shortly after and took up a teaching position later at the Assunta Secondary School (for girls) in Petaling Jaya. The school was in walking distance from the house.

Our very own family

At this stage we were in a position to start a family of our own. Rohan was born on the 11th July 1964 followed by Rienzi on the 24th November 1965. Watching the two little ones grow up was a joyful time in our lives. They were as different as chalk and cheese, but each delightful in their own way. They were easy children to manage.

Rohan and Rienzi were born at the General Hospital in Kuala Lumpur. They were both delivered by Dr. Ronny McCoy, a well respected gynaecologist who was married to one of Annette's school mates at St. Mary's. In fact, all of us were born in the General Hospital – home deliveries were no longer in practice. Annette stayed home the first two years to look after our babies.

Renan was born several years later on 16th November 1969 at the Assunta Hospital in Petaling Jaya. Renan was born in more turbulent times – the curfew was still in place following the racial riots in May 1969. In fact, I had to break the curfew to take Annette to the Hospital – with our two little boys in tow, as they were fast asleep and had to be woken up.

Bringing up our boys

Annette and I always saw our boys as a precious gift from God and we were determined that one or both of us would always be there for them, during their growing up years. I was especially conscious of my own experiences in my youth of being away from my family and in another country as well for so many years and I was not going to let that happen to our boys.

When our boys were born, Annette and I chose names for each of them without any reference to our parents. In doing so, we checked out various reference sources. We wanted each of our boy's names to be simple, yet not common. We also steered clear of emulating the practices of previous generations of giving our children Christian or Biblical names or any names that smacked of an English colonial hang-up. We felt that one forename for each of them would suffice. We were also careful not to saddle our sons with any of my forenames or the forenames of any of our male relatives. We accordingly named them Rohan, Rienzi and Renan.

Although our boys share some common features from the gene pool, they have different character attributes. Rohan is perhaps more extrovert but we tried to treat all of them equally and avoid giving any of them the impression that he was the favourite son. But Annette and I were different characters ourselves and we may have related to each of our sons differently.

When Rohan was a curly topped, tousle-headed toddler, running around in a sagging nappy hitched on both sides by a large safety pin – I used to come home from work taking care to switch off the engine and freewheel the car close to the front gate. I would then sneak up to the front door, hide behind the wall and give out a very special whistle – almost like a bird call. Rohan would recognise the whistle, get terribly excited and would rush from one room to another, hiding behind the curtains until I walked in and then he would rush toward me to be picked up. Nearly thirty years later, when Rohan was at work, I phoned him, said nothing but only gave my famous whistle – and we both started laughing.

It may well be that because Rohan was our first born, I had this special relationship with him as a child but I was never able to develop anything on similar lines with my other two sons who are just as dear to me. I have no explanation for this. When I think of our three sons and their lives, I see in our older sons some of their mother's traits while Renan, our youngest, is more like me than any of the others.

Growing up in Malaysia, our sons have always been bi-lingual – English and Malay or Bahasa Malaysia. They still are, although they have lived in Australia and other parts of the world for over forty years. Rohan especially has an aptitude for languages and also speaks Japanese – not only to the Maitre d' at Japanese restaurants but also at meetings with Japanese business counterparts in Tokyo.

All our boys attended the Methodist Kindergarten, followed by the Methodist Primary School and then the La Salle Secondary School, all of which were in Petaling Jaya. While Rohan and Rienzi were attending Kindergarten, I used to drive them to school, pick them up at lunch time and take them home. Later all three of them travelled by school bas to and from their respective schools.

Before the boys started attending Kindergarten, we had live-in house maids to take care of our boys while Annette and I were away at work. As the boys grew up, we discontinued having house maids in order to encourage our boys to be more self reliant – in fact, when they came home from school, they were expected to fix their own lunches – which they did.

When the boys started eating solid foods, I cooked daily for them and often fed them as well. The boys were very disciplined – they usually stood in front of me in a row as I fed them and never gave me any trouble. As they grew up, they got used to the same spicy food that was prepared for our main meals.

After the maids left, cooking for the family became part of my daily routine. Over the years, I became quite a good gourmet cook! The boys always enjoyed my cooking —and still do. Annette always prepared the speciality dishes. Some of these culinary traditions have been passed down to the next generation – Rohan has turned out to be quite a good gourmet cook himself. He has even emulated his mother in cake making – his Christmas cake and suji cake have turned out almost as good as his mother's efforts.

Annette and I were never over indulgent with our boys. We gave them what we could afford – which was somewhat modest. We tried to balance what they wanted with what they needed – especially in terms of birthday and Christmas presents as well as clothes and shoes. The boys were given a little pocket money but it was nothing to brag about – their mother was in charge and she was quite strict. The whole idea was to give our boys a sense of frugality – money was not easy to come by.

I think our boys grew up reasonably well balanced. Being a teacher Annette kept track of the boys as they progressed from kindergarten to upper secondary level. As I recall, their overall progress in school in scholastic or academic terms was unremarkable. Rohan however did show some promise in speech making and oratory and also in fiction writing. In fact, Rohan won a cash prize for his short story entitled "The asteroids are going to hit us" which was published in the Malay Mail on December 21st. 1978 – Rohan was 14 years old then. Fortunately, all our boys got a good grounding in maths – thanks to their mother. This may explain why all of them choose careers in engineering.

Annette and I were so pleased that none of our boys ever got caught up with any kind of substance abuse – smoking, drugs or alcohol. As adults, we enjoy a beer together or perhaps a glass of bubbly – but hard liquor – whisky, brandy, gin or arrack have never been of much interest to any of us. Their mother and I have always been partial to the sweeter wines.

As the boys grew up and became more self assured and confident in themselves, we gave each of them a brand new chopper bicycle. None of them appeared to have come a-cropper on their chopper bikes – no bruised shins or twisted bike handles. We never realised until they revealed to us as adults how widely they roamed on their choppers – we would have been more than alarmed had we known. Their mother especially would surely have blown a fuse.

Where games and sporting activities were concerned, I was more involved with the boys than their mother. As a foursome, we played badminton and table tennis at our home in Petaling Jaya and tennis at the Subang golf club. I think we enjoyed our tennis games the most.

In their adult lives however, it is only Rienzi who has retained an interest in tennis and plays tennis frequently, not only in Australia but also when he is on holiday abroad.

Rohan, on the other hand, has developed an abiding interest in basket ball and still plays the game regularly. I recall that it was their mother who took the boys to an exhibition game of the Haarlequin Globetrotters at Stadium Negara. I remember being told later that when one of the players attempted a slam dunk, the board shattered and there was quite a delay after that to get another board mounted in its place. This exhibition performance could well have been the start of Rohan's fascination with basketball. Renan by contrast, is perhaps the most promising golfer amongst us. Unfortunately, his very exacting work and travel schedule leaves him with very little spare time for golf. I have had the pleasure of golfing with my sons, but alas, not too frequently.

The boys and I also frequented the local cinemas and had a preference for the action oriented films – which were not their mother's cup of tea. Annette nevertheless joined us on occasion. Annette did try to expose the boys to the more cultural pursuits of drama and theatre but this did not seem to catch on with any of them.

During their growing up years, it was the swimming pool at the Subang Golf Club that we used most of all. We also had meals at the Club from time to time. Although I was a member of the Club for many years, I never got interested in golf. I only took up golf in Australia, long after I retired.

When our boys were growing up, we made sure they got to know their grandparents on both sides of the family. From time to time, when the boys were attending La Salle School in Petaling Jaya, they used to drop in for lunch at Grandpa and Neneh Jaya's home (Annette's parents) – which was a stone's throw away from the school. The home of my parents – grandpa and grandma to our boys – was also close to the school and our boys dropped in there too from time to time for a bit of lunch.

Since we always had stay-in maids to look after the children while Annette and I were away at work, we never had to leave our children with either of their grandparents. This was in complete contrast with my sister Jenny who left their children with Mum and Dad while she and Wence (her husband) were away at work. Dad even drove their children to school and back for several years.

I also recall a couple of enjoyable family holidays we all spent together by the seaside in Port Dickson. Both grandparents and other members of the family were present and we all got on famously. I usually rented a large bungalow by the beach where we all fitted in. The boys especially, got on very well with their cousins – Annette's brother Terrence's three daughters. There were times when we even tried a bit of crabbing (catching crabs) after dusk as well as some dragnet fishing on the incoming tide. We caught nothing worth bragging about.

Finally, I must place on record that I am eternally grateful to Annette for instilling in our boys a sense of right and wrong. Without seeming to do so, she set for them a moral compass which has guided their lives and their relationships. Even as adults, Annette was not averse to asking pointed questions – on the unshakeable premise that 'I am your mother'. By contrast, I would have cringed at doing so.

Our boys at PD with a friend

Annette and I tried to instil in our boys the basic tenets of our Christian faith. Their onward journey from there however, is very much a matter of personal belief. Within our circle of family and friends, there are those who have stayed true to the tenets of their faith, as there are those who have drifted away.

From a purely personal standpoint, having a sense of the spiritual has little to do with attendance at a place of worship or adherance to rituals and practices. More than anything else, it is a deep and personal communion with the Almighty, who is the giver of all life. I thank the Almighty every day for his bounty and his blessings. It is a mental and silent

Annette and the boys with their paternal grandparents

communion in the stillness of dawn, more than at any other time.

Now that I have more time for reflection, I sometimes wonder for what purpose I was placed on this earth? Regretfully, the answer continues to elude me. There may be many paths to the Almighty just as there are many perceptions of the afterlife. Who really knows the hereafter – for no one has ever returned to tell us.

Our own home in PJ

In 1966, a housing development project was being promoted in Section 17 Petaling Jaya. University staff members were encouraged to choose building sites within the project and select from a range of single and double storey house plans presented. I was interested but did not even have the money for a down payment.

Our boys with their maternal grandparents, Annette and Annette's sister, Chits.

The University came to my rescue and paid the down payment on my behalf, deducting a small sum each month from my salary. A low cost housing loan was also arranged. It was exciting to see our very own house being built. We moved in about a year later and settled in quite easily. This was the house the boys grew up in.

I presume that several other work colleagues who also committed to the project were extended the same assistance by the University. There is no doubt that there were key personnel within the university administration who facilitated the financial arrangements made on our behalf. I knew nothing of the real goings on. It seemed too good to miss and we were easily persuaded.

Shortly after a few of my work colleagues and I had committed to the housing project in Section 17, we were informed about another housing development project in

Pantai Hills – a much more prestigious location on the hill slopes just outside the main entrance to the University. While many of us were tempted, we did not have the financial resourced to commit to another property. Besides it would have been most awkward to opt out of our commitment to the housing project in Section 17.

Corneal graft

In the mid-sixties, Annette's eyes continued to deteriorate. She was virtually blind in one eye already. It became imperative for her to have a corneal graft on the remaining eye where she still had some degree of vision. Unfortunately, this could not be done within the country. She was advised to go to London and be treated by a Harley Street Specialist, Dr. Ridley.

This was a very costly operation then and we did not have the necessary funds. In those days there was no private insurance to fall back on. Fortunately, Dr. Ridley was able to solicit the necessary funding support for Annette's medical costs under Commonwealth Educational Funding because she was a teacher. This took care of the bulk of the costs. We only paid her air fares.

Annette was away for many months and she had to go to London all on her own. The corneal graft operation was a success. In those days, after such an operation, the patient had to lie on her back for a few weeks perfectly still. It was a truly trying experience. Annette's younger brother Brian was then a student in Bournemouth and called on her from time to time which helped.

While Annette was away, I had our two little boys on my hands, but that was no problem. We had a live-in housemaid, who did the cooking and cleaning and looked after our little ones while I was away at work. Annette's mother came over to live with us to help out. It was a nice gesture but was completely unnecessary as I was managing quite well.

For the rest of Annette's recuperation outside the hospital, arrangements were made for her to stay at one of the convents in the London area. Annette got on well with the nuns who made her life bearable.

But when Annette finally returned home to her two little boys, it must have been heart-breaking, because Rienzi then about 2 years old would start bawling if she picked him up. Even worse, Rohan used to call her Auntie. But everything soon returned to normal and all was well.

Changing course

In the mid-sixties, Malaysia and the Philippines were embroiled in a territorial dispute over Sabah. This dispute came to be popularly referred to as 'the Philippine Claim to Sabah' The dispute spilled over into the international arena and the Malaysian Government detailed the country's Permanent Representative to the United Nations – an eminent lawyer named Mr. R.Ramani (a Malaysian Indian) to prepare the country's legal defence to the claim.

For a few months Mr.Ramani visited the University of Malaya Library a few times each week to study key documents in the holdings of the University Library. I was the officer detailed to assist Mr. Ramani in identifying key documents and making them available for his research.

Mr. Ramani arrived in his chaffeur driven Rolls Royce. I met him at the main entrance and accompanied him to a special cubicle in the Library where he could carry on his research undisturbed. I was at Mr. Ramani's disposal and assisted wherever I could. In the process I became quite fascinated by the prospect of a career in Law.

I subsequently called on the Lord President of the Malaysian Judiciary – Tun Mohammad Suffian Hashim to discuss with him the prospect of taking up a career in Law. It was clear that a further period of study would be required – possibly in the UK and this was a luxury I could ill afford since I now had a young family to take care of. I gave up the idea completely and decided to stay focussed on my work at the University Library.

Sabbatical

In 1968 the University granted me 6 months Sabbatical leave with full pay. This was part of my job entitlement and I decided to take it earlier rather than later not realising that there would be another addition to the family later. Academic staff who apply for sabbatical leave are required to put forward a research proposal for approval by the University. Administrative and Library staff who are also entitled to Sabbatical leave are also required to submit a research proposal. I submitted a proposal accordingly which was approved shortly after. Sabbatical leave for administration and library staff were seen more in terms of long service leave.

Annette and I then started active planning for my impending Sabbatical and decided to take both our boys with us although they were still very young. The University paid all our air fares. We spent the first two months in the US, specifically in Honolulu, Los Angeles, San Francisco, Washington DC and New York with study visits to various universities. On the way to the US, we had enjoyable stopovers in Hong Kong and Tokyo. It was our very first experience of staying in five star hotels and ordering room service for dinner.

On our first stop in Honolulu, we stayed with Professor Edgar Knowlton at his apartment which he shared with his mother. We saw a little bit of Hawaii with our boys. From there we went on to Los Angeles where I had several study visits to UCLA (University of California Los Angeles). We stayed with Professor James Guyot and his family.

During our stay in LA, we took the opportunity for a day long visit to Disneyland. Our two little boys walked tirelessly with us everywhere. I still remember when it was nap time for them in the afternoon, they simply stretched out on a low stone parapet wall along the pathway and fell fast asleep with the two of us sitting beside them. We woke them up an hour or two later, ready to renew their 'walkathon' – no crankiness or tantrums. They were real troopers and simply delightful to have along.

In San Francisco, we visited the Berkeley Campus of the University of California. We also caught up with a friend and former colleague, Joyce Kho – who used to work with me at the University of Malaya. Joyce arranged for us to occupy the apartment of her friend (who was away on vacation) which helped greatly to cut down overall costs.

The two-room apartment had all the basic conveniences and we felt very much at home. We took in the usual sights, including the Golden Gate Bridge and Fisherman's wharf. Joyce was the very first among us to leave the country for greener pastures elsewhere and the very first to settle down and work in the U.S. She worked then at USC (University of Southern California).

It was most fortunate that I had friends in Honolulu, Los Angeles and San Francisco who allowed us to stay with them. Elsewhere in the US, we had to pay for our accommodation. This included brief stopovers in Washington and New York before flying on to London, where we spent the next four months.

My longer stint in London was to fulfil residence requirements for an M.Phil (Master of Philosophy) Degree I had registered earlier for at the University of London. I was however unable, during my brief Sabbatical, to meet the residence requirements stipulated and had to abandon my earlier plan. I did however continue with my study visits to Sussex University to complete my Sabbatical commitments. We subsequently rented an apartment in Finchley (London) and stayed there for the duration. Using London as a base, we travelled south to Bournemouth to visit Brian and stayed a few days at the house he was sharing with some of his friends and fellow students from Malaysia – Singam, Duli (or Roti Man) and Chris.

We bought our boys a nice Hornsby train set while we were there. Rienzi still has one or two of the Hornsby coaches as a souvenir of days gone by. The colourful red Norska-rug we bought still graces my study. From London we proceeded to Copenhagen for a short stay before flying on to Moscow. It was very unusual to visit Moscow in those days and I was subject to some prior scrutiny by the Malaysian Special

Branch (Police). In addition, an Entry Visa to Moscow could only be issued by Russian Immigration on the basis of a written invitation from a person already resident and working in Moscow. Fortunately, this invitation was forthcoming from my former room-mate at the University of Ceylon, Ray Forbes, who was, at the time of my visit, a member of the Ceylon Diplomatic Service and served as Second Secretary at the Ceylon Embassy in Moscow. We stayed at Ray's apartment and spent about two weeks in Moscow. It was bitterly cold though as we were there in mid-winter.

Russia was a depressing sight in those days – long queues of unsmiling people and shop windows completely empty and without any goods on display. Foreigners in Moscow however were allowed to shop in the Dollar Shop where a wide range of goods were available and where only foreign currency was accepted – in particular the US Dollar. I tried to buy a few items and joined a long queue just to pay for my purchases in advance. I was then issued with a payment coupon of sorts and joined another long queue just to collect the items I had paid for.

Annette took the opportunity of attending a performance of the Bolshoi Ballet with my friend Ray. I was not particularly interested in ballet and stayed at home with the boys. Ray had given me the phone number of one of his work colleagues in case I needed anything. I did and spoke to their maid who answered the phone. She only spoke Sinhalese and so I tried to make myself understood. She later spoke to Ray and told him that a gentleman had called and spoke in a rather strange accent! I had not spoken Sinhalese for nearly ten years.

Ray took us to visit Lenin's tomb – the queue seemed endless and it was so cold. Annette was carrying Rienzi and I held Rohan's hand as we trudged along in the snow and slush. We came in for a bit of bother with some heavily rugged Russian women speaking to us in Russian. They were waving their hands and pointing to Rienzi. Ray explained to us that we were being berated for failing to keep our two little boys in warmer clothes.

Ray owned a VW Beetle in Moscow and he took us places in it. On one occasion, we also travelled on the Moscow underground. This was an experience indeed – the main stations were so ornate and so unlike London's drab underground stations.

We left Moscow on an Aeroflot flight, (flying on one of their Ilyushins) to New Delhi. There was again a delay of several hours at Moscow airport – the plane apparently could not take off until a certain dignitary (from India) arrived to board the same flight. There were many Indians, some in turbans, waiting to board the same flight and they were not impressed. I heard one of them complain rather loudly that we all had to wait 'until his greatness arrived'.

The Aeroflot flight was quite unremarkable. The chicken served for our dinner was bland and tasteless to an Asian palate while the air hostesses looked like football players. I am sure no terrorists would dare to hijack an Aeroflot flight! In New Delhi we boarded an Indian Airlines flight to Madras where we transited to an Air Ceylon flight to Colombo. The young man who checked us through confided in us and told us that Air Ceylon had bought the aircraft (we were boarding) second hand from Manchester – not very comforting!

Back in Sri Lanka

Our final weeks were spent in Sri Lanka. We stayed at the home of Milroy Ratwatte in Colombo – Milroy used to be a fellow boarder at St Anthony's College as well as fellow hall-mate at Arunachalam Hall, University of Ceylon. Using his place as a base, we saw a bit of the country, including Kandy, Nuwara Eliya, Sigiriya and Hikkaduwa.

While we were in Nuwara Eliya, we caught up with College mates and fellow boarders, Victor and Winston Bayley. They had both become tea planters and held positions as General Managers on different tea plantations in the surrounding hill country. They were both PDs – this acronym stood for 'Peria Dorai or Big Boss in Tamil – since most of the tea pluckers were Tamils. Winston very kindly made available his new Borgward (limousine) as well as his driver for the rest of our tour in Ceylon.

When we got to Sigiriya, I was content to see the rock from below and to stay with the boys in the car. Annette was having none of that and insisted on climbing to the very top – and she did just that. I had little choice and followed her to the top. Conditions were somewhat basic then. I visited Sigiriya twice since but only made it half way up – and that too with the assistance of a guide.

While staying at Milroy's place in Colombo, a get-together dinner party was organised to catch up with some of my batch mates from the University. I remember that Ray, Cecil, Milroy, Rex and Trevor as well as Stanley Tenuwera from Boarding school days were present. It was a fun filled evening indeed.

Back to work

In 1969, at the end of my six-month Sabbatical, I resumed work at the University of Malaya Library. Shortly after, I was approached by Brian Peacock, a lecturer in the University's Department of History, as to whether I would be prepared to undertake for the Royal Asiatic Society, the prearation of a comprehensive index to the Journals of the Straits and Malayan Branch, covering the period 1878 – 1963. This was a massive task but I gave my consent and started work but it was more than I could chew as I had my normal duties to perform within the Library. I needed a collaborator to ease the load and invited a colleague – Edward Lim, who was then Head of Cataloguing to join me in undertaking the Index. Edward readily agreed to work with me. The University Librarian assigned to us the use of one of the larger Carrels to do our work, which we undertook after normal hours.

Our completed work was titled Index Malaysiana and was published by the Royal Asiatic Society in 1970. Since then we continued our indexing coverage of the Journals of the Malaysian Branch of the Royal Asiatic Society – Supplement 1, covered the period 1964-1973 and was published by the Society in 1974, while Supplement 2, covered the period 1974 -1983 and was published in 1985. Overall, Index Malaysiana covered a period of just over 100 years – it was tedious and time consuming work.

Annette went back to teaching at the Assunta Secondary School. We had a live-in house-maid at that time, mostly to look after the boys and do the cooking, cleaning and other household tasks. Our house maids were were most agreeable and got on well with our boys.

We were somewhat dependent on house maids while the boys were growing up. There was little in the way of crèches and play schools at that time while the kindergartens did not admit children until they were at least five years old. The boys' maternal and paternal grandparents were quite close by but we avoided burdening them except in an emergency. Most of our house maids were young Malay girls and sometimes, older ladies. We rarely had Indian house maids. The Chinese amahs of pre-war years were not as easy to come by and not as affordable. Most of these local house maids were later replaced by foreign housemaids from Indonesia, Sri Lanka and the Philippines – this however only happened in households that could afford to do so. We never could. We discontinued using house maids as the boys were growing up, in order to make our boys more self reliant.

On May 13th 1969 the seeming tranquillity of Malaysia's multi-racial society was shattered by violent racial riots following the defeat of the ruling cabal in the Selangor State elections. The Government's official news release then has since been proved to be a complete misrepresentation of the facts. It does appear now that unscrupulous elements within the dominant political party were using the mask of simmering racial tensions to carry out a coup d'etat to topple the moderate leadership.

This led to the suspension of Parliament and the setting up of the National Operations Council where far reaching affirmative policies were put in place. Despite the racial riots, political stability was soon restored. Parliament was back in business but most important of all the NEP (New Economic Policy) was put in place and consistently applied since then.

Within the family we began to have some concerns, not so much for ourselves but for our young sons and their future within the country. But there were too many uncertainties and it was difficult to see clearly the way ahead. We had committed to our new house and had only just begun the mortgage repayments.

Renan, Rohan, Rienzi

Our boys in our Section 17 House, PJ, 1974

Annette, under the bougainvillea

Career and Family

At this point in the narrative, I tried to recall the career development choices I had made over the years which had impacted on the family in one way or another. I did discuss these with Annette and made my choices with her fullest support. The boys were far too young then to be brought into the picture, but they were always fully in our focus. We tried to give them our best to enable them to stand tall and find their own place in the sun. We are proud of all of them.

In 1971, I was appointed Deputy University Librarian at the University of Malaya. I was 37. Life within the cloisters of academia was pleasant though not overly challenging. It was possible to build stable relationships with teaching staff from the various disciplines and also with those in the Administration. The politics of race and ethnic discrimination had not impacted on me – yet!

In 1972, I was elected President of the Persatuan Perpustakaan Malaysia <PPM> (Malaysian Library Association), which gave me some national visibility. Prior to that I had served as PPM Vice-President and Secretary. My term as President was from 1972-74 and I was re-elected again for a further term in 1975-76.

Planning for a national library

In the mid-sixties the Government had been giving consideration to the setting up a National Library for the country and established the National Library Services Unit (NLSU) within the National Archives. The NLSU was given a limited brief and a few staff were appointed. The NLSU's initial focus was on the implementation of the Preservation of Books Act and the publication of the Malaysian National Bibliography.

Following the setting up of the NLSU, steps were taken to obtain the services of a UNESCO consultant to advise the Government on the establishment of the National Library of Malaysia; to draft the necessary legislation for this purpose and to identify a suitable Malaysian capable of spearheading the development of the fledgling institution. Sir Harold White, former Head of the National Library of Australia was appointed as UNESCO Consultant to carry out his brief. Sir Harold's Report was subsequently accepted by the Government and implemented.

I knew little of the on-going developments in this regard. I did however meet Sir Harold and Lady White. Shortly after their departure, overtures were made to me to take up a position within the NLSU – I presume that Sir Harold White had something to do with this. But I declined as I was fairly well established at the University of Malaya Library and a career path in academia, particularly in a teaching capacity at the proposed Library School looked quite attractive.

It was then that the Director General of the National Archives and Library, Dato Alwi Jantan – who later became a personal friend – approached me and asked me whether I would consider joining the National Archives and Library on a two year secondment. I was still somewhat hesitant.

In February 1972, the Malaysian National Commission for UNESCO was invited to nominate a suitable candidate to participate in a Training Course in Documentation Techniques in Asia to be held in Tokyo. The course included visits to various libraries and documentation centres and was organised by the Japanese National Commission for UNESCO in cooperation with UNESCO. While it would have been quite logical for a senior member of the NLSU to be selected, the invitation was extended to me.

I could see where this was going even though I was not as yet a member of the Public Service. I realised that if I had to play a greater role in the development of library and information services in the country, the training course in Tokyo could prove useful. Consequently, I accepted the invitation and the University granted me the necessary leave to attend the training course.

On my return, I received a call from the Office of the Prime Minister informing me that the Chief Secretary to the Government who was also Secretary to the Federal Cabinet would like me to call on him. This was a bit unsettling to say the least. At the same time I realised that this may have been a logical progression to the fact that I had not as yet made any commitment to join the Public Service.

Anyway, an appointment was fixed and I called on the Chief Secretary, Tan Sri Abdul Kadir Shamsuddin. It was a very pleasant visit. He said he had spoken to the Prime Minister and would very much like it if I would take up a position within the Public Service on a two-year secondment from the University of Malaya. He also said that not only would I be able to go back to my position at the University of Malaya at the end of my secondment but that the Government was prepared 'to sweeten the deal' by upgrading the post within the Public Service to be on par with my position at the University of Malaya.

My resistance was slowly slipping and the opportunity to serve at the national level rather than at an institutional level was most inviting. Annette was fully apprised of all these developments and encouraged me to take up the appointment.

I did not realise then what great demands this would make on my person. I did however appreciate that I would need to upgrade further my competence in Bahasa Malaysia, the National Language, in order to function effectively within the Public Service. I nevertheless gave my consent and the wheels of the bureaucracy were set in motion.

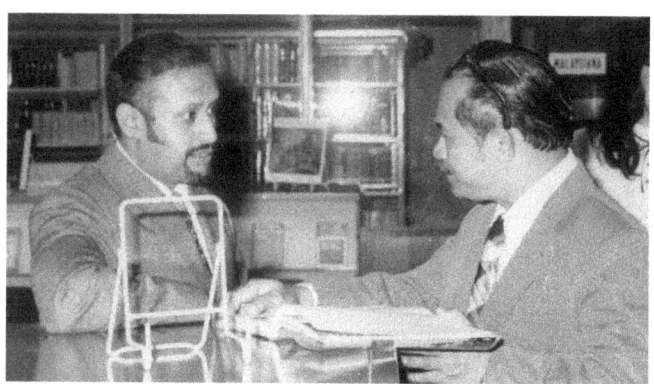

with the Chief Secretary to the Government the late Tan Sri Abdul Kadir Shamsuddin

The Public Service

In June 1972, I was seconded by the Government to serve a two-year term in the Public Service as Deputy Director,

National Library of Malaysia. A new chapter had opened in my life. In September 1972, the National Library Act (Act 80) was passed by Parliament. I subsequently attended language classes in Bahasa Malaysia for adults, sat for the appropriate examinations along with secondary school students and passed the exams with a credit grading. It did not take me long to acquire the necessary levels of competency in the language for all official purposes.

Looking back, it does appear that the policy to appoint ethnic Malays was not as well entrenched then for me to be appointed to this key position. There were two other Malays, both male who had been with me in London for professional training and were serving in special libraries in Kuala Lumpur. While both gentlemen had obtained their professional qualifications at Associate level, neither of them had a basic university degree. It may be because of this reason that they were passed over in the selection process. A male staff member at NLSU, with both academic and professional qualifications, who would have been considered 'bumiputra', was also passed over for one reason or another. Names need not be mentioned but all gentlemen passed away decades ago.

Pilot project for educational television

The same year that I was seconded to the Public Service, Annette was selected along with a few other teachers to participate in a pilot project to introduce educational television programmes into Malaysian schools. In 1974, following the completion of the project, the project team, including Annette was sent to CEDO (Centre for Educational Development Overseas) London for training in educational television production. Annette was away for nearly four months.

Managing without Annette

I now had our three boys on my hands. We did however have a live-in maid at that time who did the cooking and cleaning. We managed just fine. Renan had already begun to attend Kindergarten. A privately run school bus service picked up the boys in the morning for school and brought them back in the afternoon. As is customary among Asians, all the kids who used the same school-bus to school, addressed the Chinese bus driver as Uncle Yap – although he was not related to any of them. It was simply a mark of respect for an older person.

Similarly, my sons' Asian friends in Australia who are in their late forties, address me as Uncle, although I am not related to any of them. It is simply an Asian cultural tradition of respect for an older person.

From time to time, all four of us played tennis doubles at the Subang Golf Club (of which I was a member). The courts had to be pre-booked but sometimes when we arrived, there were others on the court well past their allocated time slot. We developed a technique for handling such situations. We simply stood outside the court – all four of us, arms akimbo and faces expressionless – this proved to be rather unsettling for the players who simply left the court. Nobody said a word but it was very effective. From time to time we also used the Club's large swimming pool.

We used to drive by Taman Selera on our way home after tennis and usually stopped by our favourite Tebu (sugar cane) seller for drinks of freshly squeezed sugar cane stalks. Light green in colour, it was such a refreshing drink. If it was darker green in colour, it meant that the sugar cane water had been prepared earlier and was not as fresh.

We also ate out from time to time or went to the cinema together – all of us enjoyed the action films very much including the Shaolin Kung–fu films. Most of the cinemas we frequented were in PJ – these included the Sentosa, Paramount and State Cinemas.

We always bought nibbles at the cinema – not the sweet stuff one gets in Australia, rather it was more exotic nibbles like stuffed tofu with a drizzle of chilli paste, crushed dried sotong or cuttle fish with a dash of chilli as well as an assortment of nuts from the kachang putih vendor or fresh fruit on skewers. The boys were sent out to buy whatever they fancied.

Annette returned after her training and worked from then on as a Producer in the ETV (Education Television Service) of the Ministry of Education. Annette greatly enjoyed her training stint in London. She even qualified for further post graduate study at Bristol University but this would have meant a further stay abroad for one or two years.

I was not too supportive of the idea largely because I was often away myself on my official duties, either within the country or abroad and felt it would be unwise to leave the boys on their own. In fact we often avoided travelling together by plane – should anything untoward happened, one of us would still be around to take care of our boys.

I recently came across a composition by Reinaldo (who was one of Annette's fellow course members at CEDO in London. Reinaldo was from South America.) I quote in full below, what he wrote, as it reflects not only some of my own sentiments when teaching or attending courses abroad with participants from all over the world but also because it brings back to mind the London I used to know with Annette in the early sixties.

THOUGHTS

Dear stranger – Dear fellow – Dear friend
The hours tick away. Very soon ETV 7 will be a memory
One more course dutifully registered in CEDO's documents
Reduced to a paper file in the secretary's hands
BUT FOR MANY OF US IT WAS MORE
Do you still remember how it all began
Wandering eyes, watching heads, black hair
Quizzing eyes, doubting looks, questions in the air
Asia? Here, Africa? Here, Europe? Here
Even a voice from Latin America answers 'Yes'
And then it came like a mighty 'zoom'
All these new technical words
Beginning with 'module' and going to 'boom'
Twirling through the mind like birds...
And then there was LONDON
Bustling – Hustling – Russell Square
Running – Honking – Euston was there
Overground – Underground –
Lights and Darks
Buses and Taxis
Coming at me like sharks
But now it was over and done
Four months of our lives have gone
Like it or not –

Now it's a history spot
No more running to the pigeon- hole- maze
No crazy fire alarm
No more friendly chats at Lily's place
No evaluation session brings harm
No more rushing a script by the hands of Marie
No cool elegance of a shining red sari
No more heated discussions and battle cries
No more freezing skin in a winter morning rise
The last page of the production schedule we had
And I tell you – my heart feels very sad
I would feel much better
I assure you
If we all could again be together maybe
When Zabedah has her twin babies...
What a joy it was to discover new friends
What sadness it is for the last time: shake hands
Most likely we'll never see again
So I ask: is there something that will remain?
Remain not only in CEDO's green paper
But remain in our hearts?
Maybe if they tell us in the future to hate
Another nation, another race
Another country, another faith
We won't give up
The respect we learned from each other
Since we know now for sure
Long away from here lives my human brother!
Let's even try to put this on tape
Before in this explosive world it might be too late!

Moving away from CEDO and London and back to life in Malaysia, a little incident comes to mind that involved Renan. It happened that Annette was away and the boys were told not to take the school bus home as nobody would be home and the gates would be locked. They were asked

*Group photograph of international participants
at the CEDO Training Centre in London
(Annette seated extreme left)*

instead to go to grandpa's house (Annette's father) which was but a 5-10 minute walk from La Salle Secondary School which Rohan and Rienzi attended but about a 20 minute walk from the Methodist Primary School which Renan attended. Rohan and Rienzi remembered and acted accordingly.

Renan unfortunately forgot and took the school bus home – only to find the house locked up. It was already evening and dusk was not too far away. I realised what had happened and drove the usual route home looking for Renan. Annette's sister came along. We back tracked and tried several alternate routes but still there was no Renan in sight. I was getting really worried.

And then on Jalan Putri – the road leading to grandpa's house, we spotted him trudging with his school bag strapped to his back. He had walked nearly 4km all the way – he could not have been more than ten years old then. It was such a relief to see him. Renan cried of course as his aunty Chitra put her arms around him. He was none the worse for wear.

Swimming lessons

Annette was far sighted and arranged for Rohan and Rienzi to take swimming lessons at a private home a few km away. It was a small above-ground pool. It was arranged that the swimming coach would pick the boys up and bring them back after each swim session. This arrangement worked very well. The boys enjoyed it very much and it stood them in good stead later on. Renan was too young then to join them.

Piano lessons

Annette came from a musical family and grew up with a piano at their family home in Jalan Inai, Kuala Lumpur. Annette, her younger sister Bridget (we called her Chitra) and her younger brother Basil all took piano lessons. Basil was quite an outstanding pianist and later won a scholarship to Durham University where he read for a music degree and trained as a concert pianist. Annette's other brothers, Terrence and Rodney, played the violin.

With this musical background behind her it was natural that she was keen to create the same opportunities for her sons. In the early seventies we purchased a brand new Rippen piano which had a middle foot pedal to create a harpsichord effect. Annette arranged a piano teacher for Rohan who took to the piano naturally. Later Renan too took up piano lessons. Rienzi however did not seem to show much interest in playing the piano.

Annette herself continued to play the piano at home. Later in 1981, we bought a Kawai Electronic organ which Annette played herself. Both musical instruments were part of a shipping container for our household goods when the family migrated to Australia in 1983. After Annette died I gave the piano to Rohan – it now sits at his home in the suburb of Malabar in Sydney.

Bayu

During the school holidays, we invariably spent time at our favourite beach–side bungalow in PD (Port Dickson) called Bayu (the breeze), about 2 hours away from KL. We sometimes also stayed at the Sri Kenanga bungalow which was on a kind of promontory overlooking the beach. Rental of the bungalow included the services of a resident cook who prepared all our meals.

We enjoyed our times there very much. The whole routine of preparing for the trip was exciting too, especially for the boys – who worked with simple check-lists in getting their little carry bags ready with swimming trunks, spades, toys etc. The drive down to PD was exciting too, especially when nearing our destination and getting first sight of the sparkling blue sea.

The beaches at PD were very gradual and safe with fine white sand and the tides changed significantly each day. At low tide, the waters receded greatly and one could walk far out but one had to keep pace with the incoming tide in order not to be caught out in too deep water. Whenever the tide was out, we spent our time in the swimming pool at the adjacent Yacht Club, of which I was a member. We often had our meals there.

The boys and their cousins, Bayu, PD, 1973

Teaching stint at Aberystwyth

In 1975 I was invited to assist in teaching a course in library development planning at the College of Librarianship in Aberystwyth, Wales. The course was fully sponsored by the British Council. Most of the participants were senior or middle level professionals from Africa, the West Indies, the Middle East, Asia and Oceania. I was away for a few weeks. Stephen Parker was appointed Director of the course. Since the participants were fairly senior professionals, I learned much from them and this helped greatly in the tasks I faced in Malaysia, particularly in the development of public library services in the country.

While at Aberystwyth, Stephen Parker invited course participants on a few occasions to join him at the local pub for a pint or two. Although these were fun filled evenings, the British practice of frequenting the pubs in the evenings for a pint and a natter never really caught on with me.

At the end of the course, a social evening was organised and the participant from Fiji – Kanti Lal Jinna put on a show about the traditional preparation of 'kava' for ceremonial occasions. All of us had to drink a bit of the traditional brew – it tasted awful. Although all of us made protestations to keep in touch, most of us never did. However I did meet up with Stephen Parker and Kanti Lal Jinna in subsequent years.

Subsequently, participants were taken to Manchester for a further stay in order to visit some of the libraries and broaden their horizons. I am sure I would have benefitted from it as well but I had already been away from home for several weeks. I wanted to get back home and since I had completed my teaching commitments, the organizers arranged for my flight back to Kuala Lumpur. Needless to say, many of the course participants I had got to know quite well– especially Kanti Lal Jinna and Ahmad Issawi –were quite disappointed. The group ceremoniously presented me with some souvenirs as a parting gift.

Saad Marzuki was Director General of the Archives and National Library at that time and he gave me his fullest support. Several years later, I was able to obtain the services of Stephen Parker in a consultant capacity for the development of public library services in the state of Sabah. A few years earlier, I had secured the services of Alexander Wilson (from the British Library), in a consultant capacity, for the development of public library services in the state of Kedah.

Fascination with flying

Whenever I have been abroad, I have always shopped around for gifts for Annette and the boys. While in Aberystwyth, I purchased a toy aeroplane for the boys. It had a motor and could fly in an arc. It was linked to the 'flyer' by a length of cord and the boys had much fun with it. I understand that even before that, I had bought a few other models as well but do not remember any of them clearly. Rohan remembers that these were rubber powered planes or gliders possibly marketed by a German company called Graupner, with names like Zugvogel or Flugzeug. Later we built our very own Cessna out of balsa wood which was very light and propelled by rubber power (rubber bands linked together and attached to the propeller) which was then wound and released into the air.

We sometimes flew our Cessna at Batu Tiga, which was on the way to Klang, where there were open spaces. The Cessna flew several times quite successfully and we enjoyed chasing after it. But one time, it took off almost vertically and then plummeted earthward – it was flattened and was beyond repair. Our flying days were truly over.

Rohan however never lost his fascination with planes. He would have liked to have become a pilot and perhaps fly those jumbo jets but his eyesight was a handicap. He ended up doing the next best thing instead – a degree in Aerospace Engineering, but he never got to apply this in his working life. Rohan later built a rather large model plane in balsa wood – which is still with us today but needs to be finished – with wings attached to the fuselage and the motor attached and tested. I would indeed like to see it fly.

Pulau Pangkor

During the school holidays, we tried to take the children to different places. On one occasion, I took Annette and the boys on a short holiday to PulauPangkor (Pangkor Island) in the Straits of Malacca, off the coast of Perak in Peninsular Malaysia. We drove to Lumut and went across to the island by launch. We spent a pleasant few days there – mostly swimming.

One day, while swimming in shoulder deep water, Renan suddenly screamed and went under. He had been stung by a jellyfish. We rushed him back to our chalet and Annette dissolved a liberal quantity of panadol in water and applied it all over Renan's body and that helped greatly to lessen the pain and neutralise the toxin from the jellyfish sting. Some jellyfish stings can be quite lethal. By the next morning, Renan had largely recovered, but we did not venture into the water again.

I never dreamed that nearly forty years later, long after Annette died, that I would be in Lumut again – for a holiday on a smaller island tucked away behind the main island called Pangkor Laut. Karen and I spent a few days at the Pangkor Laut Resort in an over-the-water-chalet with nothing but a sea-vista on three sides of the chalet. Renan made most of the bookings and very kindly paid some of the costs. We stayed at Renan's place in Lumut for a few days before proceeding to Pangkor Laut.

Renan was still with Chevron but had relocated from Houston, Texas and was stationed at Lumut where the plant for the Wheatstone (oil and gas) project off the West Australian coast was being fabricated. Renan was one of the senior project engineers – a far cry indeed from his first jellyfish experience in Pangkor, when he was just a little boy!

I visited Renan again a year or two ago, while he was still at Lumut and expressed my desire to join him and a few of his work colleagues in an off shore fishing expedition. Unfortunately, I chickened out at the last moment when I discovered that the boat might be venturing far out to sea and not just hugging the coastline – which I would have found more comforting. I was most pleased however to be invited subsequently to join them at dinner where the 'catch' was prepared by a local restaurant – which we all enjoyed very much.

Renan also arranged for me to be chaffeur-driven from his home in Lumut to the hot springs in Sungkai – which was most enjoyable. I spent a few hours soaking myself in the warm sulphur springs, as well as the cascading waters and swimming pools, followed by a nasi lemak meal in the little kiosks on site. All this while, the driver waited patiently and drove me back to Renan's place in Lumut. I am determined to visit the hot springs again with Karen – she is sure to enjoy the experience.

Boating and fishing

I have always nursed a love for boating and fishing. There was little opportunity for indulging in such activities while living in Malaysia – there was something that always militated against it. We lived too far from the sea and the rivers which were close enough to home were muddy, unwelcoming and crocodile infested. I would have liked to own a medium sized launch or boat with an outboard motor but could not afford it at that time.

I do recall being in a row-boat with Norbert, off the coast – line in Port Dickson, doing a bit of fishing. We had lots of laughs, but caught nothing – not even a tiddler. Years later, long after Annette died, I did a bit of line fishing with friends, off the beach in Rockingham, but only caught some herring.

I used to take long walks alone the shoreline in Rockingham to keep up my exercise levels. On one occasion, I noticed a number of anglers fishing off one of the long jetties. Curious, I walked over to see how they were doing. Most of the anglers seemed to be fairly well equipped – with their lines and reels but did not seem to have much success. Then I noticed this middle-aged Philippino woman, sitting on the jetty with her legs dangling over the water – she did not have any rod or reel, but merely dropped a line into the water and was hooking the fish in, one after the other. Having got her catch for the day, she gathered up her belongings and waddled away. I would really have liked to know what her secret was.

When the family first migrated to Australia, they lived in a rented property on Kent Street in Rockingham, quite close to the beach. Renan as a young lad then, used to do a bit of fishing with a neighbour, who lived in the adjoining property. Regrettably, I was still working in Malaysia then and missed this opportunity of being a part of his life in his growing up years – I did however get to see his cubby-house in the bush.

Late in my life, this desire for some boating on the Swan River has caught up with me again – perhaps a little fishing too. It may be that I am too old now to seriously consider this – but one can always dream. Now that I have the means, I may not have the strength and energy to go with it. I may have to settle instead for simple canoeing on the tranquil waters of the Swan and some off the beach fishing.

Travel abroad

In 1979, I was the sole Malaysian participant on a programme sponsored by the US Information Service which brought together selected participants from different areas of expertise within the Asia-Pacific region for an east-west interaction, which began in Hawaii and went on to Los Angeles, Dallas and Washington. While in Washington, I took advantage of the week-end to visit Annette's brother Terrence and wife Betty who were living in Falls Church in Virginia. Terrence was then a Doctoral student at Georgetown University. The programme ended with a session at the Centre for the Book at the Library of Congress. A commemorative booklet was published a year later which included contributions from a few of us.

Map of West Malaysia

Quite apart from the above, I was very fortunate to be able to travel abroad from time to time to serve on expert panels, attend meetings or present working papers at international conferences. The expert panels I served on were at

Map of East Malaysia

UNESCO, Paris while the meetings attended were in Den Haag, as a member of the Professional Board of IFLA (International Federation of Library Associations and Institutions). I also presented working papers at international conferences in London, Paris, Washington, Chicago, Tokyo, Seoul, New Delhi, Bangalore, Colombo, Singapore, Kuala Lumpur, Bangkok, Jakarta, Bali, Manila, Fiji, Port Moresby, Sydney and Canberra.

All these visits were fully sponsored by international organizations and I was usually away for only a couple of days on each trip. From a developmental point of view, some of these visits were especially important as it enabled me to successfully bid for projects and consultant assistance from UNESCO and other international organisations in pushing forward library development programmes within Malaysia. From time to time I nominated senior and middle level officers to represent the department at international conferences or meetings to give them experience and widen their horizons.

When I look back on all those trips abroad to many countries all over the world – some countries and capital cities were visited more than once – I seem to have concentrated largely on the business aspects of those trips, rarely taking time to relax or see more of the countries or cities I was visiting. On a few occasions, I even cut short my trips after the main business was over in order to return home.

As a result, on a visit to the US in the late seventies, I missed out on trips to the Grand Canyon which had been paid for by the US Information Service for delegates from the Asia-Pacific region. My thinking then was that I would visit again later but I never did – not even years and years later when Renan was living and working in Houston, Texas! This is not the only example of my failure to take advantage of these wonderful opportunities to see more of the world.

The boys enjoyed coming to the airport with their mother to see me off and to meet me when I got back, never dreaming then that in their own working life later, they would travel even more extensively. On one occasion, the whole family made a special trip to the Subang International Airport to witness the landing for the very first time of the Boeing 747 jumbo-jet. It happened to be a Qantas jumbo from Australia. We never envisaged then that one day we would all be migrating to Australia.

Although I tried as far as possible to keep Annette fully informed of my travel itinerary – especially of my return flights, I slipped up badly on one occasion on a return flight on PIA (Pakistan International Airlines) from London to Kuala Lumpur. Our departure was delayed and we missed our connection flight at Lahore.

The Airline put us up at a hotel in rather basic rooms which I had to share with another passenger I did not know and I completely forgot that Annette would be waiting at the airport on the designated date. When the plane failed to turn up, she was quite distraught, fearing the worst. When I finally arrived, days later, I got a real dressing down. She was not pleased and I made sure that never happened ever again.

Travel within the country

As part of my official duties I travelled extensively within the country – to all States in Peninsular Malaysia – often by air and sometimes by car, serving on the Boards of all State Public Library Corporations (SPLC) for several years. I also visited Sabah and Sarawak but not so frequently. Once the

SPLCs were established, staff appointed and public library services opened to the public, professional officers from the National Library were appointed to represent the Department on the SPLCs. While this did reduce my travel commitments within the country, it compromised the pace of developments at state level and I had to visit some of the states from time to time.

Trauma in Trengganu

On one of these official visits in 1976 to the State of Trengganu, I travelled by car and took the family along. Since my weekend was free, I took the family to the nearby beach. Annette was with Renan building sand castles on the beach. I was with Rohan and Rienzi who were astride a log which I was pushing along in shallow water. One minute we were fine but the next minute, all three of us were in the water, caught in an undertow (rip tide) and dragged out to sea. The boys were in their swimming trunks, while I still had my batik shirt on, the pockets full of sea shells which were weighing me down.

I still remember Rienzi grabbing me and wrapping his arms tightly around my neck. It was choking me. He was such a skinny little boy then. I disengaged his arms and vaguely remember telling him to try to float and tread water. Unfortunately, in the process the two boys were caught up in one stream of the current and swept further out to sea while I was caught up in the other.

My one thought on being separated from my two boys was that I had lost them forever. After struggling for what seemed about an hour, I worked myself out of the rip tide and moved closer to the shore. How I actually managed this is still unclear to me as I was out of condition and totally exhausted. Annette had to jump into the water and virtually drag me the last few metres onto the beach. By then, the boys were only visible as two little dots far out to sea – in deep water. I looked at Annette and told her I could go out to the boys but it was unlikely I would be coming back.

A crowd had gathered to watch the unfolding drama but there was no rescue or lifesaving facilities whatsoever available on the beach. It seemed then that out of nowhere, a young Malay fisherman turned up, bare-chested and in a pair of shorts. He knelt on the beach, prayed and then ventured into the water. But the sea was too rough and he came ashore.

He stood for a while and bowed his head and then plunged in again regardless. We could see him battling the waves, often disappearing completely from sight. Finally, about a half hour later, we could see far out to sea three tiny dots and we knew he had reached the two boys and they were still alive. But the waters were still far too choppy.

Then out of the blue, two European tourists – we thought they were German – strapping men possibly in their late thirties, plunged into the water and took off. Then there were five dots and we knew they had reached the boys. It was hard to believe but it seemed that the dots were becoming more and more distinct – they were moving closer and closer to shore. Finally, all five walked on to the beach, none the worse for wear.

Rienzi showed the signs of the ordeal the most – his skinny chest was full of welts and bruises, some bleeding. But apart from that they were as chirpy as ever and greeted both of us with a smile and the words "Hi Mum", "Hi Dad" – as if nothing untoward had happened. We wanted to thank the young men who had saved our boys but could not find them anywhere. We expressed our deep gratitude to the young Malay fisherman and gave him several hundred Ringgit – it was all we had.

The press were present and interviewed the two boys and took photographs. Renan wanted to know why the press were not interviewing him. Annette and I realised that the hand of God had been there at work that day. We talked to the boys afterwards about the whole episode and Rohan related how they had used the log to stay afloat; diving under when the log became a missile, then surfacing when the log lost its momentum, using it to stay afloat. He also kept up a conversation to distract his younger brother. We were absolutely amazed. They were barely ten and eleven years old then. Strangely, it was I who became super cautious about the sea ever since, but it never fazed either of them – they still love the beach and the sea.

An unforgettable holiday

A few years later, I had to attend a series of meetings in the northern States of Kedah and Perlis. Since this was during the school holidays, the boys came along with me in the car. The plan was that I would drop them off in Seberang Perai (which was part of the State of Penang) where they would be picked by their Uncle Terrence (Annette's brother) for a short holiday with their cousins. The boys all grew up with their cousins – all girls. Sure enough, when we arrived they were waiting for us. I left the boys and drove on to Alor Star in the State of Kedah. The boys were to fly back to KL a few days later.

It so happened that my meetings ended earlier and so I decided to stop by in Penang and take the boys home in the car. The trip back to KL was indeed a memorable one. It was raining cats and dogs and I often had to stop by the roadside so that Rienzi could dash outside, wipe the mud off my headlights and dash back inside again – all wet. I was driving fairly fast but my Peugeot 504 was up to the task.

We got to Ipoh without any mishap and stopped at about 8.00 pm for some piping hot 'murthabak' or roti and a drink each – we really enjoyed that meal and none of us forgot that trip. That same day, one of the MAS (Malaysian Airlines) flights – a Boeing 737 from Penang to Kuala Lumpur was hijacked and crashed in Johore killing everyone on board. The boys were booked on that flight MH 653, but by the grace of God, I took them home by car.

Severing ties with academia

It may be necessary at this stage to go back a little in time and touch on developments in the work place that impacted on me and consequently on the family as well. In June 1974, the period of secondment ended but was extended for a further six months. I was then asked to call on the Chief Secretary once again. He apologised profusely and said that in spite of what he had assured me of over two years ago, he felt that there was still a great deal to be done and that my continued services were very much needed. It did not seem that I had much choice in the matter.

This brought to a close my career with the University of Malaya. There was little I could do. I was subsequently absorbed within the Public Service and appointed Deputy Director General. But even this process was not painless and dragged on for several months. Whether this was done deliberately by minor minions in the Public Service to discourage me or simply because the wheels of the bureaucracy were grinding at its usual pace, it is difficult to say. During this transitional period, I received no salary whatsoever and had to depend on the generosity of my close friend and colleague within the service who kept me in funds. Arrears in unpaid salary were later paid back to me.

Developing the infrastructure

Developing an infrastructure for library and information services within the country, virtually from scratch, was no mean feat. It was virgin territory indeed, especially at State level – where officialdom, bureaucracy as well as the political masters were relatively unfamiliar and unappreciative of libraries.

It was patently clear that two years was an impossible time frame to put in place a network of state public library systems. It was a real struggle to set up State Public Library Corporations on the basis of State Legislative Enactments in all the states of Peninsula Malaysia in addition to spearheading and developing the National Library of Malaysia. Many of these developments have been well documented in my recent work: 'Contributions towards the Malaysian Library and Information Infrastructure: a historical perspective' which was published by MPH (Malaysia Publishing House) in 2011 and will not be repeated here.

Developing the National Library was by itself a major task and required a great deal of tact and diplomacy in carrying out its designated mandate. The National Library was set up on the basis of Federal Legislation (National Library Act, 1972). It was a relatively 'new' institution vested with an over-arching, pivotal role within the nation's system of libraries.

My early days in the Public Service

The National Library was also not as large or as well resourced and financed as some of the older established University Libraries which did not take too kindly towards a new institution attempting to muscle in on its turf. We were so to speak 'the new kid on the block'. It took time to build up a rapport with the University libraries and gain their trust and cooperation in pushing forward developments on several fronts.

There was concurrently the need to also bring about a culture of change, not only among professional and non-professional officers serving within the library system but also to get policy makers and those who held the purse strings – to see libraries as important components of the national information system. Within the broader society, Malaysians did not read very much and that was a matter that would need to be addressed too.

While on the one hand it seemed that my continued services within the Public Service were necessary, there were underlying forces at play to prevent me being appointed Director General – not because I was inept or incapable but because I was not 'bumiputra'. While I had the support and confidence of those at the highest levels, there were ambitious minor minions within the system who often frustrated the developmental thrust.

From my appointment in June 1972, I was the Chief Professional Officer of the National Library of Malaysia and mainly responsible for its growth and development throughout the '70's and '80's. I was the de facto head, but not the head de jure. That role and the Designation of Director General was given to senior civil servants in the Administrative and Diplomatic Service. Unfortunately those who came to be placed in the National Library after 1973 as Director General had little or no knowledge of running a library system.

During my years in the Public Service, it was a well known fact that the National Library was used as a dumping ground for senior civil servants. This was not necessarily because these officers had outlived their usefulness but because there were insufficient posts at the appropriate pay grade to absorb them.

*early days in the Public Service
with the Minister of Housing and Local Government
the late Tan Sri Ong Kee Hui*

The rationale seemed to be to just place them in the National Library – it was felt that they could do little enough damage in a library even if they stuffed up! Being the chief professional officer, I had to deal with them and copped most of the flak.

Some came in with bruised egos or a sense of betrayal. One of them genuinely tried to affect some positive developments, particularly in regard to the new site for the National Library building as well as the establishment of the National Library as a separate Federal Department, no longer attached to the National Archives.

Since my absorption into the Public service in 1975, I had been pushing for the separation of the National Library from the National Archives. I recognised early into my secondment that the National Library would be stifled so long as it was tied to the coat tails of the National Archives – an institution established nearly a decade earlier. It was most fortunate that the Director General at that time supported my efforts.

One of those appointed as Director General immediately after, gave scant attention to his responsibilities and duties as Director General and passed all official matters to the Deputy Director General (myself) for action. He slouched on his sofa throughout office hours writing his magnum opus which he said "would revolutionise the world". He only served for two years, took optional retirement and died three months later but his 'book' was never even published.

Yet another one of them was quite aggrieved at being placed in the National Library and resented my position within the Department. Nothing of any significance was achieved under his leadership. He was clearly quite unsuitable and it was necessary to make representation to have him transferred. However, before he left, he submitted to the authorities a long list of charges against me which surfaced several years later. I strongly suspect that these charges were formulated with the connivance and instigation of ambitious senior officers within the National Library itself. Years later, he did try to make amends as he realised that the allegations he had made against me were ill founded and that he had well and truly been manipulated. As far as I was concerned the matter was closed.

Doctoral studies

Looking back, it is apparent that the setbacks started much earlier. It made me realise that it might be beneficial for me to pursue further studies in order to improve my marketability and perhaps take up a teaching role elsewhere, either within or outside the country. Since my early career days at the University of Malaya, I had been involved in education and training in the library and information field. I lectured part-time at the Mara Institute of Technology and also served as Director of Courses for the Malaysian Library Association which prepared students sitting for the Professional Examinations of the British Library Association.

Although I discontinued all teaching functions on assuming duties in the Public Service, close friends of mine had been urging me for some time to undertake post graduate studies at the Doctoral level. This would have meant a period of study abroad and I knew it would be futile to request for a period of study leave for this purpose. Even with all the goodwill in the world, there was no way I could be given the necessary leave – there was simply no-one else within the Department to take over my duties.

By the mid-seventies however I had become fairly well known in the world of libraries. Loughborough University in the UK was especially keen that I consider undertaking my PhD studies at their university and approved special provisions to enable me to fulfil residence requirements.

In my Doctoral robes, 1981

In 1978, I began my research studies and for the next few years plodded on in my own time with my research. It was heavy going as I often had to burn the midnight oil and at the same time perform my onerous duties in the National Library. I had the fullest support from Annette and this encouraged me to plough on. I completed the research and submitted my thesis within the stipulated time period.

In 1980 I applied for leave and flew to London to appear before a Panel of Assessors appointed by the University. I defended my dissertation successfully before the Panel. That same night, Professor Peter Havard-Williams hosted a dinner party for me at his home in Loughborough and

I phoned Annette to tell her that I had been awarded the PhD and that she could call me 'Doctor' in future. Annette was delighted.

I never bothered to inform the Public Services Department of this. But the information leaked out eventually. Curiously, this information only came to light a year later at a conference in Singapore when I was first addressed as 'Dr' at one of the public sessions!

At the Convocation the year after, I was conferred the PhD in absentia while Sir Harry Hookway, the CEO of the British Library was conferred an honorary PhD. It would have been quite an event but it was far too expensive for me to fly to the UK yet again to attend the convocation. Professor Havard-Williams was most disappointed that I was unable to attend the convocation as it was a unique occasion where the CEO of the British Library and the Deputy Director General of the National Library of Malaysia were both being conferred the PhD on the same occasion.

When I look back on my life, I realise that I have never attended the Convocations in the Universities I earned my academic degrees. They were always conferred in absentia! The reasons were the same in each case – I could not justify to myself the expenses involved.

When I obtained my PhD however, I wanted to attend the Convocation, cost considerations aside, but I knew that conditions in the work place were far too dicey and I felt it would be unwise to be away from the country.

The year after my doctorate at Loughborough University, Professor Peter Havard-Williams urged me to apply for one of the Professorial posts that had fallen vacant in Loughborough University. Needless to say, I was flattered but did not pursue it as the family had already applied for migration to Australia and so the timing was just not right. While working in England could have been a career opportunity for me, I had long taken England out of the equation for possible migration for the family – it was overcrowded and job opportunities were limited. As one of my English colleagues put it, the country was undergoing a period of 'reverse colonialism' with former colonials now colonising the mother country.

National accolades

In 1978, I was awarded the Bintang Cermerlang Negeri Kedah (Kedah Distinguished Service Star) for my work in promoting the development of public library services in the State of Kedah. The late Dato Shuaib Othman, Chairman of the Perbadanan Perpustakaan Awam Negeri Kedah (Kedah State Public Library Corporation) was especially appreciative of my efforts in relation to the enactment of state legislation for the setting up of the Kedah Public Library Corporation and the development of public library services in the state of Kedah.

It was my very first experience of receiving a royal decoration and it took me completely by surprise. It was unexpected and totally unsolicited. I was simply doing the job I was brought in to do. I had served as a representative of the National Library on the Board of the Kedah Public Library Corporation since its establishment. Dato Shuaib relied heavily on me. Several years later, I had facilitated a substantial Federal grant to the Kedah Public Library Corporation which was officially presented by the Chief

Secretary to the Government, Tan Sri Kadir Samsuddin at a formal ceremony in Alor Setar Kedah. I was proud to be present on the occasion and to witness the beginnings of Federal Government endorsement.

I took Annette and the boys to Kedah for the investiture ceremony. We stayed at one of the hotels in Alor Setar. However only Annette and I were allowed to attend the investiture itself. His Royal Highness, the Sultan of Kedah who graced the occasion later became the Duli Yang Maha Mulia (DYMM) the Yang di Pertuan Agong (King).

The day after the investiture, Dato Shuaib took the whole family by boat to the Langkawi Islands. We stayed at the Country Club and spent a few pleasant days there. The Country Club was regarded as up-market accommodation at the time. Today the Langkawi islands are dotted with many up-market resorts and tourist attractions. I have been back a few times as a tourist long after my retirement and am amazed at the changes that have taken place.

In 1979, I was awarded the Kesatria Mangku Negara (KMN) by DYMM Yang di Pertuan Agong(King). The Sultan of Pahang had now become the DYMM Yang di Pertuan Agong. Annette and I attended the investiture ceremony at the Istana Negara (Royal Palace) in Kuala Lumpur. The KMN is one of the orders of chivalry and is accompanied with a scroll which carries the Royal seal. The KMN is a Federal Award unlike the earlier state level award.

In 1981, Annette was conferred the PPN (Pingat Pankuan Negara) by DYMM the Yang di Pertuan Agong (King). Annette had been part of the pilot project to introduce educational television services in Malaysian schools.

In 1987, I was nominated for the SDK (Setia Darjah Kinabalu) by the State of Sabah which carried the title of Dato. The Secretary General of the Ministry of Culture, Dato Hamzah Majid had asked me to call on him and as soon as I entered his office, he informed me of the award and asked me whether I was willing to accept the award. It was indeed a great honour and I told the Secretary General that I would be pleased to accept the award. He then congratulated me and told me that the Ministry would be taking the necessary action.

Had this matter been taken up immediately, I would have been the very first Director General of the National Library of Malaysia to be made a Dato. My predessor Dato Hashim Sam Abdul Latif actually became a Dato long before he was posted to the National Library.

Unfortunately, the award had to be deferred as I was due to leave shortly after to take up an appointment as Visiting Professor at the Department of Library and Information Studies at Curtin University in Western Australia. Several months earlier, Curtin University had extended to me an invitation to serve as Visiting Professor, Department of Library and Information Studies for a period of six months. The Public Services Department deemed this to be a great honour and granted me the necessary leave to serve as Visiting Professor. I was hopeful that the appointment would lead to a permanent appointment at Curtin University on my retirement. This however did not eventuate. I proceeded abroad and served my term at Curtin University. It felt good to be back in the cloisters of academia again.

On my return, I realised that the initial award of SDK had been downgraded to ASDK (Ahli Setia Darjah Kinabalu) – which did not carry the title of 'Dato'. Quite obviously someone had thrown a spanner in the works. I am quite sure who it was, but I took it all philosophically. There would always be the small minded – the 'flies in the ointment' so to speak or in Australian parlance 'the tall poppy syndrome'.

State authorities told me that they would resubmit my name for the SDK award the following year. However as I would be retiring then and living in Australia, I saw little point in pursuing the matter as such a title would be meaningless in Australia. I flew to Kota Kinabalu for the investiture ceremony and spent a few pleasant days there.

Malaysian nationality

My paternal grandfather came to the Malay States in 1890 as a young man. Grandmother came shortly after. My father was born in Seremban, Negeri Sembilan in 1905 and was a subject of the Ruler of Negeri Sembilan. His Certificate of Registration, which he had carefully preserved over the years, attests to this fact. My mother too had a Certificate of Registration under the Constitution of the Federation of Malaya, Citizenship Rules 1960.

In my own case, I had a Certificate of Citizenship, issued under Article 30 of the Constitution. All my brothers and sisters were also born in the Malay States after 1932 and were therefore second generation citizens of the country. My three sons, all of whom were born in Malaysia, were citizens by operation of law and were third generation Malaysians. All of us held Blue Identity Cards (IC) which conferred on us citizenship status or 'Warga Negara Malaysia'. Malaysia was our home. We gave the country our allegiance and always identified ourselves as Malaysians. I sometimes still do.

Not long after Independence in 1957, the seeds of political disunity began to seep in. These were the years of my early working life in Malaysia. Cocooned as I was within the portals of academia, I failed to appreciate the political ferment that was beginning to bubble under the seeming tranquillity of interracial harmony within the country. My two years in London soon after, on post graduate studies kept me further shielded from political realities back home.

Many of my professional colleagues at the University of Malaya, saw the writing on the wall very much earlier. They migrated to the United States, Australia, Canada and New Zealand long before I even considered doing so. The Government's 'Bumiputra' policy was not as yet full blown at that time. Little purpose would be served in a discourse on 'Bumiputraism' at this stage. My sons are very well aware of what it means. In any case, the Internet is replete with information on the subject.

The blight of bumiputraism colours all aspects of Malaysian society and has led to a continuing brain drain of its non-bumiputras to greener pastures abroad. One only has to read the recent writings of Zairil Khir Johari, Azli Rahman, Bakri Musa, Mariam Mokhtar and other writers to get a fuller picture of the malaise that Malaysia is in today - spearheaded by a political and ethnic blunted steam roller that has been rolling downhill since independence. It seems likely that the downward propulsion may take decades to run out of steam and for a new course to be charted for the benefit of all

Malaysians. There has been a refreshing change of government, at long last, but so far the political leadership has done little to slow down the downward spiral of bumiputraism.

Malayanisation

At the time of Independence or 'Merdeka', key positions within the public service were held by British expatriate officers who saw to it that British interests in mining, agriculture and other key areas were safeguarded for England and Her Britannic Majesty!

It took time to put in place a policy of 'Malayanisation' – to replace British expatriate officers with competent locals. Unfortunately, over the following decades, 'Malayanisation' came to be progressively distilled into a more and more 'pro-Malay' ethnic interpretation.

We were becoming increasingly concerned about the prospects for our sons within the country. We knew that our sons were very intelligent and bright but their chances of realising their full potential in Malaysia were dismally slim. We doubted very much whether they would even be able to make it to the local universities.

We knew that we could only afford to support one of them for tertiary study abroad but could not afford to do so for all three. We felt that if we could not do it for all three of them, we should not do it for only one.

We realised therefore, that we had to take our boys out of the country of their birth if they were to reach their full potential. This was a very difficult decision to make. We both held fairly secure positions in the public sector and realised that one or both careers would have to be sacrificed. It took many years for us to make up our minds.

The migration option

Annette and I both worked and earned a reasonable wage. This was the norm in most families. We were reasonably comfortable but never considered ourselves wealthy. Annette took up editorial work on the side from time to time to supplement the family income. As a family, we were never able to afford even a single holiday abroad.

When we began to seriously consider migrating, we did have several choices, but a return to our ancestral roots was never one of them. At that time Sri Lanka was immersed in a seemingly unending ethnic conflict with little resolution in sight. The UK, US and Canada were too far away and therefore not worth considering. Besides, our parents were still alive then and we did not want to be too far away from them.

Australia seemed to beckon – it was safe; it was close enough to Malaysia; it was underpopulated and seemed a land of opportunity. Australia was indeed worth exploring as a possible new home for the family. We also had the advantage that members of the family, including my sister as well as my wife's brothers had migrated to Australia in the early seventies and had assimilated into the work force without any hiccup. Australia is a beautiful country to live in and we have never regretted our decision to migrate.

Despite my long period of dedicated service and my performance record, I recognised the many road blocks placed in my way. But I was determined to do the job I was brought in to do. The accolades and awards to Annette and me failed to detract us from our resolve to migrate and seek greener pastures elsewhere, especially for our boys. We did just that. In 1981 we submitted an application to the Australian High Commission in Kuala Lumpur for Permanent Residence in Australia.

Our application was sponsored by Annette's brother Lionel who had migrated to Australia nearly ten years earlier. This was granted in 1982 and the family was given until October 1983 to take it up. Annette took Optional Retirement and left with the boys in February 1983. I deferred my own departure largely because the Director General would be retiring in a month or so and there were indications that I would be appointed the next Director General, notwithstanding the intrigues of minor minions closer to home.

I had no inkling at that stage that serious charges had been formulated against me by a previous Director General and were 'fermenting' within official circles. These charges were officially communicated to me only after the next Director General also retired – in March 1983. Had I migrated with the family in February 1982 (before even being appointed Acting Director General) my departure would have been exploited to the fullest as an admission of guilt. It is also quite likely that I would have forfeited all pension rights. This would have been a very bitter pill to swallow, considering the energy and years I had invested in building up the infrastructure of libraries within the country.

Although it was a portentous decision not to accompany Annette and the boys to Australia in February 1983, it was at the same time a decision seemingly directed from on high. I put on a brave front but it pained me very greatly to see the family leave. My only consolation was my supreme confidence in Annette – she was a very capable person and none of our boys were problem children in any way.

This was a gamble which may have paid off in career terms but it did little for togetherness and family life. Our two older boys were young men and could cope well enough but I failed to realise that my absence would be felt more strongly by their mother. Families need to stay together. No career goals are worth pursuing at the expense of family.

In retrospect, my decision to accept the invitation to serve within the Public Service, specifically within the National Library, may not have been the best decision I could have made from a family standpoint. From a long term career perspective too, it was questionable. National Libraries are unique to each country and when one migrates, one is likely to find work opportunities rather limited in the same line of work. Whereas, had I remained at the University of Malaya, not only would I have reached professorial pay grades so much earlier but I would have found so many universities abroad – in my case Australia – that I could have readily fitted into at the highest executive levels.

Serving in the National Library may have given me some national visibility, royal awards and decorations and opportunities for international travel but it did take a lot out of me and detracted from the attention I should have lavished on my family.

Dad's passing away

My Dad never got to see me reach the very top position at the National Library. On the 21st November 1982, tragedy struck. My Dad died. He was seventy seven. Mum called me that morning and told me that Dad had been coughing all night through and was in a bad way. I could hear my Dad's voice in the background: "tell Donny it's serious!" My Mum asked me to come right away and I did. We took him to the Assunta Hospital barely 2km away. He was attended to straight away by Dr. Noronha whom Dad knew very well.

Dad's condition was stabilised soon after and we were told that he was being moved to the ward on the floor above. We were all present – Mum, myself, Clarence, Basil and our families. Jenny, Irene and Norbert lived abroad and hence could not be there. When we reached the ward, we noticed a flurry of activity in one of the cubicles. The curtains were drawn and a doctor was attempting to revive my Dad. Minutes later, they announced that my Dad had gone. My mother bowed her head and rested it beside Dad's head on the pillow for a few minutes in a final gesture of parting. It was so very sad but at the same time so very dignified.

I was very upset when Dad died. It was all so very sudden. Dad was perfectly fine the day before. He had done the shopping in readiness for Mum's birthday on the 22nd November and even baked a birthday cake himself. But as it turned out, there was no birthday celebration. It was a quiet passing for a gentle man.

I would say that Dad had a good life. He kept in reasonably good mental and physical health all his life. He and my

Escorting my Parents to the reception hall, La Salle, Brickfields

Mum holding court at the anniversary celebrations

mother were able to celebrate their 50th wedding anniversary or Golden Jubilee on the 1st August 1981. We were all there.

It has been well over thirty years since Dad passed away and I can still picture him in his stained and battered felt hat and baggy shorts working on his beautiful orchids in the garden.

The family at Mum and Dad's 50th wedding anniversary

In our Christian tradition we believe in the resurrection of the body and life everlasting. In other religious traditions, there is belief in an after life or in rebirth and reincarnation in some other life form. But who really knows what happens when the flickering light of our lives finally flutters and fades away.

Mum's twilight years

When I retired from the Public Service in November 1989 and took up permanent residence in Australia shortly after, my mother continued to live on her own for many years after that and managed very well. I used to phone her every Sunday morning at a specified time and she would wait by the phone for my call. Mum was most fortunate that Basil and Elaine lived fairly close by in Petaling Jaya too and were able to assist in many ways, including Mum's pension payments.

I am happy that I was able to spend so many years with my mother in her home after my father died. I may not have been the best company for her as my energies and my preoccupation may have been focussed on two fronts – in Australia where my family lived and in Malaysia with all the problems on the job front. My mother however was very happy to have me on hand and probably understood the stresses I was subjected to.

Whenever I had the opportunity, I took my mother on trips with me – usually by car to Singapore so that she could spend time with Irene. Earlier, when my father was still alive, I took them both on trips with me. After I retired and moved to Australia, I continued to visit Malaysia two or three times a year, mostly to visit my mother and stay with her and attend to other matters. I always caught up with other members of the family too and also with some of my friends. On one or two occasions, my mother visited Perth and stayed with us in Rockingham. I took her to the Fremantle cemetery to visit Clarence's gravesite – he died in 1992.

In 1994 Annette and I visited Sri Lanka on holiday. Rohan came along with us. We stopped over in Kuala Lumpur so that my mother could accompany us to Sri Lanka. It was a good trip for all of us. My mother stayed with her sister Sally while we toured the country. She was also able to catch up with Sister Mary Clementa – her youngest sister, who was a nun in the convent. We met many of our cousins, nephews and nieces for the first time.

A few years later, I took my mother to Sri Lanka for what turned out to be her last visit. I flew from Perth to KL first in order to accompany her to Sri Lanka. The plan was for her to stay for about three months with her youngest sister, who was at that time in an Old Age facility in Kegalle. Both my mother's sisters were alive then. I was to fly back in three months time to bring my mother home. Unfortunately, my mother fell quite ill and I had to take her back to KL shortly after to her own home. She lived there on her own for a few more years.

Unfortunately, Mum had a fall in her bathroom and hurt her knee badly which required knee surgery. While Mum recovered from the surgery, she was never able to walk again and had to be placed in a nursing home where she also suffered a stroke and lost her speech. Despite all the setbacks, she still had that ready smile. She even tried to say a few words very slowly and sing along after a fashion.

I visited her from Perth a few times and so did Rohan and Rienzi. Fortunately, Basil and Elaine were able to visit her almost daily. Arjuna – their son also visited frequently when he was in town.

My mother died on the 8th October 2000 – just short of her 90th birthday. Basil phoned me in Perth to inform me that Mum was poorly and had been readmitted to Hospital. I made arrangements to fly over right away but arrived after she passed away. There was a High Mass at St Xavier's Church and Bernard Wijasuriya (one of my first cousins) read the eulogy (none of us were up to the task). My mother's ashes were interred in my father's grave in the Petaling Jaya Cemetry. My mother truly enriched our lives. She was a very special lady.

I have visited my parents' grave at the Petaling Jaya Cemetery from time to time over the years. In Malaysia, non–Muslim cemeteries are very poorly maintained and are an absolute disgrace. It is in stark contrast to the Fremantle Cemetery in Western Australia where both Annette and Clarence are buried. I visit these graves too from time to time and reflect on our shared lives in days gone by.

The family's departure

Annette's departure with the boys in tow in 1983 ushered in the beginnings of the family split-up. This did not mean that the family had broken up, rather that members of the family were now dispersed in cities thousands of miles apart. The Australian component was part of our new horizon and will be narrated further down the track.

After the family left for Australia, I moved into my mother's house so that she would not have to live alone. I had another six years to serve before I retired and I immersed myself in my work, but it was no bed of roses. When the incumbent Director General retired shortly after, I was appointed Acting Director General and confirmed a few years later. I served in that capacity until my retirement in November 1989.

The continuing saga

My years in the Public Service were the most challenging in my entire career. There were difficult times too, especially from 1978 – 1981. During this period, I seriously considered resigning once, but this I realised would seriously impact on the family's wellbeing. As I was not yet 50, I could not apply for Optional Retirement and would have lost all service benefits. I decided therefore to stay put and tough it out. I am glad I did, for the tide began to change soon after.

In 1984, just to complicate matters, the Registrar's Office, La Trobe University in Melbourne, Australia, contacted me by phone and enquired whether I would be prepared to fly to Melbourne for a short visit to be interviewed for the post of University Librarian as Dietrich Borchard, the University Librarian would be retiring shortly and had recommended that I be considered for the position. While I knew Dietrich Borchard, I did not know that he was retiring and had not applied for the post. The visit to Melbourne was fully sponsored by the University.

Although I attended the interview, I was in a real dilemma. I realised that if I left the National Library at that stage, it would not only have greatly set back developments but there was a grave likelihood that the post of Director General would be filled by senior civil servants or PTD Officers once again. None of the 'senior' officers in the Department at that time had the maturity and standing to be seriously considered. It had taken many years for the post of Director General of the National Library to be categorised as a professional post to be filled only by professionals from the library and information sector. In hindsight, would this have really mattered?

When I phoned Annette to inform her of this unexpected development, she did not dissuade me in any way but merely said "you will be as far away from us as you always were!" I do not think that she was only talking in geographic terms. Annette's remark weighed very heavily on me.

Taking up the appointment at La Trobe University would have meant at least another 15 years in the service of the University and since I was already 50, I could take Optional Retirement from the Public Service. While this may have appeared to be an attractive proposition, I had serious misgivings as Annette and I would continue to remain far apart. I am also sure that while we would have visited one another from time to time, the ties were bound to grow weaker over the years and it is quite possible that Annette and I would have gone our separate ways. This was a prospect I was simply not prepared to consider.

The Vice-Chancellor, who chaired the selection board, appreciated my sense of uncertainty, thanked me for taking the time to present myself before the board and wished me a safe return to Kuala Lumpur. I was later informed in writing that a local candidate had been appointed. Dietrich Borchard was especially disappointed that I was not appointed as his successor at La Trobe. I continued to keep in touch with Dietrich until he passed away a few years later.

We may delude ourselves into thinking that we are masters of our own destiny and that our footsteps and the direction they take are our very own. In reality however, I believe that our progression in life is preordained. Loyalty and commitment have always been driving forces in my life although these have not always seemed to have worked to my personal advantage. Admittedly, there may have been lost career opportunities but hindsight is always 20-20 and I have no regrets.

Surviving in officialdom

On the job front, there was no end to intrigue perpetrated by a devious and unscrupulous staff member. This compromised the development of key projects and much time and energy was expended to minimise the negative fallout. Tact and diplomacy have always been a part of my management style and I could not bring myself to initiate disciplinary proceedings. Eventually it was necessary to effect a lateral transfer of the staff member to a position of lesser importance in another building – away from the focus of power. This helped greatly to get on with the tasks at hand without irritating distractions.

I had taken the decision to stay on in the service – not just to survive and mark time until my retirement but to complete what I was brought in to do. It was a portentous decision not to accompany my family when they migrated to Australia in 1983 and this cost me dearly.

At the Ministry level, there was a need from time to time to adjust to new Ministers appointed with Cabinet reshuffles. There were five different individuals who served for varying periods as Minister of Culture, with changes and portfolio additions to the Ministry.

Anuar Ibrahim was easily the most charismatic and outstanding Minister of Culture I had the honour of working under, who gave me his fullest support. I remember mooting the idea of setting up the National Centre for Malay Manuscripts at the National Library and obtaining the Minister's endorsement to enable the Department to proceed further and turn the idea into reality.

This included a Ministerial directive for small collections of Malay manuscripts in other institutions within the ministerial purview to be transferred to the National Library. The Department even purchased a rare Malay manuscript at an auction in Sotheby's in London. The preparation of a Cabinet Paper for the setting up of the

National Centre for Malay Manuscripts at the National Library followed by Cabinet endorsement soon after led to staffing and funding support to facilitate the development of a research centre for Malay manuscripts at the National Library.

Unfortunately, with successive Cabinet reshuffles, other individuals were appointed as Ministers of Culture who seemed to be more comfortable with the portfolio areas of culture, youth and sport and paid somewhat superficial attention to the library sector. This bias is understandable as the culture, youth and sports sector offered the potential of voter support whereas 'libraries' represented a somewhat strange animal – a nice environment where school children could do their homework! It was an uphill task indeed to change these perceptions.

A few years later, Anuar Ibrahim (who had since become Minister of Education) had called for a meeting of the Vice-Chancellors (VCs) of the various universities to consider the question of mainframe computer support for the university libraries. The Minister however also directed that the Director General of the National Library (myself) should also be invited to attend the meeting.

I dutifully attended the meeting and sat unobtrusive at the far end of the table set up for the meeting. The Minister finally arrived, nodded to those assembled and took his place at the opposite end of the table. Before the meeting commenced, the Minister, to my complete surprise, addressed me directly across the table and said "Dr. Wijasuriya, have you read the book 'Information and the Muslim World' by Ziauddin Sardar". I confessed that I had

With Anwar Ibrahim, Minister of Culture.

not. The Minister then said "You should, for you have been quoted in it several times". He then walked across the room, handed me a copy of the book in which he had written in his own distinctive handwriting 'Dr Wijisuriya, ikhlas dari Anuar Ibrahim' and signed it in my presence. Thirty years later, the book has pride of place on the bookshelves in my private study.

Apart from the Ministers, there were also new Secretary Generals transferred from within the Public Service to head the Ministry. It was like having the same fiddle but having to play a different tune every time – it could become quite tedious at times but I had no problem with any of them.

I recall as Director General, presenting to the then Minister of Culture (who was the previous Prime Minister) draft revisions to the National Library Act for submission to Cabinet and Parliament. It was a high level meeting held at the Ministry and the legal boys from the Attorney General's Chambers were well represented – all in readiness to poke major holes in the draft legislation. The Minister listened carefully to my presentation and at the end of it he just said two words: 'very clear'. These words virtually set the stage for the onward progression of the draft legislation – the revised Act was passed by Parliament in 1988 and has remained on the Statute Books ever since.

In Malaysia, the Federal Cabinet met every Wednesday morning and the Prime Minister at that time, Dr. Mahathir Mohammad initiated the practice of requiring all his Cabinet Ministers to hold post cabinet meetings with the Ministry Secretary General and all Director Generals falling within the Ministerial portfolio in order to apprise all of them of important matters that may have been discussed at Cabinet.

One minister in particular virtually bored us to death by reading long-winded cabinet papers that were of little interest to most of us. In fact, it was so boring that the Director General of the National Museum fell fast asleep at one of these meetings and was even snoring quite loudly – we had to kick his legs under the table to wake him up!

There were also other key agencies of Government to deal with in order to push through major developments. These included not only the Office of the Prime Minister but also other agencies within its ambit, namely the EPU (Economic Planning Unit) and Mampu (Malaysian Administrative Modernisation and Management Planning Unit).

This was the height of the economic recession and many key projects had been frozen. Particularly important were funding for the National Library building and the mainframe computer for the National Library. I decided to make representation on these projects to the EPU myself and not entrust the task to any of my officers.

Major funding for the new National Library building was one thing but it was familiar territory for EPU officers as they had dealt with issues such as this before, but major funding for a mainframe computer system however and in a Library no less was unheard of. In those days large computers were only installed in agencies with large number crunching needs, such as the Statistics Department or Income Tax. As it turned out, it became necessary to accept some cost cutting but funding was finally approved for both projects.

But there was still one more major hurdle to go through and that was Mampu approval for the mainframe computer system itself, without which we could not go ahead. A proposal for the computer system had been submitted somewhat hastily to Mampu and a date was set for its consideration. The day before the scheduled meeting, National Library officers were in a panic as the assistant Director scheduled to make the presentation was taken ill. They suggested that the Mampu meeting be postponed but I disagreed. It was difficult enough getting Mampu to set a date to consider the National Library's mainframe computer proposal. If the Department lost its allocated slot, there was no telling when a new date could be fixed.

Having decided to represent the Department in person, I called for the proposal paper which had been submitted to Mampu and was horrified when I read through it – it was weak, poorly presented and unconvincing. Mampu officers who had read the department's proposal earlier had predicted that the proposal would be totally rejected.

At the Mampu meeting subsequently, I was accompanied by several of the National Library's Divisional Heads. I apologised for the Department's proposal paper which had been prepared and submitted somewhat hastily and asked for it to be set aside. I then made the presentation off the cuff as I had been involved in the preparation and approval of the system specifications and had an overall grasp of what we were aiming to achieve.

There were some queries on specific aspects of the Department's proposal. I readily conceded on features which were desirable but not critical. and contrary to predictions by Mampu officers, the entire proposal was approved. Senior officers of the National Library who were with me at the meeting congratulated me for pulling it off.

Several years earlier, based on the architectural brief I had prepared, the principal architect and design team had conceptualised the building and had completed all the physical planning including the internal layout. The piling work had also been completed, the construction of the building had commenced and several floors were already up.

The revisions to the National Library Act and the new Deposit of Library Materials Act had been passed by Parliament. The mainframe computerised system had also been set up. At the State level, all States in Peninsula Malaysia except the State of Johore had passed the necessary legislation for the setting up of State Public Library Corporations and public library services were slowly developing in the country.

The year before I retired, the National Policy for Library and Information Services was approved by the Federal Cabinet. I had chaired the Policy Drafting Committee under the purview of the Ministry, with senior representatives from sectoral interest areas including the Universities and facilitated the onward transmission of the final policy document to the Ministry and to the Federal Cabinet.

I felt that I had not only completed what I had been brought in to do, but had put far more into place. It was time for others to put their shoulders to the wheel. I was confident they could do the job. I was well and truly done.

The many key developments initiated or put in place during my tenure in office or on my 'watch' as the saying goes have been well documented. Within the ambit of my authority, I called it as I saw it and treated all fairly, discounting colour, creed and gender.

In Malaysia, Public Service personnel are required to take mandatory retirement on reaching the age of 55. Although overtures were made by the Secretary General, Ministry of Culture for my reemployment on a contract basis after retirement in order to see through the completion of the new building for the National Library of Malaysia, I formally declined in writing to do so and assured him that there were capable officers on the staff who could take over. I felt I had been away from the family long enough.

Official farewells

Continuing the chronological thread, the farewell party organised by the Department on my retirement in November 1989 was unprecedented. It was organised with all the traditional trappings with drummers and dancers and held at the Harlequin Ballroom of the Merlin Hotel (one of the leading hotels in Kuala Lumpur). There was a fair turn-out of staff not only from the National Library of Malaysia but also from the various library and information components of Federal Ministries and Departments.

During the Farewell Programme, refreshments, savoury preparations as well as kueh Melayu (Malay cakes) were served while a concert was put on by staff members, which included chorus singing, traditional dances and drummers – all to honour their retiring Director General. I was also presented with commemorative presents from the Department including my framed portrait painted by a local artist. I was touched. It was a clear recognition by all and sundry of the contribution I had made. I was told years later that it was an honour accorded to no other Director General of the National Library, before or since.

At the farewell reception for the Director General

Earlier that month, the President, Persatuan Perpustakaan Malaysia (PPM) (Malaysian Library Association) organised a Farewell Tea Party in my honour, acknowledging my three terms as its President and my many years of continuing service on the Council as well as Chair of various committees. Ch'ng Kim See, Head of the Library at ISIS (Institute of Southeast Asian Studies) – a former colleague and friend, flew down from Singapore to deliver the commendation address. It was a fun filled, light hearted and unforgettable evening.

Later that month, a farewell dinner party was hosted by the Secretary General, Ministry of Culture in my honour and a commemorative plaque was presented to me as well as a letter of commendation for my services to the nation. The letter of commendation (Surat Penghargaan) signed by the Director General, Malaysian Public Services, has been framed and has taken pride of place in my private study alongside other academic and professional awards and decorations both at the national and international level. It helps me remember that I may have left a discernable footprint after all.

The future

Since my retirement in 1989, there have been over eight Director Generals of the National Library of Malaysia – seven were women and two were men – all of whom reflect the ethnic bias, not only within the National Library itself, but within the entire Public Service. The National Library can do little to correct the situation as it is not a recruiting agency. The answers lie elsewhere at the upper echelons of the Public Service and finally at policy levels of Governmant. Malaysia cannot afford the brain drain to continue. Talented Malaysians have been leaving the country for greener pastures abroad since the 1970s.

For the key position of Director General of the National Library of Malaysia – a position provided for in Federal Legislation, it is indeed short sighted to keep appointing professionals from within the service if they lacked the leadership, vision and drive not only to move the institution forward but more importantly to effectively manage change in a rapidly changing society.

For the National Library to stay relevant, effective leadership is a critical ingredient. The human resources of the nation's institutions need to be tapped, not necessarily the resources of the National Library alone. It may even be necessary at times to recruit individuals from the international arena to serve on contract and inject fresh blood into the system.

The gender imbalance at professional and sub-professional level also needs to be corrected. This is a complex problem. While recruiting agencies have a crucial role to play in this regard, perceptions of the profession within the broader community tend to make the men shy away to more lucrative and higher profile areas of work.

The National Library revisited

I visited the National Library of Malaysia in August 2011 – nearly 22 years after my retirement. I had stayed away the previous two decades to enable the 'succession' to find their feet and chart the institution's onward progression. Three staff members in full suits (in the tropical heat) – one of whom was my close associate nearly two decades earlier, were waiting at the steps of the main entrance to greet their former Director General.

It was a moving tribute and was followed by receptions, speeches and gifts to commemorate my visit. Karen who accompanied me on my visit was treated as a visiting dignitary and presented with a gift in crafted pewter.

There was even a suggestion by the incumbent Director General, Dato Raslin Abu Bakar that I might consider coming back for a short-term consultancy to assist the institution in its ongoing developments. While I would have welcomed the opportunity to assist the institution in its further development, prudence dictated that I stay away – my experience of the past had not been forgotten.

Following the visit, an official car was placed at our disposal and we were taken on a tour of the opulent facilities of the Government's new centre of administration at Putrajaya. It was most impressive.

Malaysia is a good country. It was the country of my birth and I served it faithfully. My grandfather came to the Malay States in 1890 in his youth while I left Malaysia in 1990 on my retirement. Members of the family have served in various capacities in the public sector over a period of 100 years.

It is indeed the end of an era for my own family in the Malay States.

Family Doings

Culinary tradition

Outside the workplace, I was glad that I was able to be around for my mother. She was still very independent and did all the cooking. She had a gardener named Arumugam who also undertook small errands for my mother. I did most of the grocery shopping or marketing – especially the purchase of fish or meat as well as vegetables and fruit. Mum was an excellent cook. I watched her sometimes and learned a great deal simply by watching.

My mother at 79 in her own kitchen

My own culinary skills were honed over many years as I did most of the cooking when the boys were growing up. When the boys were much younger, we had live-in house maids who did most of the cooking and cleaning. Once we began to seriously consider the prospect of migrating, we gradually discontinued all domestic help and began doing things for ourselves – this applied to all of us.

Looking back, I must acknowledge that when I first got married, I could hardly cook anything – Annette did all the cooking and learned her skills in her mother's kitchen. Annette's mother was an excellent cook too but she was a very critical and a hard taskmaster. Annette used to tell me that she could do nothing right in her mother's kitchen. But she learned a great deal and I learned a lot from Annette.

When we lived in London, we had a rule that whoever got home first cooked and so began my early lessons in the culinary arts. Once the kids came along and we stopped having maids, I prepared most of the meals while Annette did the special dishes, especially for Christmas family gatherings. Kiribath (rice cooked in coconut milk) was a traditional breakfast at Christmas or the New Year and was eaten with pol sambal (coconut sambal), kiri hodi (grated coconut squeezed and cooked with a dash of turmeric), sugar or jaggery.

In Malaysia freshly grated coconut was readily available – this was so in Sri Lanka too, but in Australia, one had to settle for grated coconut in packets or blocks of coconut cream. A more convenient alternative is canned coconut milk. Annette was also quite successful in her preparation of seeni sambol – small shallots cooked with maldive fish chips (umbalakata), spices and drizzled with a sprinkling of sugar.

We never tried preparing 'hoppers' or 'string hoppers' (putumayam) as it took up too much time. We had our fill of these whenever we visited Sri Lanka on holiday. At grandma's house in Kossinna, in days gone by, string hoppers or 'iddi appe' as well as hoppers or 'appe' including 'biththara appe' or egg hoppers were often made, simply because the tedious work involved was done by the 'kussi ammah' or cook woman. We sometimes had 'pittu,' which was a granular rice flour and coconut mixture steamed in a bamboo cylinder and was usually eaten with kiri hodhi. It could also be eaten with a sprinkling of 'jaggery' or coconut sugar in brown coloured 'cakes'.

When I consider the culinary skills of many of my relatives, I remember especially my own mother who would have brought to the Malay States a wealth of experience in cooking Sri Lankan style meals. But she was not unique in this respect. Both Annette and her mother were excellent cooks too as were my own sisters as well as my aunts on both my father's and mother's side. It seems that most Sinhalese women were taught early in life how to cook but this tradition does not seem to have been continued in successive generations.

It is not usual for Sinhalese or Sri Lankan men to have culinary skills, but I was an exception and so were two of my brothers. Uncle John too was an excellent cook. Two of my sons are fairly good cooks and so is my nephew Arjuna.

I still rarely use cook books and neither did my mother. It is more convenient to use pre-blended spices in packets for cooking fish, seafood or meat dishes. But in my mother's kitchen, spices were ground separately and then blended at the cook's discretion for a specific dish or culinary creation.

Christmas celebrations

When the boys were growing up in our Section 17 home in Petaling Jaya, Christmas time was always a time of special celebration. Quite apart from the celebration of the birth of the Christ child and the attendance at Church services, there were also the joys and excitement of putting up the Christmas tree as well as Christmas lights and decorations. Shopping for new pyjamas for the boys as well as the buying of presents for one another as well as for our parents and other members of the family gave us much joy.

Annette usually started getting into gear months in advance. Getting ready for baking the Christmas cake took a lot of time and effort. Annette enjoyed doing all this. I helped a little – mostly in wrapping the Christmas cake in colourful cellophane paper.

Making dodol

Making 'dodol' was another 'must' at Christmas time. My role was mostly in stirring the 'thachuva' (large metal pan with a curved base) on an 'anglow' (open fire) – usually set up outdoors. Several squeezes of freshly grated coconut – separated into several containers, categorised as first milk and second milk were first prepared. This concoction was then continuously stirred over a strong fire into which dissolved jaggery or 'hakuru' was added. The end result was 'dodol' a dark brown coloured pudding or cake which was cut up into square or rectangular pieces. We all loved eating dodol.

Preparing 'seeni sambal' and sometimes 'acharu' took a lot of time as well. Those of us who were around assisted in one way or another, Annette was the expert. I have never attempted to do any of this myself – this was outside my culinary repertoire. On one occasion, when grinding the fresh chillies for the seeni sambal, Annette failed to put on a pair of gloves resulting in a severe burning sensation on all her fingers, so much so that she had to keep her hands submerged in cold water for several hours after completing the grinding in order to alleviate the severe burning sensation. She never made that mistake again.

Christmas eve dinner was very special and only for our little family – Annette and the boys. Christmas dinner for family and friends at our home on Boxing Day – both in Malaysia and in Australia was always well attended and became almost a fixture on the family calendar. Christmas day lunch and dinner was usually spent at the home of my parents or Annette's parents – while we were still in Malaysia. All of this came to an end when Annette and the boys migrated to Australia in 1983. We continued with the Christmas tradition for family and friends in Australia too until Annette had her stroke in 2004.

Life without the family

When the family migrated to Australia in 1983, I missed having the family around. I missed going on holidays with them; the trips we took together; playing tennis and going to the cinema. It was a very difficult period in our lives. There were many things significant and momentous going on but I could hardly discuss any of it with my mother. I could not fall back on Annette either – she was no longer there and some issues were simply not suited for discussion over the phone.

There were some highlights for my mother during this period. Mum's sister Sally (she was Aunty Sally to us) came down for a visit and stayed a few weeks with my mother. Aunty Sally's youngest daughter Noeline lived in Singapore with her husband Kingsley and family and so her visit to Kuala Lumpur was organised from Singapore.

Both sisters spent many pleasant times catching up. It would have been a golden opportunity for me to tap their collective minds. Alas I was far too preoccupied and tied up with official matters and so that golden opportunity was lost forever.

It was good to hear conversations between the two sisters – jabber, jabber, jabber – in a mixture of English and Sinhalese.

In the mid eighties, Mum and I discussed the possibility of organizing a visit of her youngest sister (Sister Mary Clementa) to Malaysia, which required special permission from the Head of the Religious Order as this was Sister Clementa's very first and only visit abroad. Permission was finally granted on the condition that Sister Clementa was accompanied by a responsible member of the family. Fortunately, my first cousin Sybil was able to accompany Sister Clementa on the visit to Malaysia. Mum paid the air fares for both of them. It was a very pleasant get together for both sisters as they had not met since our family visit to Sri Lanka in 1950.

In the late eighties, Mum's step sister Gladys and son Ranjith came over for a visit. It was good to catch up with them and share memories of pleasant times long gone – in Grandma's house in Kossinna as well as their own home in Gampola. Clarence and I used to visit them there after Mass on Sunday. Ranjith was then just a little boy and had a little sister called Ranjini. Later two other siblings were added to the family – Chrisantha and Darius – they were my first cousins.

This brings to mind my visit to Sri Lanka in 1985 to attend an International Conference at the Bandaranayake International Conference Centre in Colombo. Conference delegates stayed at the Oberoi, Colombo. It so happened that my cousin Darius who worked at the same hotel saw my name on the guest list. Darius introduced himself and told me that he was my cousin. It was great catching up with his mother and family who subsequently joined me for dinner at the hotel.

Picking up the threads of the story once again, over the next five or so years, I flew down to Perth a few times a year, spending a week or two on each visit. This was not a very satisfactory arrangement but it was the best I could do.

Balancing the needs of the family in Australia; making sure my mother was OK while I was away and coping with the demands of the work environment proved tricky and difficult but I coped well enough and stayed on an even keel. From time to time I tried to fit in brief visits to Sydney too to keep in touch with Rohan and Rienzi. Renan was still in school then and so I saw him every time I came to Perth.

Catholic heritage

My background has always been very Catholic. I grew up in a Catholic home; I went to a Catholic boarding school and so being Catholic was part of my inner being. When I got married in the Methodist Church, that delicate thread got somewhat frayed but never disappeared. In our early years of marriage, I went along with Annette whenever she attended one of the churches in London.

When the boys came along, we attended services at the Methodist Church in Petaling Jaya while the boys attended Sunday School. The boys were baptised there. I was still very Catholic but did not want to pull the boys in a different direction. Their mother was an excellent role model and I relied on her firm guiding hand as our boys were growing up.

After the family migrated, I began going back to the Catholic Church once again, initially to take my mother for Sunday mass but latterly I realised that I had in a way returned to my roots. This never left me again and I tried to fit it in with my life back in Australia – but it was still a tightrope of sorts.

Our little family on the pier at Port Klang

I still have misgivings about some of the beliefs and practises in the Church – but I was not prepared 'to throw out the baby with the bath water'. There was much in the Church that was good and wholesome and I found no alternative religious persuasion that appealed to me.

Home ownership headaches

When the boys were growing up, we tried to inculcate in them a sense of frugality. Whatever they were given in pocket money was rather modest when compared to what their school mates were given. Their mother was in charge and she was quite strict.

With Annette and the boys, half a lifetime ago

We both recognised early on that our boys would have to strive on an uneven playing field. Whatever surplus funds we were able to save we invested in property. Our thinking was that we should try to own at least three properties which we could leave to our sons – to ensure that at the very least, they would have a roof over their heads.

Our family home or bungalow was built (on freehold land or land held in perpetuity) in Section 17 in Petaling Jaya – the boys virtually grew up in it. Apart from the master bed room and attached bath room, each of our boys had their own rooms. There was a lounge room, a separate dining room and a carpeted study we all used which also served as the TV room. There were two other bathrooms for the use of the boys as well as guests while the maid had her own room and bathroom.

There were other unique features to the house too which were put in by us and were not part of the original architectural plans. This included a feature wall of broken Italian marble in the main lounge, yellow ceramic bathroom fittings, wood floors in herringbone design in the lounge room and quality kitchen fittings.

One irritating feature of the house however was a poorly designed carport which collected water in the flat roof enclosure and leaked through, leaving chalk deposits on the car. The roof of the house was also poorly designed with a roof gradient which was quite inadequate to cope with the heavy rainfall. It was a real nuisance to keep placing buckets at various points in the house to collect water dripping from the ceiling.

Despite these irritations, it was still home and a focus for family gatherings. Poker sessions were held from time to time for the adults and Annette's parents joined in on occasion. Darts were also played in the study as was carrom. From time to time, we also played badminton on the front lawn and table tennis in the carport. Periodically, the boys and I got together to mow the lawns and trim the bushes. Many family gatherings and dinner parties were held at the family home.

Our next property investment was a two storey terrace house in Damansara Utama with an unusual sunken bathtub upstairs. This property was rented out to Indian tenants – a brother and sister who shared the house. They were lovely people.

When the family migrated to Australia in March 1983, I was unable to sell the family home as the real estate market was depressed and I had to rent it out for a few years. This proved to be a real headache as some of our tenants were rather demanding. I had German, Japanese and Malay tenants at various stages in the family home. There was much work to be done in each property – especially in repairs, recarpeting and repainting – prior to placing them on the market.

Our last property investment in Kajang was a bit of a disaster. The terrace house was badly designed and rather cramped but it was low cost housing and for that reason alone, it offered the prospect of easy rentals. Irene readily joined up as co-owner of the property and shared in the financial investment required.

Unfortunately, continuing problems with the developer caused us to opt out of the project and put it up for sale. This proved to be quite problematic as there were a number of caveats on the property that I was not informed of at the time of purchase. Consequently, the property could not be sold without approval from the relevant authority. This took many years and was eventually sold well below the original purchase price.

While I was able to write off the loss as a bad investment, I greatly regretted that I had got my sister involved in a most unprofitable investment. The final sale price was so low that it was only possible to reimburse her with only a fraction of her original investment. This weighed very heavily on me and I tried to make up for her loss by making financial contributions to her from time to time in the years following.

New Horizons

Our Australian family home

The planning of our new home in Australia had to be left entirely to Annette. She was very capable and managed everything very well without troubling me much. Annette would have faced many difficulties herself but I fear I may have inadvertently allowed her to carry too heavy a load. But all that is now history. We all make decisions and choices in life – some not the best.

When Annette and I first made up our minds about migrating to Australia, we each came on separate visits to get a feel for the country. Australia seemed like a nice place and we felt that the family could fit in nicely. We have not been disappointed. Every member of the family has travelled very widely but for all of us, Australia is truly our home. Malaysia is still a favoured travel destination but none of us retain any sense of allegiance to the old country. Despite the many years I spent in Sri Lanka, I have no special allegiance for Sri Lanka either.

While Annette and the boys were granted Permanent Residence when they first migrated to Australia in 1983, each took up Australian Citizenship at different times – Annette became an Australian Citizen in 1987 and the boys took up Citizenship before 1990. I was the very last as I only came over in 1990 as Permanent Resident and did not take up Australian Citizenship until 1999 – after my mother died.

Initially the family stayed in rented accommodation in Rockingham while our house was being built. They rented first in Andromeda Street and later in Kent Street in Rockingham. The choice of Rockingham as a suburb to build our home and put down roots was obviously influenced by the fact that Annette's brother lived and worked there. In hindsight, we could have done so much better by picking a choice river front block in a suburb closer to the city centre.

Our first building block which we purchased in Shallow Close, Safety Bay was later sold because of difficulties with the Council. Annette then purchased a larger block in Cooloongup and we built our home on this site. Annette reckoned that this was to be our very last home – and for her it was.

Annette put in a great deal of time and effort in planning and building the family home, working closely with Brian Stanley, an architectural draftsman who faithfully reflected Annette's ideas in the architectural plans. With four bedrooms, a study, a games room, a family room, a sunken lounge, a dining room, kitchen and laundry – it was a fairly large home. The high roofs, timber rendered ceilings, exposed rafters, feature slate walls and use of quality brickwork gave the house a distinct elegance. Added to this was a two car garage with roller doors, a front and rear lawn, a covered rear patio as well as a below ground pool. It was indeed a high maintenance property and remained the family home for over thirty years.

School and university

The boys enrolled in Rockingham Senior High and later went on to university – Rohan to the University of New South Wales, Rienzi to the University of Technology in Sydney while Renan went to the University of Western Australia. The boys all chose engineering studies and graduated with Bachelor of Engineering degrees; Rohan in Aerospace Engineering, Rienzi in Computer Systems Engineering and Renan in Resource Engineering.

When Rohan sat for the TAE (Tertiary Admissions Exam) at Rockingham Senior High, he obtained the second highest score at the school and qualified for entry to the University of Western Australia (UWA), the University of New South Wales (UNSW) and the Royal Melbourne Institute of Technology (RMIT). He chose engineering studies at UNSW and left for Sydney shortly after, residing initially at Warrane College and then at International House.

Rienzi left home the year after – he was barely 20 years old. Rienzi's departure had nothing to do with tertiary studies. Rienzi always wanted to be his own person and to be completely independent. He showed signs of this even earlier in life when he wanted to join the Royal Military College (RMC) in Port Dickson. Both Annette and I were somewhat relieved that this did not eventuate. When he eventually left for Sydney in 1985 on his battered old motor cycle, sleeping in a very basic tent as he crossed the Nullabor and managing with some very basic meals along the way, Annette and I were more than anxious. But he made it and survived for many years entirely on his own, working in a bakery and in other jobs before joining Telecoms where his expertise with Ericssons telecommunication systems took him on contract to many countries. Not surprisingly, Rienzi 'retired' in his early fifties and travels abroad very often. Along the way, Rienzi obtained an engineering degree at the University of Technology in Sydney – but I suspect that this was mostly to please his mother. His degree did little to advance his career.

Despite shaky beginnings, Renan's academic and scholastic achievements, following his return to university, were the most impressive. He is the only one in his own generation as well as the previous generation, not only to take a First Class Honours degree in Engineering but also to receive scholarship awards from the private sector which carried job guarantees even before he completed his Degree.

The boys have since gone on to other post graduate qualifications in Business Administration and in Oil and Gas and have carved out careers for themselves which have taken them to different parts of the world. I am proud of all of them and so was their mother – who has since passed away.

Like most migrants, our boys faced some initial irritations from a few of the local yokels, but their excellent grounding in English and maths soon saw them through. Their school years in Rockingham coincided with the years I continued to work in Malaysia so I knew little of the difficulties they may have faced. I am confident that Annette would have helped them over the rough spots if any. Rohan and Rienzi left home for the Eastern States within a year or two after their arrival in Australia. Renan stayed at home with Annette until he moved out to his own home in his mid-twenties.

Annette's work life down under

Annette herself faced many challenges and applied for many jobs shortly after her arrival but without success. She managed to get some media work, in script writing and in theatre and stage production. She was employed by the Audiovisual Education Branch of the Education Department, Western Australia as a freelance script writer and produced a few educational television programmes. She also wrote plays for public performances for the Western Australian Theatre Company and for the Australian Bicentennial Authority as part of the programme of activities for the Bicentenary in 1988, which were designed to reflect multicultural Australia.

In 1984, Annette got a job in Rockingham at Chesterfield House – which was a home for wayward kids. Annette worked there as cook and cleaner and did two shifts a day. On the weekends, Annette taught Sunday School at the Baptist Church in Rockingham. Her talents as a school teacher were soon recognised and she was invited to take up a teaching position at the newly established Maranatha Community College. In a very special way, Annette had come home – doing what she loved best – teaching and moulding young minds. Annette taught maths and science at upper secondary level for nearly ten years and also served briefly as Principal.

In 1987, during term break at Maranatha College, Annette was able to realise a long cherished dream to visit the Holy Land and to traverse the paths that Jesus walked during his brief ministry on this earth. She was able to travel to the Holy Land on her Australian Passport. I was unable to join

Annette

her as I was still a Malaysian Citizen and Malaysian Passport holders had a travel ban to Israel and a few other countries stamped on their passports. I did however meet up with her in Singapore on her return journey to Perth.

Annette retired in 1994, bringing to a close a teaching career that had spanned nearly 40 years – in Malaysia and Australia. But even after her retirement, she continued to teach Christian education in selected schools in Rockingham but on a strictly voluntary basis. She also tutored a few students. Teaching was in her blood and brought her a sense of fulfilment. Annette always was a very dedicated teacher. She also was one of the most popular teachers in the school. Her students kept coming back to see her long after leaving school.

It is most surprising that when she retired – she was relatively young at 61 – she did not decide to do a degree at one of the local universities. She would have been readily admitted and no doubt done very well. It is something she felt deprived of in her youth and I still feel twinges of regret that I failed to encourage her enough. I left her to make up her own mind as to what she intended to do when there should have been more discussion and communication. I fear that our physical separation over the years had forced each of us into separate grooves where we faced our challenges and made our choices entirely on our own.

Special mention needs to be made about Annette's deteriorating eyesight – a problem that she had to cope with from her early twenties. It is a drama she fought silently and seemed never ending. Annette is seen wearing glasses in most of the photographs in the family album.

Although Annette and I were in correspondence during my undergraduate days in Ceylon, she never burdened me with her eyesight problems. I have touched on Annette's eyesight problems in earlier sections of this narrative – and the corrective measures taken over the years in London, which improved her eyesight and enabled her to continue teaching. Teaching was her passion and her calling – and she was good at it.

But very few realised that Annette was functioning on one eye only. She never let that restrict her movements or her mobility. She just kept on going. She also continued driving her car and compensated for her limited vision by avoiding driving at night, preplanning her route and identifying specific landmarks on it – which always took her to her destination and brought her home safely. Looking at Annette close-up, she looked normal enough and no one could tell that she was blind in one eye.

Alas, by the turn of the century, her sight in her 'good' eye was beginning to fade as well. Dr. Morlet who was her eye specialist decided to operate on her 'blind' eye and perform a corneal graft operation. This was however dependent on a 'donor' cornea becoming available. Annette resigned herself for a long wait. Quite unexpectedly, a 'donor' became available. Annette was informed and arrangements were made for Annette to undergo a second corneal graft operation, but this time in Australia. Dr. Morlet performed the operation successfully and for the very first time in her life and at the age of 72, it seemed that Annette would have sight in both eyes.

But Annette was not out of the woods yet. She still did not have sight in the operated eye as the lens had been removed and she had to wait for nearly a year for the removal of stitches and for the insertion of a plastic lens. It is probable that all of this preyed on her mind, so much so that she suffered a TIA (transient ischemic attack) the year after, followed by a major stroke. When I did take Annette for the removal of stitches and the insertion of the plastic lens, she was in a wheel-chair and partly handicapped – but she was determined to go through with the procedure.

Finally, in the last two years of her life, Annette had sight in both eyes. I hope our boys have been infused with some of their mother's traits, particularly her determination and her tenacity.

Post retirement blues

Knowing that I would have to retire in November 1989, I gave some thought to what I would do after retirement. Considering that I had devoted the greater part of my career to working in libraries – something I drifted into, rather than by choice – firstly within academia and then within the public sector, I was keen to meet new challenges.

This was indeed a tall order and was made doubly complicated by the fact that I was attempting to do this not on home territory where I was known but in a new country to which I was migrating. Unfortunately, the prospect of working in libraries in Australia did not interest me at all. I could see that having worked in the library world in Malaysia at the highest executive level and in a national institution set up by Federal legislation, it would indeed be difficult to find any equivalence abroad.

I knew also that I would find it difficult to fit in at a subordinate level in libraries. In any case, top level appointments in libraries were few and far between and I doubted very much that I would be prepared for the level of commitment required – so I stayed away from libraries completely. I was happy to simply be a user of libraries.

Prior to my retirement in November 1989, I called on the Chief Secretary to the Government to pay my respects, to thank him for his cooperation and support and to wish him farewell as I would be leaving the Public Service shortly. He enquired then as to what my plans were after retirement and asked if he could help in any way to set me up in some organisation within the purview of the Government.

I realised that this could be a further 3-4 year commitment within the Public Sector. While this would have ensured that I was gainfully employed for a few more years, it would most likely have been in areas of little interest to me personally or professionally – my expertise and long experience in the library and information sector in the country would have gone to waste.

I told the Chief Secretary that I had planned to take up a teaching appointment abroad and thanked him for his interest and concern. This is the route I eventually embarked on – but I only accepted short-term commitments, in order not to be away from my family for too long.

Many of my colleagues, both within the country and abroad, expected me to continue my professional interests and commitment at the international level. This is something I would have welcomed, but I realised it would have meant longer term commitments abroad – most likely in UNESCO (UN Education Science and Cultural Organisation) in Paris. I did not want Annette to give up her teaching career in Australia to be with me, wherever abroad I ended up.

Private Sector interests in Malaysia wanted me to spearhead the expansion of their business interests in Singapore. Various inducements were thrown my way but I declined their offer as it would keep me away from my family in Australia. Besides, the business and commercial world had never held any interest for me.

I had time on my hands but so little to do. Retirement in Australia for me was for many years quite frustrating. Part of the reason for this was self-imposed constraints I had placed on myself.

Consultancy work

Having painted myself into a corner in deductive terms, I thought that I should take a stab into consultancy work in Third World countries where the need was greatest and where my own Third World experience could be meaningfully brought to bear. I set up the mechanics accordingly and drew together three other well known consultants from the USA, India and Singapore, working in tandem, to address Third World issues.

But we only had limited success. While the need was there and while we had the collective experience to draw from, Third World countries were rather poor paymasters and depended greatly on international aid agencies (for funding support) – who themselves had their own established panels of consultants from the Developed World.

Nevertheless, a few consultancy missions were undertaken in the Asia-Pacific region on behalf of international aid agencies.

The cloisters of academia

My choices were limited indeed. I eventually accepted short term stints in academia both within the country and abroad. Most significant of these was my appointment in the early nineties as Rufus Putnam Professor at the Centre for International Studies at Ohio University, United States of America. This was a most interesting and rewarding experience. Ohio University wanted me to take up a longer term teaching stint at the Centre for International Studies. But I did not pursue this as Annette was still teaching at

Maranatha and I knew she would not want to give this up to be with me in America.

There were other teaching opportunities too – at the University of Addis Ababa, following immediately after my stint at Ohio University. This involved another two year stint at Addis Ababa which was quite out of the question. I realised that I had already spent nearly 8 years away from my family when they first migrated to Australia and the prospect of spending even more years in my retirement away from them seemed quite unwise.

The boys were all grown up and had long flown the coop. I am sure that my continued absence would not have impacted negatively on them. But I simply could not leave Annette alone any longer. I realised that I simply had to come back home and learn to get used to a life style seemingly lacking in mental stimuli and sense of purpose.

In the mid-nineties I served a four year stint as Adjunct Professor (Research) at the Department of Library and Information Studies at Curtin University. This was my second stint at Curtin but it was not a teaching role and only involved the supervision of research students. I did not find this stint at Curtin University challenging or rewarding at all and was glad when it was over. During this period, I also conducted a short term course in research methodology at the University of Papua New Guinea and served briefly as External Examiner for Masters Degree students at the University of Malaya and Monash University.

International commitments

Apart from short-term consultancy missions I touched on earlier, I also continued to serve on the Professional Board of IFLA (International Federation of Library Associations and Institutions) and served as Special Advisor for Asia and Oceania for many years. At the regional level in South East Asia, I had earlier served as Chairman, CONSAL V (Congress of South East Asian Librarians). For some years after retirement, I continued to accept invitations to present working papers at international conferences – in Budapest, Jakarta and Fiji – the very last being in Japan and in Papua New Guinea in 1997 and 1998.

Commemorative publication

As we approached the end of the century, I thought it might be appropriate to bring out a collection of my published works. Since the mid-sixties I had written and published extensively – and I thought it would be appropriate if a select collection of my papers could be produced. It was a tedious task to begin with. I had nearly a hundred published papers over the years and needed not only to track them down but to re-read them and make a judicious selection.

Annette gave me her enthusiastic support and even agreed to take on the exacting task of keying-in the entire work onto the computer in a format ready for the printers. A limited edition was subsequently published by Bistari Mediabuku in 1999 with the title "The National Infrastructure for Libraries: selected papers" and distributed to friends – in particular to my first Boss and mentor, Wilfred Plumbe – who was ailing at that time in England. Despite his failing health and sight impediments, Wilfred had his son Anthony read selected passages from the book. Wilfred has since passed away.

Annette's participation was invaluable. I could not have asked for a higher level of professionalism, which coupled with her critical comments greatly helped in completing the work. The same work, with a slightly different content and titled "Contributions towards the Malaysian Library and Information Infrastructure: a historical perspective" was published by MPH Publishing in Kuala Lumpur in 2011. With the advent of the 21st century, I ceased all professional interest in the world of libraries.

Holidays together

When Annette retired in 1994, we had more time on our hands and we took the opportunity to travel abroad – to Bali, Langkawi, Kuala Lumpur, Sri Lanka and also to Uppsala in Sweden. We also took many long trips by car but mostly in Western Australia – with pleasant stays in comfortable self contained chalets in Denmark, Augusta, Albany, Esperance, Manjimup, Nannup, Pemberton, Bunbury, Busselton, Carnarvon and Broome.

Golf

Conscious of the need for regular exercise, I decided to take up golf and grew to enjoy the game. I became a member of the Rockingham Golf Club and began playing 2-3 times a week with a group of friends. I even took part in competitive golf within veteran circles and this kept me reasonably occupied. In the early stages I played alone and Annette walked the nine holes with me to encourage me.

Having a hit with the boys

I shall be 85 this year. I still enjoy my golf and play with my friend Peter Moxham each week.

Volunteering

I also undertook volunteer work for a brief spell providing transport help for the elderly to keep medical or hospital appointments. I used my own car for this purpose and transport costs were reimbursed.

Later, I signed up to assist in literacy and reading programmes. The latter programme involved a period of training. Clients with reading or learning difficulties were assisted on a one to one basis at a designated time slot at the Murdoch University Library in Rockingham. Annette gave me some invaluable help in fashioning suitable programmes for each student.

This was followed by a stint with the Samaritans, which was also preceded with a period of training. The Samaritans operated a call centre in Perth, mostly for clients who were lonely, distressed or who were suicidal. Volunteers manned the centre on four-hour shifts once a week as well as an overnight shift once a month. There were several volunteers manning the call centre at any one time. I discontinued further involvement with the Samaritans when Annette fell ill.

Painting

My interest in art, drawing and painting go back to my school days. I picked up the rudiments of water colour painting at art classes in High School Klang. My parents were very proud of my artistic creations, a few of which were framed and hung up. When the family home was sold after my mother died, most of the contents were given away. I must admit that while I had some artistic flair, painting was never a passion and my creative output has been disappointing – my paintings have been few and far between. My painting of the Last Supper in oils was done in London in 1961 and is now in Rohan's home in Malabar in Long Bay, Sydney. More recent landscape paintings in oils adorn my private study.

With more time on my hands, I am hopeful of increasing my creative output in painting – but in acrylic paints, a medium I am unfamiliar with. I have attended an introductory workshop in acrylic painting but I am yet to motivate myself to start painting in earnest.

Supporting aid programmes

During Annette's working life in Australia, she regularly tithed a sum from her wages to the Baptist Church in Rockingham and later to the Church of Christ. Annette also supported the Christian Blind Mission and a few other aid organisations. When Annette died, I decided to support some of the programmes myself.

I started with child sponsorship programmes under World Vision and contributed regularly to several other programmes including CBM Australia (for the visually handicapped), Royal Flying Doctor Service, Caritas, Silver Chain and Medicins Sans Frontieres. While I continue with this support and respond to emergency relief appeals from time to time, I do so in good faith and in the belief that the bulk of funds collected are expended on the designated programmes. Whatever the shortcomings of these agencies, I recognise that they are at least doing something concrete to alleviate the lives of the disadvantaged.

Passive support however does not involve any direct participation and from that perspective it is not very fulfilling. At one stage after Annette died, I did consider greater participation in these programmes by serving in the field. The fact that I did not may be providential. It could also be that I was getting along in age and was reluctant to move beyond my comfort zone.

Annette's own support and contribution to some of these programmes – especially for the visually handicapped predated my own involvement. And then quite suddenly, the leisurely pace of life for Annette and me changed completely when she suffered her first stroke.

Annette's illness

Annette had her first stroke in 2004. It was called a TIA – transient ischemic attack or a mini-stroke. I had just returned from my morning round of golf and found her on the carpet in her study. At first I thought she was resting after her exercise routine, which includes head-stands and some yoga routines but soon realised she was in trouble. I phoned Renan who came over immediately and we managed to get her to her bed. We called the ambulance and she was taken to the Rockingham Hospital where she was attended to immediately. Annette remained completely lucid throughout her ordeal and recovered fully by evening.

Although Annette recovered, she remained fatigued but continued with her usual activities. About eight months later she suffered a major stroke. Renan was fortunately still around. We called for the ambulance and Annette was taken to the Rockingham Hospital. When we left her that evening, she was quite normal.

However, when we visited her the next morning, we found her condition had changed dramatically. Her legs were wrapped in some kind of stretch –stockings. The previous evening she had complained of headaches which were treated with pain-killers. Early the next morning, Annette was scheduled for a brain scan and it was then discovered that she had extensive bleeding over the brain. She was already semi paralysed on her left side and there was a flurry of activity to have her transferred to Charles Gairdner Hospital for emergency surgery.

A Chinese neurosurgeon performed the operation and told us he had done all he could. We just had to wait. Annette remained in a coma for almost a week – we did not think that she would come out of it, but she did. All of us were there when she recovered consciousness. She could not speak however, with all the tubes attached to her nose, and mouth, not to mention the tubes in her wrist.

She nevertheless made us understand that she needed a laptop to communicate. We did so, but Annette was too weak to use it effectively. Later a tracheoscopy (incision in the throat to facilitate insertion of oxygen tubes) was performed to enable Annette to talk normally, which resulted in partial damage to her larynx. While Annette was able to speak very softly, it took a few years of voice therapy at the Peel Medical campus in Mandurah before Annette was able to speak normally again. I drove Annette down for all these sessions and we treated these visits to Mandurah as an outing.

We tried hydrotherapy too for Annette, which involved weekly visits to Perth. Annette was in a wheel-chair and her main carer, Christine accompanied us and helped Annette to get in and out of the little capsule where she received her treatment. Annette got little benefit from this treatment. Usually, after her weekly treatment sessions, we stopped by the riverside, off Mounts Bay Road for sandwiches and refreshments. This helped to restore a small measure of normalcy to her life.

A year or two later, I arranged for Annette to be treated by an acupuncture specialist in Rockingham – who had been trained at the feet of the Masters in China. This treatment benefitted Annette to some degree. Her left arm however remained paralysed and despite all her determined efforts, she was unable to regain its use. The acupuncture however did enable her to partially regain the use of her left leg. This gave her limited mobility and she was able to 'walk' with the aid of a quad stick – but only for short distances.

But Annette's loss of personal independence and abhorrence of having to depend on others was difficult for her to come to terms with. While Annette remained mentally as sharp as ever, I failed to realise that as the ailment dragged on, her personality attributes began to change too – she was no longer the generous and fair minded person she used to be and it became more and more stressful coping with Annette and looking after her. Annette really never came to terms with her condition. For Annette, partial recovery was not enough. She either recovered fully or not at all. Half measures at anything was simply not part of her psyche.

Following surgery at Charles Gairdner Hospital and a period in the ICU (Intensive Care Unit), Annette was transferred to Shenton Park Hospital for further treatment and rehabilitation. After a few weeks of treatment, the Doctors there determined that Annette's recovery had 'plateaued' and that she was unlikely to recover any further. Annette was then moved to a slow stream recovery facility at Bicton.

During this entire period, I drove down from Rockingham every morning and spent as much time as I could with Annette. This proved to be very exhausting. On one occasion when I visited Annette in Bicton, she was not in her usual room. Annette had been moved to a common room for some group physiotherapy. When I reached the room, I found Annette slumped in her wheelchair looking utterly despondent. I knew then that the best chance she had of recovery was for her to be cared for in her very own home.

So I brought her home and was her principal carer for the next four years of her life. Placing her in a nursing home would have been easier but was an option I was not prepared to consider. The carers at Silver Chain helped enormously. I could not have managed without them. In particular I must mention Christine Hulme – to whom I am eternally indebted. Annette and Christine got on famously. Annette was physically handicapped, but was mentally still as sharp as ever and she inspired several of her carers – a few of them went on to nursing studies at university because of her urgings and encouragement.

These were the most difficult years of our lives – for the first three years I did not have a single day of respite. This took its toll on my health. A slight twinge in my chest while playing golf resulted in my being referred for exercise stress tests which pointed to severe blockages in three major arteries. Surgery was recommended. In December 2008, I underwent quadruple heart by-pass surgery. I recovered fully and have not had any negative symptoms since.

Annette however had to be placed in a nursing home for about a month while I was in hospital. None of the boys were around. Renan was working in Houston, Texas at that time while Rohan and Rienzi were working in Sydney. Annette's brother and his wife were on holiday in Malaysia.

Rohan flew over from Sydney and had me admitted for the operation. After I was prepped and was being wheeled away, I raised my hand – I was really saying good-bye as I did not expect to come out of the operation. I was so thoroughly exhausted and I knew the boys would take care of their mother. Rohan stayed until I came out of surgery and was placed in the intensive care unit, following which he flew back to Sydney. Just before I was discharged a week or so later, Renan flew in from Houston and stayed with me for a month until I was well enough to be on my own.

Renan and I visited Annette frequently at the nursing home during the time I was recovering at home. We brought her home for a home cooked meal on Christmas day and New Years' day. Renan put up the Christmas lights – just as Annette herself used to do in days gone by.

We jointly bought her a Christmas gift – a bottle of her favourite perfume but I could sense that Annette was losing heart, not only because there seemed to be no respite or prospect of recovery for her but also because of a realisation that looking after her at home had worn me out.

Renan and I brought Annette home again for lunch on 10th January. Renan went to see her again on the 11th. before his flight back to Houston Texas later that day. It was the last time he was to see his mother alive. On 14th January Rohan flew over from Sydney on business and we planned to take Annette out for lunch on Saturday 17th January.

But on Friday 16th January when I visited her she complained of head pains – I knew the signs and got the ambulance to take her immediately to the Rockingham Hospital. Rohan came with me and was with his mother before she was sent for a CT (brain) scan. This revealed extensive bleeding on the brain and we were advised that there was little that could be done.

Palliative care was the best treatment possible in order to keep her as comfortable as possible. She was slipping away. It was very sad for me especially and the recollection of it still is – so many years later. Rohan was the last to talk to her but already her mind had gone back to the days when they were little boys. Rienzi came over from Sydney on 17th January to be by his mother's side. Renan was informed and he made arrangements to fly back from Houston.

Rohan, Rienzi and I stayed by Annette's side the next couple of days and took turns staying overnight as well. Each of us talked to her but she could only respond by squeezing our hands. Annette struggled on for several more days and passed away quietly at 12.30am on 22nd January 2009. Renan arrived shortly after she had passed away. The funeral service for Annette was conducted by Rev. Peter Moyle at the Church of Christ that Annette used to attend. Rohan delivered the eulogy which was jointly contributed by the "four men in her life" as Annette used to refer to us. Annette was interred at the Fremantle cemetery on 28th January 2009.

Annette was an inspiration. She touched the lives, not only of those students who passed through her hands both in Malaysia and in Australia but also of countless people from all walks of life, from different age groups and across religious, ethnic and cultural divides. She continued to do so even after she was stricken. She was sincere, honest and forthright in all her dealings.

Despite the frustrations and the challenges Annette faced especially over the last few years of her life, Annette never wavered in her determination to overcome her situation. Annette has always been a fighter. Tenacity, downright stubbornness and an absolute unwillingness to yield were key to her fighting spirit and the inner strength she always seemed to possess. She also had a deep and unwavering faith that stood her in good stead all her life.

An ending and a beginning

When Annette died, I resigned myself to the fact that my life was over too. I had had a good life but it was time to gracefully fade away. But Rohan got me to see things differently. He said "Life is not over for you Dad, so live again". He also suggested that I put up the Rockingham house for sale and move to Sydney.

I subsequently spent some time in Rohan's home in Alexandria and this helped me to get over the trauma of losing Annette who had been a part of my life for nearly fifty years. Maria – Rohan's partner at that time and later his wife, was especially helpful. Rohan and Maria even arranged for me to take up membership in the Lawn Bowls Club in Alexandria – which I did.

As it turned out, I decided against moving to Sydney. I realised that with job volatility in the private sector, there was no guarantee that Rohan would remain in Sydney. If he needed to go elsewhere to take advantage of job opportunities, I did not want him to hold back simply because of me.

I have always been independent and felt quite confident that I could survive on my own. I decided to stay put in Perth but was reluctant to put the house up for sale as the real estate market was still in the doldrums. The house was eventually sold in December 2014 – nearly six years later.

Music in our lives

From early days when the boys were growing up, music and singing have been a part of our lives – especially at family parties. Piano accompaniment was usually provided by Annette or her sister Bridget. Everybody joined in singing along.

I remember Rohan as an 8-year old – he was somewhat of an extrovert even then – announcing "… and now we shall have a song from Uncle Terrence". I also still remember Rohan's rendering of "When you're going to San Francisco", Rienzi's unexpected contribution of a cheeky limerick at another party as well as Renan's confident piano rendition of "Fur Elise". Renan was only about eleven then and we were absolutely flabbergasted! Outside the home, Annette was a member of the Selangor Philharmonic society and took part in a few public performances.

Long after the boys had flown the coop, Annette played the piano from time to time and I sang along – but only for our own entertainment. We had purchased a really nice Kawai Electronic Organ in 1981 which we brought over to

Australia. Annette taught herself to play the organ too and I sang along from time to time. Now that Annette has gone, there is no one else to play the organ and I plan to donate it to one of the smaller churches – I am sure she would approve.

Our Rippen piano I have given to Rohan – he still plays the piano and keyboard – and it now sits in Rohan's home in Malabar, Long Bay in Sydney. We sing along there too from time to time.

Over the years, I have on a few occasions – mostly with Rohan – gone to Karaoke Bars and have sung solo a few times. After Annette died, Rohan encouraged me to take up singing again. I did and turned up for rehearsals at the Catholic Church in Erskinville in preparation for Midnight Mass on Christmas Eve in 2009. I sang with the Church Choir for the Midnight Mass and Rohan joined us too. It was the beginning of new pathways for me.

When I got back to Perth in January 2010, I began scouting around for choirs I could join. I subsequently joined a small choir in Perth, participated in a few rehearsals and got to know of a larger choir, which at that time was conducting auditions for new members. It was the Rejoyce Choir which met once a week at the Callaway Auditorium at the University of Western Australia.

I turned up for the auditions, was assessed by the two choir directors who decided that I would fit in nicely as a Tenor 2. They asked me to go and join the tenors – the rest of the choir were already assembled. I did so and met Karen there – she was also singing the tenor line. I introduced myself and as I got to know Karen in the months and years following, my life changed completely. I have been with Karen ever since.

Karen is originally from Denmark. She is very talented and plays several musical instruments – including piano, electronic keyboard, accordion, dulcimer and glockenspiel. Our world is full of laughter and music and we travel together often, both within the country and abroad. The boys (young men now) have all met Karen and I have met Karen's two daughters in Australia and a son in Denmark – all of whom are married with families.

Karen and I are no longer with the Rejoyce Choir. We did however participate in two of their public performances. The Rejoyce Choir has since been discontinued. Following this, Karen and I joined the Churchlands Choral Society, again

Singalong

singing with the tenors and we took part in two of the Choir's public performances. We have dropped out of this choir too because of the necessity for hip replacement surgery for Karen – which has since been undertaken.

Four of us from the Rejoyce Choir have now formed the Out of the Blue singers. We rehearse regularly and perform from time to time. Geoff (the only true blue Aussie) and Michelle (from French speaking Switzerland) are the other members of our 'quartet'. Karen provides the piano/keyboard accompaniment, sings the alto line from time to time and functions as the programme director.

Barbershop singers

It is indeed somewhat intriguing that my introduction to "barbershop" or 4 part harmony singing came about because of my renewed interest in learning to play the piano. I had seen an advertisment on piano playing, based on some revolutionary new method which assured students that they would be able to play a specified number of songs within a relatively short span of time. I was hooked. Classes were held once a week in one of the churches in Fremantle. I registered and attended classes for a few months. While I did manage, after a fashion, to play a few bars of a poular number, it was simply not what I was looking for. Reading music was not part of the training, neither was familiarity of the scales a necessity. I dropped out.

It so happened that Ken Richens, a fellow participant in these training sessions, was an established barbershop singer and asked me whether I would be interested in attending one of the practise sessions of the West Coast Chordsmen. I did so and in May 2010, I became a member of the West Coast Chordsmen. I had to go through an audition after which I was placed with the Lead singers – who usually sing the melody line. The WCC are four part harmony or Barbershop singers. The WCC are very active and do at least two public performances each month, mostly at Citizenship ceremonies and retirement villages. I continued as a member of the West Coast Chordsmen for about five years but have taken a break to cope with other interests. I may consider rejoining the Chordsmen within the next few years.

A new generation

In April 2015, Rohan and Maria's son – Jordan Asanka was born. What will your world be like, Jordan? Hopefully, I will see some of it with you and you will get to know your grandfather. Regrettably, I never got to know any of my own grandfathers.

the family 2017

Jordan

The Jayatilaka lineage

When I first began writing and trying to piece together the family story, I was focussed on my own life and my ancestral threads from the paternal as well as maternal side. I was fortunate to be able to draw from documentary sources and old photographs as well as from my own recollections.

Annette's side of the story has only been related largely in terms of her role as wife and mother (of our boys) as well as her career, training, family life and deteriorating eyesight wherever these impacted on the life of the family.

It would have been ideal if the writing of the family story could have been undertaken jointly. The personal interaction and opportunity for checks and balances would have been invaluable. Alas this did not happen.

Annette as an officer with St John Ambulance

Annette with her youngest siblings

However, a perusal of Annette's personal papers after her death in 2009 has revealed that her own attempts to piece together the family story and trace her own ancestral threads predate my own efforts in this respect by about twelve years.

The Jayatilaka Family tree that Annette prepared was based on information in her paternal grandfather's Bible. Annette's motivation in tracing the Jayatilaka lineage was simply because she wanted our sons to know a little bit more about their ancestry. Unfortunately, Annette was only able to write a few pages before illness struck her down. Based on what she wrote, I have attempted to provide a fuller picture as Annette wrote so little about herself during her growing up years and nothing at all about her grandparents.

In doing so, I have relied on discussions I have had with her siblings, especially Lionel who has provided me with some additional information. I have also drawn from documentary sources among Annette's private papers, including her birth certificate and School Leaving Certificate and have brought back to mind aspects of Annette's family life she has touched on, in conversations with me over the years.

Annette's paternal grandparents were born in Ceylon but it is not known which part of the country they originated from. John Simon Jaya Tilake (dob 15th Aug 1871) married Alice Maud de Silva (dob 6th Mar 1878) in Ceylon on 21st March 1900. Where exactly the marriage took place is not known. There were 11 children from this union, 3 of whom died early in life. What is unusual is that the family with the first few children in tow, including her Dad (Lloyd Cremlin dob 20th June 1907) and his elder sister (Ada Maud <Leena> dob 13th Aug 1901) – both of whom were born in Ceylon – took ship to the Malay States, before the outbreak of WW 1.

The Jayatilakas, taken at Calton Lodge circa 1932 [2]

What motivated the move to the Malay States is not known. It is very unusual to say the least. Migration was a concept relatively unknown in the early years of the 20th century. Young people mostly moved out of their homeland as single persons and not with their young families – John Simon did just the opposite. I can well imagine the scenario in his family circle – several sari clad ladies, chewing betel leaf and wringing their hands in anguish – 'apoi', 'apoi' their 'putah' was going away and taking the family too; madness! madness!

John Simon had received some level of education but there are no details available. He spoke several languages and was a deeply spiritual person. In the Malay States he worked in

---

[2]
Back L to R : Lloyd, Wolly, Cyril, Banda, Stanley.
Seated L to R : Annie, Leena, Mukta, John Simon, Alice Maude (de Silva), Soma (standing), Stella, Grace (Tiny).
Front L to R : Gerry, clarry Boy, Leela, Seria, Hector, Charlie (slave boy)

the Public Works Department. Annette never knew her grandfather as he died long before she was born. She did however know her grandmother who stayed with the family during her growing up years. Annette's grandmother suffered from dementia and so there was little meaningful interaction.

There are no details available of Annette's maternal grandparents, apart from the fact that her maternal grandfather was named Magnus Perera.

Annette's father Lloyd Cremlin Jayatilaka was an educated and cultured person. He trained as a teacher and worked in the Methodist Boys' School, Kuala Lumpur all his working life. He was a very popular teacher and was well respected by his colleagues. He was also the cricket master and was well known as a sports announcer. When he retired, he was conferred the AMN (Ahli Mangku Negara) by DYMM, the Yang di Pertuan Agung (King) for his services to the nation in the field of education.

Earlier in his career, he won a scholarship to the prestigious Raffles' Institution, apparently to undertake medical studies but was unable to take it up as his father died, leaving him to take care of the family. This is a task he undertook willingly and was fortunate to have the full support of his wife Annie Perera. Annette's parents got married in Kuala Lumpur on 6th Dec 1930.

As related to me by Annette, a proposal was made, following the conventions of the time, for a brother and sister from Ceylon (Walter and Annie Perera) to take in marriage a sister and brother in the Malay States (Ada Maud <Leena> and

Lloyd Cremlin Jayatilaka). Who exactly facilitated this 'arrangement' is not known.

Annette's parents, Lloyd Cremlin Jayatilaka and Annie Perera

Annette's paternal grandparents, John Simon Jayatilaka and Alice Maud de Silva

Large families were still the order of the day. Annette had 7 brothers and 1 sister. Annette's older brother Clarence died when he was barely 2 years old. Annette's mother was then expecting her second child (Annette) and felt the death of her first born very deeply, so much so that she used to say, seemingly in jest (though she probably meant it) that she had to be rid of the eldest in order that Annette could come into the world. Unfortunately, Annette as a little girl was greatly troubled by this and carried this hurt well into her adult life. Little is known about Annette's mother's background. I have heard from my mother that Annie Perera came from the Convent in Morotuwa, south of Colombo. Annie Perera would surely have had a modicum of education in the Convent in her native tongue Sinhalese. It is also likely that some English would have been taught in the convent while in the Malay States she learned to speak colloquial Malay and Tamil.

I do recall Annette telling me about her mother's attempts at sundry trading during the Japanese occupation in order to supplement the family income. Annette's parents were the driving force in 'arranging' the subsequent marriages of most of her father's brothers and sisters. Most of them married partners from within the Sinhalese community domiciled in the Malay States and lived out their lives in the Malay States except for one who returned to Ceylon and another who migrated to Australia.

According to her mother, Annette was born on the 24th September 1933 under a very bright star – whatever that meant but her birth date was only registered over two months later on the 27th November 1933. Annette mentions Vesak which is a Buddhist festival held earlier in the year but it is more than likely that she was born on a Poya day or a day of the full moon.

Annette schooled at St. Marys, Kuala Lumpur – one of the leading schools for girls at that time. It was a Government aided school run by the Anglican Mission and was established in 1912. According to Annette's School Leaving Certificate, she was admitted to the school in 1940 and left in 1951, having obtained the Oversea School Certificate with a Credit grading in all subjects taken, including maths and science – later to become her specialist subjects in her teaching career. Annette appeared to have continued her schooling during the Japanese occupation without any setbacks unlike my own case as I dropped out of school for several years.

Annette was very active in school – she was House Prefect, School Prefect and House Captain. She was also Vice Captain of the School Hockey team, a member of the netball and badminton teams, vice-chair of the Literary & Debating Society as well as Secretary of the School Magazine Committee.

Soon after leaving school, Annette took up teaching and enrolled in Normal Class, which was set up by the Department of Education for teacher training within the country. She passed the Final Normal Examination in April 1955 and was registered as a qualified teacher in secondary schools. Annette subsequently taught at the Bukit Bintang Girls School in Kuala Lumpur but resigned in October 1961 to join me in London.

On returning to the country in 1963, Annette taught for a further ten years in secondary schools in Petaling Jaya, firstly at the Assunta Secondary School (for girls) followed by the Sultan Abdul Samad Secondary School (for boys). This was followed by a further ten years in ETV (educational television) as a producer of educational television programmes for schools. Even after migrating to Australia in 1983, Annett continued teaching for a further ten years at the Maranatha Community College.

Several of Annette's siblings took up teaching as a career line, following the footsteps of their father. Lionel, Basil and Terrence attended teacher training colleges in the UK – specifically in Kirkby and Brinsford and taught in Secondary schools in Kuala Lumpur and in other parts of the country. Much later, Bridget graduated with a Bachelor of Science degree from the University of Malaya, followed by a Diploma in Education and a Masters Degree and taught in Schools in Selangor and Pahang.

Long after migrating to Australia and prior to his retirement, Annette's brother Basil obtained a Doctorate from the University of Western Australia. Basil's twin brother Terrence later graduated with a BA from the University of Malaya and went on to a Doctorate in linguistics from Georgetown University.

Rodney, the youngest brother, obtained a degree in Electrical Engineering, from Adelaide University, on a Colombo Plan scholarship while Brian studied at the Bournemouth Technical College and qualified as a quantity surveyor. Justin, who passed away a few years ago was sent for flight training at RAF Cranwell (UK) but was unsuccessful and returned to work in managerial positions in rubber and oil palm plantations in Malaysia.

More on the Jayatilakas and their lives in various parts of the world will need to come from the hand of one of them – either from Annette's own generation or the next.

Epilogue

When I began writing the family story, I had little to go on. There were a few documentary sources, but for the most part, I had to rely on my personal recollections of persons, places and happenings from my earliest years. I have never maintained a personal diary in my growing up years. That came years later – mostly in connection with my working life. I have long discarded these diaries – they could have been invaluable sources.

In exploring the ancestral roots of the family, I had even less to go on. While there were some documentary sources, including several old photographs, it was necessary to make assumptions that may not be accurate. I also had to depend on oral communication, especially with my mother, my remembrance of which may be flawed.

There may have to be corrections and additions as new information comes to light. There may also be a need for further research into the family's ancestry and its roots in Sri Lanka. This may require some research in Sri Lanka itself.

I am in the twilight of my life and may not have the time or the energy to continue the story. It is my hope that one of my sons and perhaps my grandson too, will pick up the threads and continue the narrative as life unfolds for each of them. In doing so, I hope they will feel the urge and the need to visit the ancestral country and appreciate their cultural heritage.

My sons and I are familiar with Malaysia – it is the country where we were born and where we grew up. Malaysia will always be 'tanah ayer ku' (homeland) and one of our most favoured tourist destinations. We live in Australia now and owe the country our fullest allegiance. Australia has been a land of opportunity for our boys – to spread their wings and reach their full potential. I wonder where it will take you, Jordan?

A modest dossier of framed photographs, photo albums, documents, paintings and other paraphernalia, including my writings over the years, I have left behind as part of my earthly footprint. More importantly, my three sons and grandson are a living, vibrant part of that footprint, while in Malaysia I left behind a footprint in terms of the physical infrastructure for libraries as well as the National Library of Malaysia.

I have been fortunate to be able to tell my story. Alas millions are born, exist and fade away – with hardly a footprint; their stories sadly untold.

My friend and colleague at the University of Malaya in the mid-sixties – the late Professor Emeritus Khoo Kay Kim, whose autobiography was published in 2017 ended his narrative by stating:

> "Little seems to have been done to solve communal problems. Instead, the political process thrives on ethnicity... I fear for the future if the situation is allowed to subsist. Today, I am indeed a sad man" (I, KKK: the autobiography of a historian, 2017)

While I share KKK's sentiments, I am confident the country will pull itself away from the morass and emerge onto a more level playing field. But the process will take time and I doubt I will be there to see it. But, I am not a sad man. I did what I could within my area of work while I was in the country and still have close friends across the ethnic spectrum.

Additional Information

For a select list of my writings over the period 1967-1992, see

D.E.K.Wijasuriya: a select list of publications in

The Information Challenge: a Festschrift in honour of Dr. Donald Wijasuriya. Edited by Ch'ng Kim See. Kuala Lumpur, Knowledge Publishers, 1995. p248-254

see also

D.E.K.Wijasuriya

Contributions towards the Malaysian Library and Information Infrastructure: a historical perspective Kuala Lumpur, MPH Publishing, 2011. 397p

For biographies on the life of the author, see

Who's Who in the World. 16th Ed. Marquis Who's Who, NJ 1999.

ALA World Encyclopedia of Library and Information Services. Chicago, American Library Association, 1986

Who' Who in Malaysia. Various editions, 1983-1988.

International Who's Who

References

Mills, Lennox Algernon. British Malaya, 1824 — 1967. Kuala Lumpur, Oxford University Press, 1966

Andaya, Barbara Watson and Leonard Y. Andaya. A history of Malaysia. Honolulu, University of Hawaii Press, 2001

De Silva, K.M. A history of Sri Lanka. Delhi, Oxford University Press, 1981

Peebles, Patrick Social change in 19th century Ceylon. Colombo, Lake House Bookshop, 1995

Appendices

Wijasuriya Family Tree

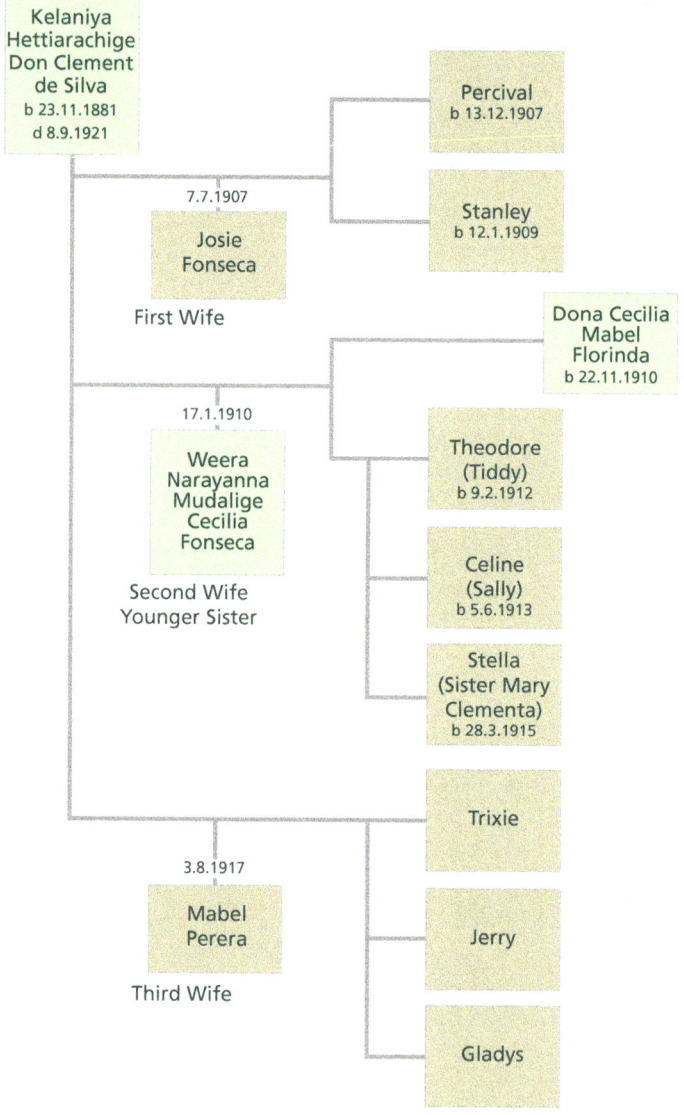

Wijasuriya Family Tree

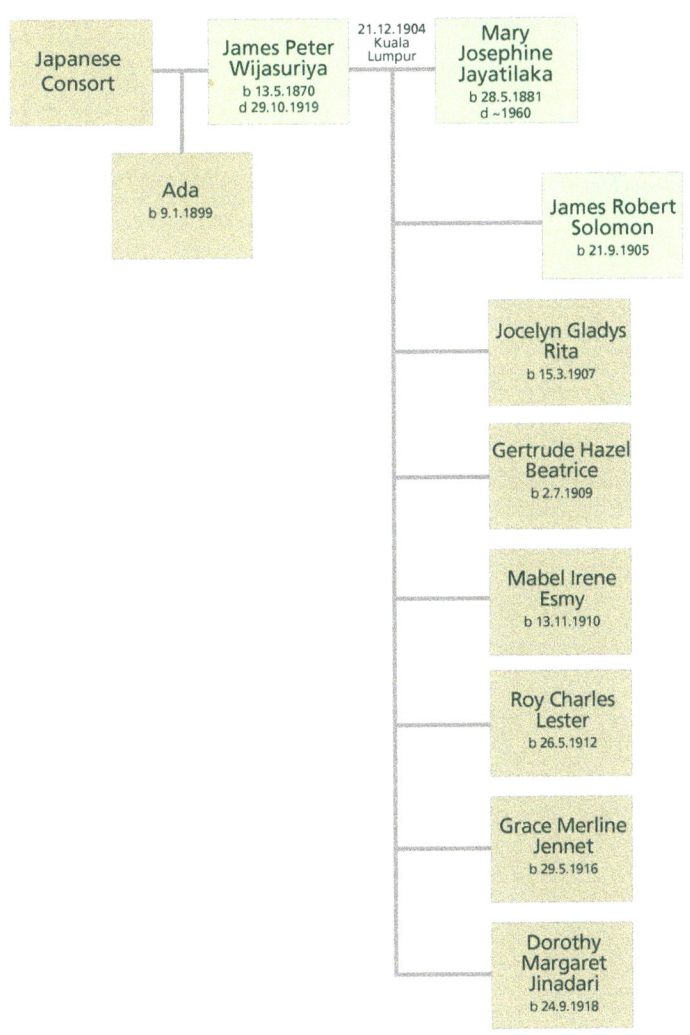

Wijasuriya Family Tree

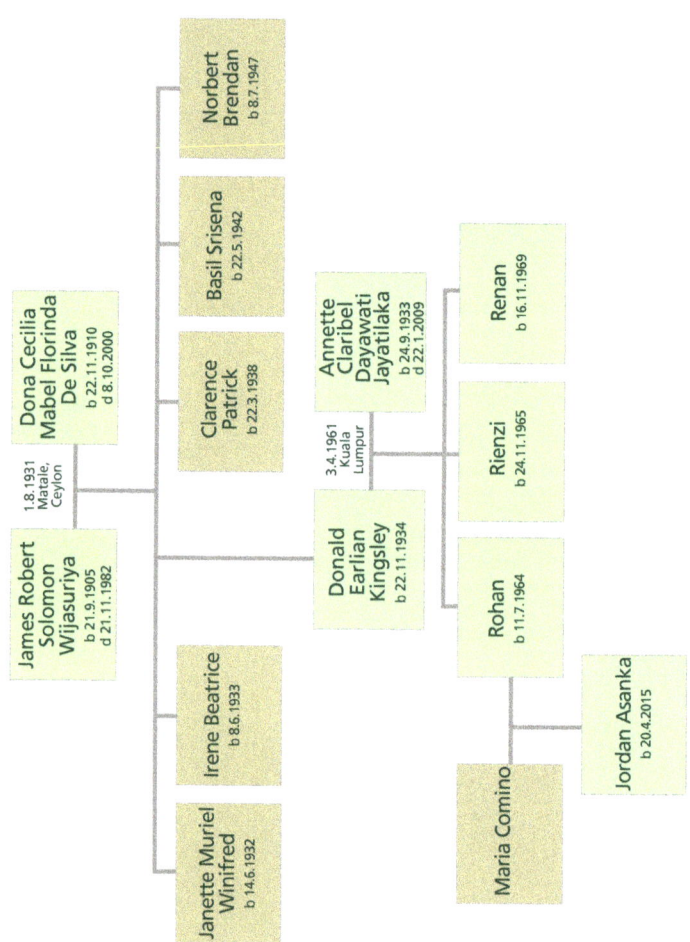

Jayatilaka Family Tree

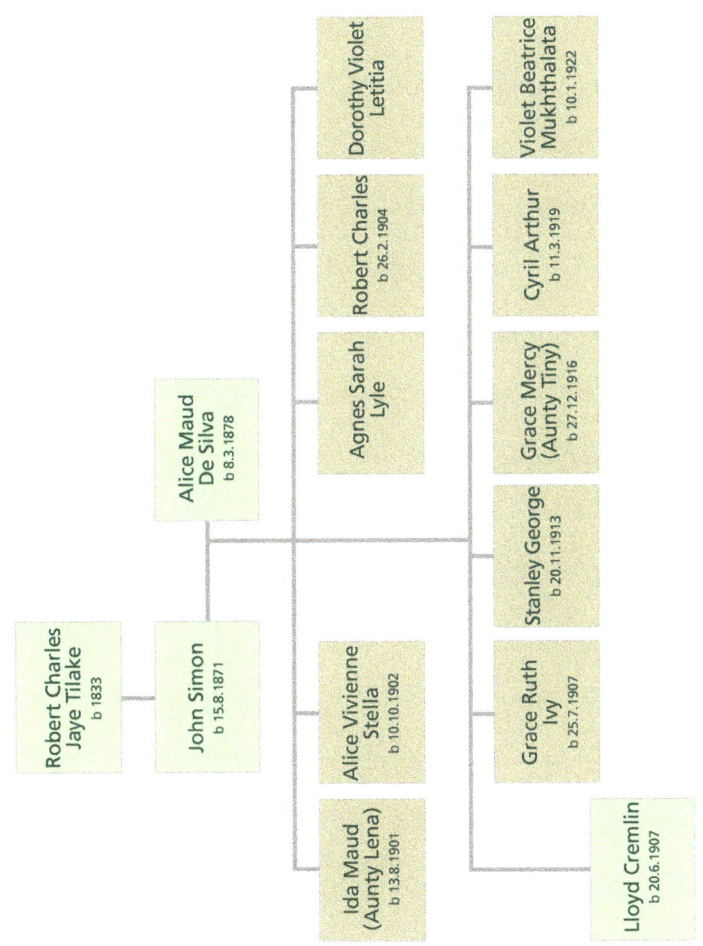

Jayatilaka Family Tree

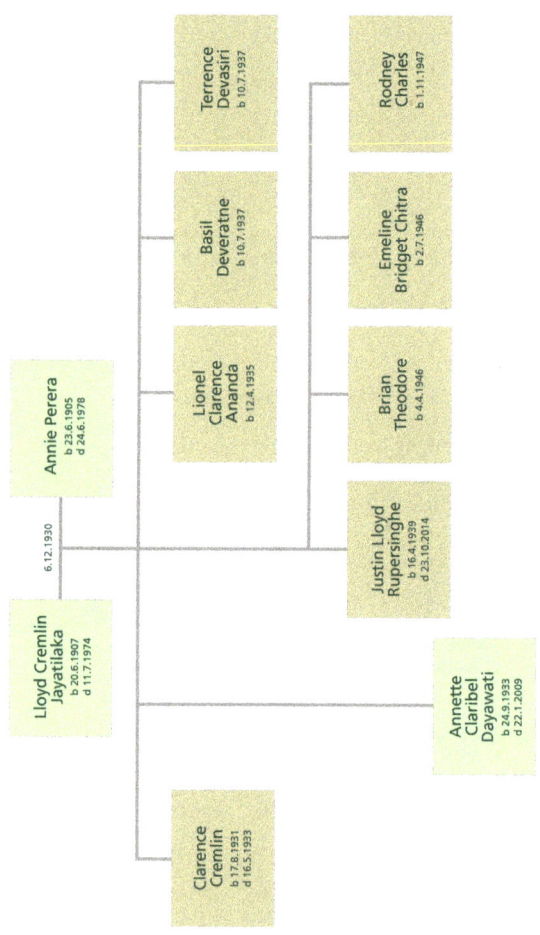

Birth Certificates

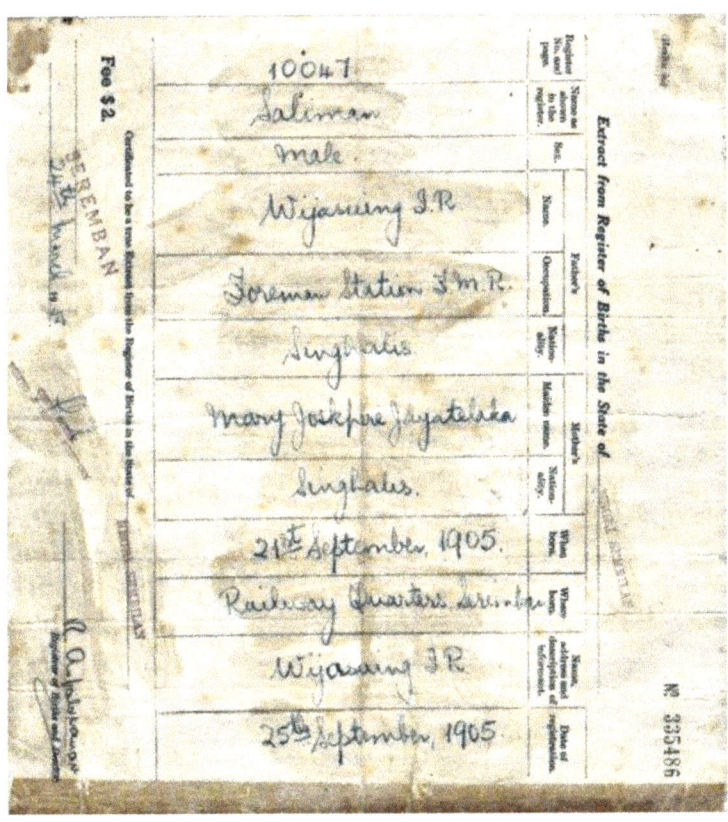

Birth Certificates

Birth Certificates

FORM M
FEDERATION OF MALAYA
CERTIFICATE OF BIRTH
The Births and Deaths Registration Ordinance, 1957
(Sections 32 (I) and 33 (5), Rule 16)

No 194777

30106/60.
(B. & D. 24)

Register No. 356490

Registration Area: KELANGOR
Sub-area: General Hospital K. Lumpur.
Full Name of Child: DONALD EARLIAN KINGSLEY
Sex: M
Where Born: General Hospital K.L.
When Born: 22.11.34 6am

Father's:
- Name: JOSEPH STANISLAUS WIJASURIA
- Occupation: Clerk
- Race: Singhalese

Mother's:
- Maiden Name: FLORENCE de SILVA
- Age: —
- Usual Place of Residence: —
- Race: Singh

Informant's:
- Name: E.A.B.
- Occupation: —

Date of Registration: 22.11.34.
Name of Child if added after Registration of Birth: —

CERTIFIED TO BE A TRUE COPY OF THE ENTRY IN THE BIRTH REGISTER

FEE $2

NOV 29 1960

Superintendent Registrar of Births and Deaths
Registrar-General/Superintendent Registrar

Birth Certificates

Baptism Certificates

Baptism Certificates

School Leaving Certificates

St. Michael's School.
IPOH.

LEAVING CERTIFICATE.

Name: Stanislaus J. Wijasuriya
Age: 21 years
Admitted: 2nd December, 1918
Withdrawn: 10th January, 1927
Name of former School (if any): Convent, Ipoh.
Last presented in Standard: Senior Cambridge
Now in Standard:
No. of Attendances since last Inspection:
Amount due:
Conduct: Excellent
General Progress: Excellent
Reason for leaving: Going to work.
Remarks: He was vice-captain of the School football team and also School Librarian and an Assistant Scout Master of the Ipoh 3rd Troop.

P.S. I hereby certify that Master Stanislaus J. Wijasuriya is the same person as James R.J. Wijasuriya whose index No. at Cambridge Junior Exam was 9...

School Leaving Certificates

No. 203/47

St. JOHN'S INSTITUTION.

CERTIFICATE.

NAME Donald Wijesuriya

Admission Number 830

Date and place of birth 22/11/34

Date of admission 20/1/47

Name of former school (if any) —

Date of leaving 6th December 1947

In what Standard at time of leaving Passed Std. III

Reason for leaving Going to Klang

Fees due (or Free place authority) Free by govt.

Attendance during the School Year Regular

Games and Athletics

Cadet Corps Record

Conduct V. Good

Remarks Promoted to Standard Four

KUALA LUMPUR.
30th December 1947.

M Matthias
Director.

Marriage Notices and Certificates

Marriage Notices and Certificates

DIOCESE OF KANDY
MISSION OF MATALE
CERTIFICATE OF MARRIAGE

I, the undersigned, do hereby certify that W. A. Stanislaus Koska Joseph Wijesuriya
son of W.A James Peter Wijesuriya
and of Maria Josephine Wijesuriya
was married to Dona Cecilia Mabel Florinda de Silva
daughter of Don Clement de Silva
and of Cecilia Fonseka
on the 1st day of August 1931
by the Reverend Fr. D.C. Mani, O.S.B
The Witnesses Were { John Simon Jayathilake
W. M. William Fonseka

As shown by the Register of marriages of the Mission of Matale.
Given at St. Thomas' Church, Matale, on the 21st day of August 19 2013

A. Fernando, S.S.J
Parish Priest

Marriage Notices and Certificates

Statutory Declarations

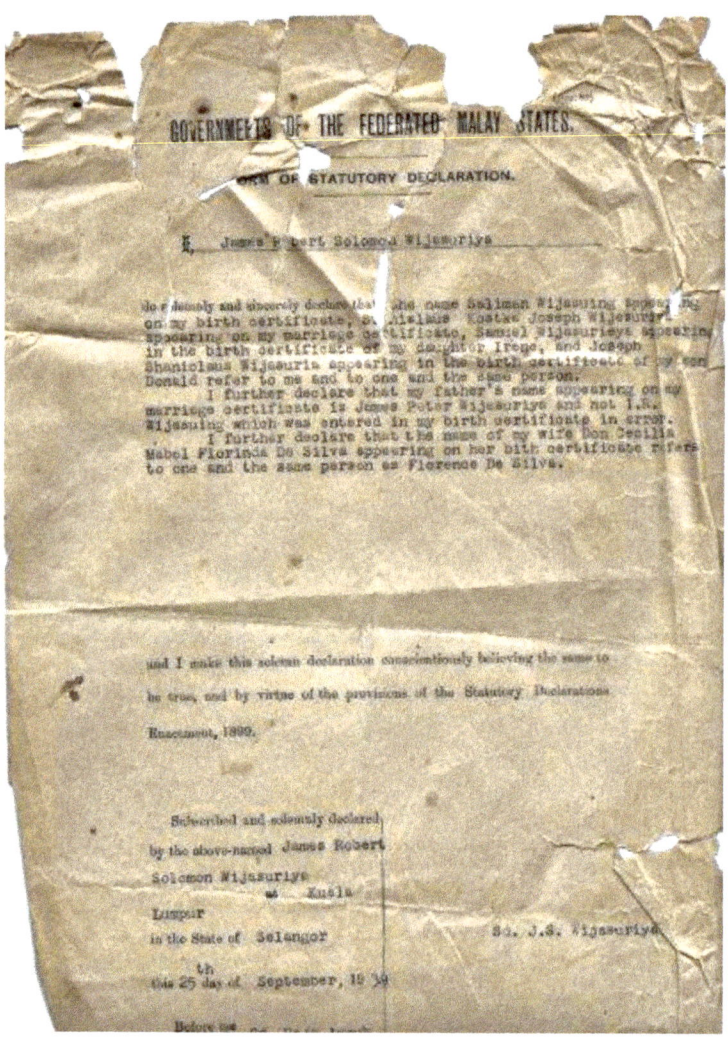

Statutory Declarations

FORM OF STATUTORY DECLARATION MADE IN A MALAY STATE.

I, James Robert Solomon Wijasuriya do solemnly and sincerely declare that the name SALIMAN appearing on my birth certificate, STANISLAUS KOSTKA JOSEPH WIJESURIYA appearing on my marriage certificate, SAMUEL WIJASURIEYA appearing on the birth certificate of my daughter Irene, JOSEPH STANISLAUS WIGASURIA appearing in the birth certificate of my son Donald Earlton Kingsley and J.S. WIJASURIA appearing on the birth certificate of my son Clarence Patrick refer to me and to one and the same person.

I further declare that my father's name appearing in my birth certificate should be James Peter Wijesuriya and not I.K. Wijasuing and my mother's name should be Mary Josephine Jayatilake and not Mary Joskpene Jayatelaku.

and I make this solemn declaration conscientiously believing the same to be true, and by virtue of the provisions of the Statutory Declarations Ordinance, 1949.

Subscribed and solemnly declared by the above-named James Robert Solomon Wijasuriya at Kuala Lumpur in the State of Selangor this 22nd day of March 1956.

Before me

Statutory Declarations

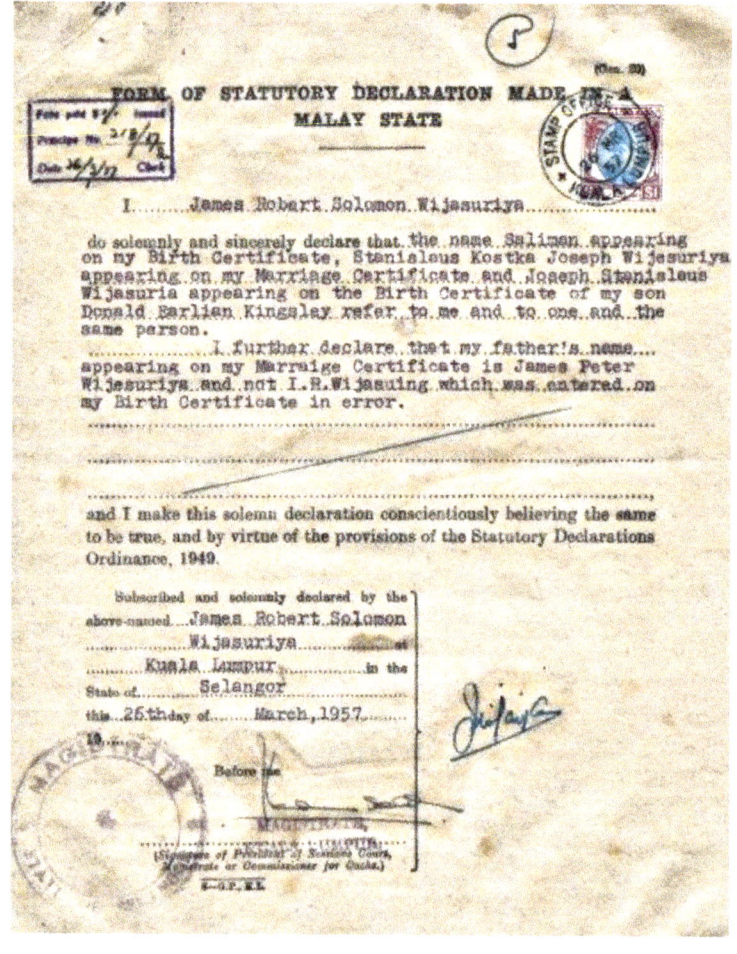

Pension Records

```
                          MEMOGRAPH

From Secretary, Widows & Orphans' Pension Office, Kuala Lumpur.

To Mr. J.R.S. Wijisaurya, Forest Office, Klang.

Copy to
```

File reference.	Date.	Your reference.	Date.
W.&.O.P.S./PM/875/79.	26.6.1954.		

Re James Peter Wijisaurya deceased
W.&.O.P.R. 875.

With reference to your enquiry my records show that you Mr. James Robert Solomon son of James Peter Wijisuris, deceased who was born at Matale Central Province, Ceylon on 13.5.1870.

2. Your deceased father enrolled as a contributor on 1st January 1904 – retired on 11.8.1919 and died on 29.10.1919.

SECRETARY.

Certificates of Registration / Citizenship

S 3990

FORM B2.

THE Negri Sembilan NATIONALITY ENACTMENT, 1952.
[Regulation 3 (3) and (4).]

CERTIFICATE OF REGISTRATION AS A SUBJECT OF THE RULER OF Negri Sembilan

I HEREBY CERTIFY that James Robert Solomon Wijesuriya of District Forest Office, Kuala Lumpur, particulars of whom are set out below, has been registered as a subject of the Ruler of Negri Sembilan under the provisions of Section 5 (1) of the Negri Sembilan Nationality Enactment, 1952.

Date 29th November, 1955

Signed
Designation

PARTICULARS RELATING TO APPLICANT.

Full name and sex ..... James Robert Solomon Wijesuriya — Male
National Registration Identity No. SL 552115 Klg
Address ..... District Forest Office, Kuala Lumpur
Occupation ..... F.M.S. General Clerical Service
Date and place of birth ..... 21st Sept.
Single, married, etc. ..... Married
Name of husband/wife: Florence Mabel Cecilia Wijesuriya (nee De Silva)
Names of parents — Father: James Peter Wijesuriya
Mother: Mary Josephine Jayatilake
Names of adoptive father and/or

Certificates of Registration / Citizenship

(Fed. Co. 44)
(Rev. 10/60)

ENTRY N° 19428

CONSTITUTION OF THE FEDERATION OF MALAYA
CITIZENSHIP RULES, 1960
Rule 17—Form M

Certificate of Registration

Whereas FLORENCE MABEL CECILIA WIJESURIYA has applied to the Federal Government for registration as a citizen of the Federation of Malaya under Article....17.....of the Constitution of the Federation of Malaya alleging in respect of himself/herself the particulars set out herein and has satisfied the Federal Government that the conditions laid down in the said Article have been fulfilled:

Now, therefore, I, KHOO BOO HOCK a Registrar of Citizens of the Federation of Malaya, on behalf of the Federal Government, grant to the said FLORENCE MABEL CECILIA WIJESURIYA this Certificate of Registration and declare that from the date hereof he/she shall be a citizen of the Federation of Malaya.

In Witness whereof I have hereto subscribed my name this 25th day of January, 19.63 at PETALING JAYA

Seal. Signed on behalf of the Federal Government.

Certificates of Registration / Citizenship

Marriage Advertisements

Marriage Advertisements

Donald Wijasuriya shares his life story in a simple and readable style. It is written mainly for his sons and grandson and draws from his incredible recollections of long ago. It also draws from a dossier of documentary and photographic sources and is on the whole chronological and factual.

The author attempts to trace the family's ancestry from it's origins in the hill country in Ceylon to migration to the Malay states in the 1890s. He also traces his own growing up years in the Federation of Malaya and to his working life in Malaysia, firstly in academia followed by a distinguished career in the Public Service.

The author reflects on the many years spent away from the family – first in boarding school in Ceylon and then at the University of Ceylon. In a fascinating life, including post graduate study in London, the family migrated to Australia in 1983. All three sons have graduated as engineers and have carved out successful careers for themselves in multi-national corporations.

Copies of this book can be purchased by
contacting Graphic Elements:
peter@graphicelements.com.au

9 780646 953274

www.ingramcontent.com/pod-product-compliance
Lightning Source LLC
Chambersburg PA
CBHW051534010526
44107CB00064B/2717